iPhone and iOS Forensics

iPhone and iOS Forensics

Investigation, Analysis and Mobile Security for Apple iPhone, iPad, and iOS Devices

Andrew Hoog

Katie Strzempka

Technical Editor

Robert Maxwell

ELSEVIER

AMSTERDAM • BOSTON • HEIDELBERG • LONDON
NEW YORK • OXFORD • PARIS • SAN DIEGO
SAN FRANCISCO • SINGAPORE • SYDNEY • TOKYO
Focal Press is an imprint of Elsevier

SYNGRESS

Acquiring Editor: Angelina Ward
Development Editor: Heather Scherer
Project Manager: Jessica Vaughan
Designer: Eric DeCicco

Syngress is an imprint of Elsevier
225 Wyman Street, Waltham, MA 02451, USA

Library of Congress Cataloging-in-Publication Data
Hoog, Andrew.
  iPhone and iOS forensics : investigation, analysis, and mobile security for Apple iPhone, iPad, and iOS devices / Andrew Hoog, Katie Strzempka.
     p. cm.
  Includes index.
  ISBN 978-1-59749-659-9
  1. iPhone (Smartphone) 2. iPad (Computer) 3. iOS (Electronic resource) 4. Data recovery (Computer science) I. Strzempka, Katie. II. Title.
  QA76.8.I64H665 2011
  005.8'6–dc23

                                                                                              2011013050

British Library Cataloguing-in-Publication Data
A catalogue record for this book is available from the British Library.

ISBN: 978-1-59749-659-9

Printed in the United States of America
11 12 13 14 15   10 9 8 7 6 5 4 3 2 1

For information on all Syngress publications visit our website at www.syngress.com

Contents

Acknowledgments

When making the decision to co-author this book, I was well aware of the impact it was going to have on my life, but did not fully realize all of the others that would be directly or indirectly involved. Luckily, I have this section to show my appreciation.

I must first thank my family and friends for being so understanding on those many nights and weekends where I was M.I.A. Specifically...thanks to my dad for editing Chapter 2, even though "the Linux stuff was kind of way over my head," and to my mom for always trying to convince me that I am way smarter than I actually am. Thank you to my brother, Danny, for caring for my dog when I was unable to. Jill, thank you for your encouragement throughout the entire process, especially when it involved cupcakes filled with cookie dough. An additional thank you to my friends for convincing me to take occasional breaks to eat sushi and play darts.

To Dr. Marcus Rogers and Purdue's Cyber Forensics program: thank you for helping me prepare for a career in this field and to continue to advise me on professional decisions.

I also owe a great deal of gratitude to the viaForensics folks, mainly for putting up with Andrew and my constant talk of the "wordcount meter." Big thanks to Ted for his ability to concatenate my iPhone simulator photos, Catherine for letting me vent on a daily basis, and Chris for forcing me to invent new ways of analyzing the iPhone, even when I laughed at him and said, "there is NO WAY we can recover those videos!"

This book would not have been completed without the help of my co-author, Andrew Hoog, who has taught me that everything can and should be done using command line (even if there is a GUI that can do it 10 times faster).

Preface

This book is intended for individuals who are interested in the iPhone and other iOS devices and, more importantly, in the type of data that is stored and can be recovered from these devices. The demand for mobile forensics has grown tremendously with the release of smart phones. Communication on these devices is now documented because people are no longer using their phones for just talking. Whether people use their iOS devices to send text messages, check their personal and work e-mail, browse the Internet, manage their finances, or even take photos and videos, what they do not realize is that this data is being stored on their devices. When they delete a piece of information, it is expected that data is gone forever. This book not only explains why this data can still be recovered but also provides detailed methods on how a forensic examiner can extract this information from an iOS device.

The book is organized in a manner that allows the reader to independently focus on one chapter at a time. If a Corporate Security Officer is only interested in whether the data stored on an iPhone or iPad is secure, he or she can jump straight to Chapter 4 – iPhone Data Security. If an experienced mobile forensic examiner understands all the files stored within the iPhone's file system but is interested in learning more about some advanced analysis techniques, he or she can skip through the first few chapters and focus on Chapter 6 – Data and Application Analysis.

The following paragraphs contain a brief summary of each of the chapters.

Chapter 1 provides an overview of the iPhone, including a timeline of events leading up to its development. Details related to the various models are outlined, including a definition of many of the hardware components within the device. The forensic acquisition of an iPhone device is introduced by defining the various ways in which data can be extracted. The chapter concludes with an introduction to Linux, showing how the use of these command-line tools can be extremely powerful in a mobile examination.

Chapter 2 introduces many of the popular Apple devices running iOS, as well as the features unique to these devices. Software updates, an introduction to device security, and the various operating modes are among the topics covered. Also covered are techniques describing the performance of system upgrades and downgrades and booting of the devices into different operating modes. The interaction between iTunes and an iOS device is discussed, including the functions it provides to support these iOS devices.

Chapter 3 discusses the type of data that is stored on the iPhone, the general locations of this data storage, and the format. Common file types recovered from an iOS device are described in detail in order to provide the examiner with an understanding of how the data is stored so that he or she can more efficiently recover data from these files. The type of memory contained on an iPhone is also outlined, in addition to the operating system, file system, and disk partitions contained on the device.

Chapter 4 provides mobile device administrators within companies options on the protection of user data. The reader is walked through the process involved in the testing of these Apple devices in an effort to determine the type of sensitive data that can be recovered from them. Also covered in this chapter is the development of secure mobile applications, strongly encouraging testing from both the user and developer perspective. Finally, some general recommendations for device and application security are provided, allowing users and administrators to proactively secure the devices used within their company.

Chapter 5 covers the various types of forensic acquisitions that can be performed on the iPhone, iPad, and other iOS devices. The importance of forensic imaging is discussed, followed by an explanation of the different ways in which a device can be imaged. Two different methods of data retrieval through the iPhone's backup files are stepped through in detail; this is followed by a logical acquisition and, finally, a physical extraction of the device. The possibility of imaging other iOS devices, including the iPod Touch and Apple TV, is also outlined.

Chapter 6 encompasses the analysis of the data contained on an iPhone. It starts out by introducing the reader to several different analysis techniques. Some basic methods are discussed, such as the mounting of a disk image, as well as more advanced techniques including the analysis of an image within a hex editor. Practical scenarios are applied for each technique in order to show an examiner all the steps needed to duplicate the command. Following the analysis techniques, the file system layout is discussed. From this section, the reader can gain an understanding of the location of each type of data. The chapter concludes with a mobile app reference section. Here, examiners can look through a list of specific applications and learn where the data for each is stored.

Chapter 7 covers the use of various mobile forensic acquisition tools, showing how they compare with one another. The data population process, which involves the preparation of an iPhone test device, is outlined. The methodology used for testing is explained in detail, followed by an overview of each of the software products used for analysis. A significant portion of this chapter is devoted to an examination of the test device using each of the tools listed. From start to finish, the reader is stepped through the installation, acquisition, and analysis, as well as a final table for each section contains the findings for that particular tool.

WEBSITE

For companion material including code, programs, and updates, please visit: http://viaforensics.com/education/iphone-ios-forensics-mobile-security-book/

About the Authors

Andrew Hoog is a computer scientist, certified forensic analyst (GCFA and CCE), computer and mobile forensics researcher, former adjunct professor (assembly language), and owner of viaForensics, an innovative computer and mobile forensic firm. He divides his energies between investigations, research, and training about the computer and mobile forensic discipline. He writes computer/mobile forensic how-to guides, is interviewed on radio programs, and lectures and trains both corporations and law enforcement agencies. As the foremost expert in Android Forensics, he leads expert-level training courses, and speaks frequently at conferences.

Katie Strzempka is a technology consultant with viaForensics, a computer and mobile forensics firm. She performs forensic investigations, security audits and research, and has trained investigators around the world in mobile forensics. She is also a co-author for a white paper on iPhone Forensics, an analysis of the various iPhone Forensics commercial tools. Ms. Strzempka received her Master's degree from Purdue University in Cyber Forensics and has a B.S. in Computer and Information Technology. Prior to working for viaForensics, she worked for 3 years in Information Security for a Fortune 500 company, handling firewall administration and assisting with internal and external network connectivity.

About the Technical Editor

Robert Maxwell is the Lead Incident Handler for University of Maryland (UMD), College Park, and the Founder and Managing Director of the Digital Forensics Lab at UMD, focused on education and curriculum development. He also coaches UMD's competitive CyberSecurity team, and is a Senior Contributor to Byte magazine. He lives with his wife and two children in bucolic Damascus, MD.

Overview

INTRODUCTION

Mobile devices have come a long way over the past few years. For a while, cell phones were simply used for making phone calls. As they continued to mature, the capability to send and receive text messages, create calendar events, and save contacts became readily available. Fast forward to the present day, and mobile devices are now being used extensively and serve many purposes. Around 4.6 billion individuals owned cell phones as of early 2010, and the number was expected to reach 5 billion by the end of the year (CBS, 2010). With this increase in popularity came an enormous demand for mobile forensics.

The iPhone was first released to consumers in June 2007. Ever since the first release, the device has increasingly gained in popularity, partly due to its advanced functionality and usability. With the iPhone, individuals now have the capability to check e-mail, take photos, browse the Internet, and do much more. These activities make the iPhone take the place of personal computers (PCs) and digital cameras. In addition to the standard capabilities that exist in the iPhone, endless applications are also available for download to assist with finances or organization, or simply for entertainment.

In the late 1980s, the Newton platform was the company's main focus. This platform was a personal data assistant (PDA), which never really took off. The project ultimately failed in 1998. One year prior to that, Steve Jobs became the CEO of the company. Before the idea of the iPhone was actually formulated, Jobs decided to have Apple start focusing on the idea of touch-screen development rather than PDAs and tablet PCs. Believing that cellular devices were going to become very popular, the company began developing a mobile device that could display pictures and videos and would ultimately have the capability to sync with iTunes. On November 2006, a patent was granted for the Apple iPhone, and in January 2007 Jobs announced the release of the iPhone at MacWorld (Wired, 2008).

Strategy

Apple's strategy over the past few years has shifted away from traditional computing. New and innovative ideas have been developed, disrupting the existing business model. In the music and video genre, several different applications and devices have been developed including the Apple TV, iTunes, and various iPod devices. The mobile category includes the iPhone, while the class of delivery channel items includes both iTunes for synchronization and downloads and the App Store. Finally, the development of the iPad (and previously the Newton device) falls within the Tablet category.

Many of these newer devices have been consolidated onto the iOS platform, with the exception of the Macintosh workstations, which are running OS X. There has been some debate in the past on whether Mac OS X will transform to iOS or perhaps a platform more similar to iOS. The Mac OS X Lion is to be released in the summer of 2011. This operating system is said to have similar qualities as the iOS devices, with the exception of a touch-screen feature. A Mac App Store was released in January of 2011, which enables Mac users to purchase software straight from their computer, similar to the way applications can be purchased through the iTunes App Store (Apple Inc., 2010).

As of 2009, the iPhone had taken third place in smart phone sales worldwide, which constituted 4.4% of the market share (McGlaun, 2010). During the first quarter of 2010 alone, 8.75 million were sold, which was more than half the number for the same period in 2009. Just prior to the release of the iPhone 4, over 50 million iPhones had been sold, and statistics from Q4 2010 show that Apple controlled 25% of the smart phone market in the United States (Slashdot, 2011). With the extreme popularity of the iPhone and the increasing number of devices sold, this mobile device has become one of the main focal points of many forensic investigations.

Development community

Apart from sales, the iPhone has an active hacking community, which has yielded research and tools that support forensic investigations. Some of these tools and techniques were originally used to assist with forensic imaging and are currently used for testing in order to better understand the device. Cydia is a popular application used for these purposes. It allows users with a modified phone to download and run iPhone or iPad applications that are not available in the App Store. More specifically, applications can be found here that may allow an examiner to better understand the iPhone file system and other data contents, such as Mobile Terminal. Jailbreaking, or modifying an Apple device, is not suggested, as it is not a forensically sound method; however, having the capability to remotely connect to a test device for educational purposes can be an invaluable learning experience for an examiner.

Another technique that is commonly used on the iPhone is referred to as "unlocking." From 2007 to early 2011, AT&T was the only provider that offered service for the iPhone in the United States. In order to function properly, an AT&T SIM (subscriber identity module) card had to be placed into the device to identify itself on the carrier's network. In February 2011, the iPhone 4 became available through another carrier, Verizon. With the device being so exclusive and only available under these two carriers, many iPhone users search for other options. Unlocking an iPhone is a method that allows the device to be used on alternative networks, and various Apple tutorial sites, such as iClarified, provide steps on how to do this. The process typically involves installing an application, running it, and replacing the AT&T SIM card with that of a different carrier. As Verizon is on the CDMA (code division multiple access) network rather than GSM (global system for mobile communications), its version of the iPhone does not come with a SIM card. For this reason, unlocking the iPhone 4 from Verizon's network is impossible using the current methods. Having said that, the Apple user community will undoubtedly develop an alternative method in the future.

The Apple developer site is another resource that can benefit developers, examiners, or individuals interested in the iOS or OS X environments. Once a registered Apple developer, an individual can download Xcode and the iOS software development kit (SDK) to assist in application development. Included in this development suite are an Xcode integrated development environment (IDE), iOS simulator, and additional tools required for iPhone, iPad, and iPod touch application development.

Once the Xcode and iOS SDK are downloaded, the installer must be run in order to use the tools. Once installed, the tools and files shown in Figure 1.1 can be found in the following path: /Developer/Platforms/iPhoneSimulator.platform

One of the most useful tools within this package is the iOS simulator (as shown in Figure 1.2). This program allows the investigator to select an Apple device and

FIGURE 1.1

iPhone Simulator and Xcode Files.

FIGURE 1.2

iPhone Simulator – Screenshots.

version and use the simulator to test this particular model. For this example, the iPhone running firmware version 4.2 was selected. Among the other options were versions 3.2 (for the iPad) and 4.0.2 and 4.1 (for the iPhone). The software is memory intensive, so one can expect the testing to be a little slow. The simulator starts up with just a few general apps, including Photos, Settings, Game Center, Contacts, and Safari. The user is able to go into these apps, use them as though they were a real device, and even perform additional functions including Toggle In-Call Status Bar, Simulate a Memory Warning, Simulate a Hardware Keyboard, and Lock the device. Lacking from the simulator are some of the more common apps, such as SMS, Calendar, Camera, Notes, and the App Store in order to download additional applications.

The main purpose of the simulator is to be used by application developers in conjunction with Xcode. When Xcode is used to develop an iPhone or iPad application, the code can be tested and run using the simulator on various firmware versions. Testing on the simulator will ensure that the application is performing the way it is expected to.

iPHONE MODELS

The original iPhone 2G was released in the United States in June 2007. Simultaneously, iTunes version 7.3 was also released, which would support synchronization with this device. Subsequent models were released in the following years: the 3G in July 2008, 3G(s) in June 2009, and the iPhone 4 in June 2010.

Table 1.1 iPhone Models

Device	Model	Available iOS Versions
2G	A1203	iOS 1.0
3G	A1241	iOS 2.0
3G(s)	A1303	iOS 3.0
4G	A1332	iOS 4.0

Each device arrives with its own firmware version, which can be found by navigating to Settings > General > About > Version. The purpose of the firmware is to enable certain features, fix bugs or security holes, and assist with the general functioning of the device. Apple will occasionally release new firmware upgrades to resolve some of these issues.

Table 1.1 displays the model number and the initial iOS versions for each device.

In order to identify the device model with the phone powered off, there are a few different things to consider. The first to look for is the model number etched at the back of the casing. Also, the original iPhone had a metal casing, whereas the 3G and 3G(s) had a plastic casing. The 3G(s) has the writings at the back etched in silver to differentiate it from the 3G, which has only the Apple logo in silver. Finally, the iPhone 4 has a unique square design. The corners are less rounded, making it easier to differentiate between the earlier versions. Apple's knowledge base articles can be helpful for this purpose. Details on identifying iPhone models can be found at the following link: http://support.apple.com/kb/HT3939

Table 1.2 shows the specifications and features of each of the models, depending on the storage size (Costello, n.d.).

There were three main differences that separated the 3G from the original iPhone device. One of these features is the addition of the CDMA cellular protocols. W-CDMA is the air interface standard for 3G networks. The intent of adding this protocol was for increased connection speed as well as more efficient support for a greater number of users. The second feature to differentiate the 3G from the 2G is the integrated global positioning system (GPS), which is also found in the 3G(s) and iPhone 4. Finally, the amount of NAND Flash memory increased by a factor of 2 (Semiconductor Insights, n.d.).

iPhone hardware

The iPhone, like most complex electronic devices, is a collection of modules, chips, and other electronic components from many manufacturers. Due to the complex and varied features of the iPhone, the list of hardware is extensive. Table 1.3 consists of a list of many of the components of an iPhone 3G(s), including the manufacturer and model or part number.

The Samsung CPU is an RISC (reduced instruction set computer) processor that runs the core iPhone processes and works in conjunction with the PowerVR

Table 1.2 iPhone Specifications

	iPhone (8 GB/16 GB)	iPhone 3G (8 GB/16 GB)	iPhone 3G(s) (16 GB/32 GB)	iPhone 4 (16 GB/32 GB)
Songs held	2,000/4,000	2,000/4,000	4,000/8,000	4,000/8,000
Screen size	3.5	3.5	3.5	3.5
Resolution	480 × 320	480 × 320	480 × 320	960 × 480
Connectivity	Wi-Fi, GSM, Bluetooth	Wi-Fi, UMTS/ 3G, GSM, Bluetooth	Wi-Fi, UMTS/ 3G, GSM, Bluetooth	Wi-Fi, UMTS/ HSDPA/HSUPA/ 3G, GSM, Bluetooth
Integrated GPS?	No	Yes	Yes	Yes
Support for App Store	With OS 2.0	Yes	Yes	Yes
Camera (Megapixel)	2	2	3	5
Records video?	No	No	Yes	Yes, 720p HD at 30 fps
Weight (in ounces)	4.8	4.7	4.8	4.8
Size (inch)	4.5 × 2.4 × 0.46	4.5 × 2.4 × 0.48	4.5 × 2.4 × 0.48	4.51 × 2.31 × 0.37
Battery life	Talk/Video/ Web: 8/7/6 hours Audio: 24 hours	Talk/Video/ Web: 5/7/5 hours Audio: 24 hours	Talk/Video/ Web: 5/10/9 hours Audio: 30 hours	Talk/Video/Web: 7/10/10 hours Audio: 40 hours
Price (as of Q1 2011)	Discontinued	Discontinued	US$49	US$199/$299

Table 1.3 iPhone 3G(s) Hardware Components

Function	Manufacturer	Model/Part Number
Application processor (CPU)	Samsung	S5L8900B01 – 412 MHz ARM1176Z(F)-S RISC, 128 Mbytes of stacked, package-on package, DDR SDRAM
3D graphic acceleration	Imagination Technologies	Power VR MBX Lite
UMTS power amplifier (PA), duplexer and transmit filter module with output power detector	TriQuint	TQM676031 – Band 1 – HSUPA, TQM666032 – Band 2 – HSUPA, TQM616035 – Band 5/6 – W-CDMA/HSUPA PA-duplexer
UMTS transceiver	Infineon	PMB 6272 GSM/EDGE and W-CDMA, PMB 5701

Table 1.3 iPhone 3G(s) Hardware Components—cont'd

Function	Manufacturer	Model/Part Number
Baseband processor	Infineon	X-Gold 608 (PMB 8878)
Baseband's support memory	Numonyx	PF38F3050M0Y0CE – 16 Mbytes of NOR Flash and 8 Mbytes of psuedo-SRAM
GSM/EDGE quad-band amp	Skyworks	SKY77340 (824- to 915-MHz)
GPS, Wi-Fi, and BT antenna	NXP	OM3805, a variant of PCF50635/33
Communications power management	Infineon	SMARTi Power 3i (SMP3i)
System-level power management	NXP	PCF50633
Battery charger/USB controller	Linear Technology	LTC4088-2
GPS	Infineon	PMB2525 Hammerhead II
NAND Flash	Toshiba	TH58G6D1DTG80 (8 GB NAND Flash)
Serial flash chip	SST	SST25VF080B (1 MB)
Accelerometer	ST Microelectronics	LIS331 DL
Wi-Fi	Marvell	88W8686
Bluetooth	CSR	BlueCore6-ROM
Audio codec	Wolfson	WM6180C
Touch-screen controller	Broadcom	BCM5974
Link display interface	National Semiconductor	LM2512AA Mobile Pixel Link
Touch-screen line driver	Texas Instruments	CD3239

co-processor for graphics acceleration. The CPU is underclocked to 412 MHz (from a possible 667 MHz), presumably to extend battery life. Many of the internal components vary depending on the iPhone model. Semiconductor Insights is a significant resource in understanding the inner workings of many different types of devices. Their device library includes many mobile devices, including the iPhone. A report is completed for each device, which includes a description of the product, details on how to disassemble and reassemble the device, tear down photos, hardware components, and much more (Semiconductor Insights, n.d.).

The baseband is another essential component on the iPhone. The baseband manages all the functions that require an antenna, notably all cellular services. Unlocking the device was mentioned earlier. During this process, the baseband is the part of the device that is hacked in order to allow the iPhone to connect to a different cellular network. There are different baseband versions, which is why the unlocking process must constantly be modified. When a new device comes out, such as the iPhone 4, it will arrive with a different baseband version. The baseband version can be found under Settings > General > About > Modem Firmware, as shown in Figure 1.3.

FIGURE 1.3

Baseband Version – Modem Firmware.

The baseband processor has its own RAM and firmware in NOR Flash, separate from the core resources. It functions as a resource to the main CPU. The Wi-Fi and Bluetooth are managed by the main CPU, although the baseband stores their MAC addresses in its NVRAM.

The images displayed in the next page, courtesy of Semiconductor Insights, were taken after an iPhone 3G(s) was manually dismantled: Figure 1.4 is an image of the top of the device and Figure 1.5 is of the bottom.

FORENSIC EXAMINATION APPROACHES

Similar to any forensic investigation, there are several approaches that can be used for the acquisition and analysis of information. A key aspect of any acquisition, arguably the most important, is that the procedure does not modify the source information in any manner. Or, if it is impossible to eliminate all modifications, which is the case with many live systems or mobile devices, the analyst must detail the changes and the reasons why it was necessary. Unlike traditional computer forensics, in the mobile world you cannot simply remove the hard drive, attach it to a write blocker, image, and finally analyze the data. However, the characteristic of NAND

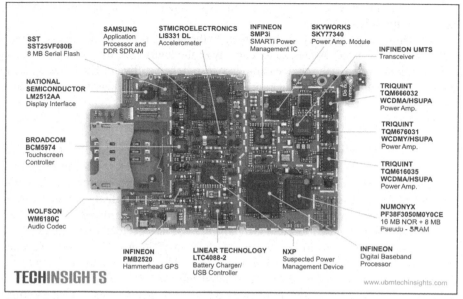

FIGURE 1.4

iPhone Tear-down Image – Top.

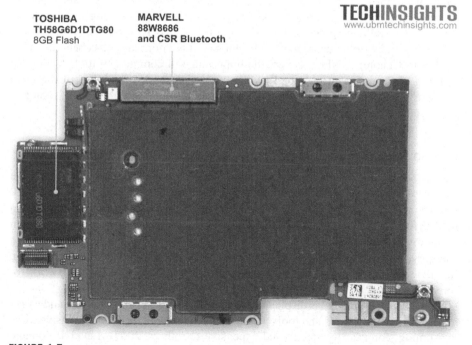

FIGURE 1.5

iPhone Tear-down Image – Bottom.

memory, the primary storage mechanism, is to retain data on the device, which heightens the forensic value.

As mentioned above, any changes made to the device must be thoroughly understood and documented. As an example, many of the logical acquisition tools write a small amount of data to the device in order to install their software. The program then gathers information from the other applications on the device and transports the data over a physical or wireless connection. Understanding what programs or files are being copied to the device as well as where they are being copied to is vital information for a forensic investigation.

The National Institute of Standards and Technology (NIST) has instituted the Computer Forensic Tool Testing Program. The intent of this project is to ensure scientific reliability and validity across the tools used in computer forensic investigations. Many of these tools are used internationally and are relied upon to provide electronic evidence for criminal cases. Since there are no standards set in the field to test the accuracy of these tools and techniques, NIST has decided to define requirements and test assertions to be used in this manner. Dating back to 2008, several different mobile device acquisition tools have been tested and validated. In Chapter 7, these tools will be discussed in detail and it will also be discussed whether each tool has been validated through NIST's Computer Forensic Tool Testing Program (NIST, 2010).

In addition to NIST, viaForensics has also performed independent testing of each tool that supports the iPhone device. This research reviewed techniques and software for retrieving data from an iPhone 3G device. Involved in this testing were the analysis of the installation process, acquisition of the device, reporting capabilities, and finally accuracy of the data recovered. Much of this information has been incorporated into Chapter 7, which covers the importance of commercial tools testing. In addition to the information found in this book, independent rankings of the tools are also provided in the iPhone Forensics white paper, which can be found at http://viaforensics.com/education/white-papers/iphone-forensics/

iPhone leveling

Understanding the various types of mobile acquisition tools and the data they are capable of recovering is paramount for a mobile forensic examiner. A mobile device forensic tool classification system was developed by Sam Brothers, a computer and mobile forensic examiner and researcher, in 2007. The objective of his classification system is to enable an examiner to place cell phone and GPS forensic tools into a category, depending on the extraction methodology of that tool. This categorization facilitates the comparison between different tools and provides a framework for forensic examiners.

The classification tool is displayed in Figure 1.6. Starting at the bottom and working upward, the methods and tools generally become more technical, invasive, time consuming, forensically sound, and expensive (Brothers, 2007). Level 1 (Manual Extraction) involves simply scrolling through the data on the device as any user does

FIGURE 1.6

iPhone Classification Tool.

in a traditional manner. Level 2 (Logical Analysis) is used by most investigators today, as it is only mildly technical and requires little training. Level 3 (Hex Dump) is where many forensic examiners have moved over the last 2–3 years, and it has been gaining quickly in popularity and support in the forensics community. Level 4 (Chip-Off) is the "new frontier" for most examiners, as formal training classes teaching this type of analysis have only just become available. Finally, Level 5 is rarely performed and is not well documented at this time, as it is extremely technical, very expensive, and highly time consuming.

It should be noted that there are pros and cons to performing analysis at each layer. The forensics examiner should be aware of these issues and should only proceed with the level of extraction that he/she has been trained to operate at. Evidence can be permanently destroyed if a given method or tool is not properly utilized. This risk increases the higher you move up in the pyramid. Thus, proper training is critical to obtaining the highest success rate in data extraction and proper forensic analysis of these devices (Brothers, 2007).

Each existing mobile forensic tool can be classified under one (or more) of the five levels. The following text contains a detailed description of each level as well as the methods that are used for data extraction at that given level (Brothers, 2007).

- Level 1 – *Manual Extraction*: A manual extraction involves viewing the data content on the phone directly as viewed on its screen through the use of the device's keypad. The information discovered is manually documented (generally using a digital camera). At this level, it is impossible to recover deleted information. Some tools have been developed that aid an investigator to easily document a manual extraction. These tools capture what is shown on the device, which is then captured digitally for future reference and storage (Brothers, 2007).
- Level 2 – *Logical Extraction*: Connectivity to the mobile device is generally established via a cable to either a piece of forensic hardware or a forensic workstation containing specialized software. The examiner may also choose to use Bluetooth for connectivity instead of a cable. Once connected, the software tool initiates a command to request and then extract allocated files on a given device. As explained by Brothers, the command is initiated by the computer and sent to the device, which

is then interpreted by the processor in the device. Next, the requested data is retrieved from the device's memory and sent back to the forensic workstation to be reviewed by the examiner. Most iPhone forensic tools currently available perform at this level of the classification system, and are described further in Chapter 7. It should also be noted that several of these tools are capable of performing an analysis of iPhone backup files saved on a user's computer (Brothers, 2007). This type of extraction is described further in Chapter 5.

- Level 3 – *Hex Dump*: A hex dump, more commonly referred to as a "physical extraction," provides the investigator with more data than was available at the lower levels. To perform this type of extraction, the device is connected to the forensic workstation generally via a cable. Occasionally, this connection to the computer is either through the device's data port, JTAG (an internal test connection), or even via Wi-Fi. Instead of initiating a command, unsigned code is copied to the device (most commonly into memory), instructing the phone to copy user data to the computer. The resulting data is copied, transferred, and stored as a raw disk image. Since the resulting image is in binary format, technical expertise is required for analysis at this level (Brothers, 2007). The currently available tools that will perform this type of acquisition on an iPhone are discussed in detail in Chapter 5.
- Level 4 – *Chip-Off*: Chip-off refers to the acquisition of data directly from the device's memory chip, which in the case of the iPhone is the NAND Flash memory. The chip is physically removed from the device and data stored on it is extracted by a chip reader. Brothers points out that this type of acquisition is analogous to imaging a hard drive from a computer or laptop using traditional hard disk imaging techniques. As the pyramid describes, this method is much more technically challenging than the manual, logical, or hex dumping acquisition techniques. The amount of required investigator knowledge greatly increases at this level as does the acquisition time. Some of the aspects that make this technique so advanced include the wide variety of chip types used, the myriad of raw binary data formats, and the risk of causing physical damage to the chip during the extraction process (Brothers, 2007).
- Level 5 – *Micro Read*: This process involves manually viewing and interpreting data seen on the memory chip. By analyzing the physical gates on the chip, the examiner can then translate the gate status to 0's and 1's to then determine the resulting ASCII characters. The process is time consuming and costly, and requires extensive knowledge of all aspects of Flash memory and the file system. There are currently no commercial tools available to perform a micro read on an Apple device (Brothers, 2007).

Acquisition types

The following points break down the most commonly used acquisition techniques used on an Apple device. These methods may have some overlap with a couple of the levels discussed in the section on iPhone leveling, but will provide more details on the techniques and how they are used in conjunction with an iPhone.

Backup

One common approach to iPhone forensics is to analyze the backup directory. There is a difference between syncing an iPhone and backing it up. Basically, syncing makes sure that files on your computer and iPhone are in sync and some key information is backed up. On the other hand, a backup will make copies of SMS, Call Logs, Contact, and other application data. For a forensic analyst, the backup information can be very important, especially if he or she does not have access to the iPhone directly.

This procedure for this type of acquisition will read files from the iPhone backup files created through iTunes using Apple's synchronization protocol. The only data that can be acquired using this method are those files that have been explicitly synchronized by the protocol. Backup analysis is beneficial when the device is either unavailable or unable to be imaged for any particular reason.

Many key pieces of information can be retrieved in this way. Common data is stored in SQLite databases and Property List files, which are both supported by the synchronization protocol. Most allocated data or, in other words, data that still remains on the device, can be retrieved through a backup analysis. In addition, by querying the SQLite databases directly, additional data such as deleted SMS, Call Logs, and Contacts can generally be recovered.

Logical

This approach acquires data directly from the iPhone and is preferred over recovering files from the computer the iPhone was synced with. Many of the available commercial tools perform a logical acquisition. However, the forensic analyst must understand how the acquisition occurs, whether the iPhone is modified in any way, and what the procedure is unable to acquire.

Using the logical approach, active files and folders from the iPhone's file system are recovered; however, data contained in unallocated space (or slack space) is not. The following items include some of the common data that can be acquired from a logical acquisition: SMS, Call Logs, Calendar Events, Contacts, Photos, Web history, Synced e-mail accounts, and more. From these files, only data that have not been deleted from the phone can be fully recovered. For certain applications, it is sometimes possible to query the SQLite database file and extract some deleted data. Chapter 3 covers data storage in SQLite database files, and Chapter 6 demonstrates methods of extracting deleted data from these and other files.

Physical

A third method of imaging an iPhone is through a physical acquisition. This process creates a bit-by-bit copy of the file system, similar to the approach taken in most computer forensic investigations. While this approach has the potential for the greatest amount of data recovered (including deleted files), the process is more complicated and requires sophisticated analysis tools and techniques. Any type of data contained on the device can be recovered using this method. Advanced data analysis of the resulting disk image file also has the potential to recover GPS coordinates, cell tower locations, and even deleted text and multimedia messages.

Many times, the metadata extracted from various files can be pieced together in order to produce additional results. An example of this might be to compare the timestamps recovered from a photo taken on the device with the timestamps of an SMS record in order to show which recipient a photo may have been sent to. While this sort of analysis is also possible using information from a backup or logical acquisition, there is greater potential using a physical image since much more data is recovered with this technique.

Nontraditional

There are also some less common, and somewhat controversial, methods that allow an investigator to extract data from an Apple device which otherwise may not be able to be acquired. These methods involve modifying the firmware on the device in order to allow greater functionality.

Jailbreaking is one of these techniques. To jailbreak a device, the firmware partition is replaced with a hacked version. The hacked firmware partition contains an installer package that allows the user to download tools and other programs that are normally not available through the App Store. Apple took the stance that this technique would cause an increase in piracy as well as technical support costs for the company (Moren, 2010). For this reason, any device that has been jailbroken is no longer covered through Apple's manufacturer's warranty and, up until early 2010, was actually illegal.

NOTE

Jailbreaking

Jailbreaking an Apple device replaces the firmware partition with a hacked version, allowing the user to download software that is not explicitly available through the App Store. Jailbreaking also voids the manufacturer's warranty on the device.

The Digital Millennium Copyright Act (DMCA) has supported companies like Apple through the contained section regarding anti-circumvention of technology. Created in 1998, the DMCA includes a section on "Circumvention of Technological Protection Measures." This portion of the document states that circumvention of technology that has been copyrighted is prohibited. Since jailbreaking an Apple device bypasses the standard firmware partition and modifies it to allow increased flexibility on the device, this technique was not exempt from the DMCA for several years (United States Copyright Office, 1998). Every three years, the DMCA is measured and reviewed in order to determine whether specific technologies still apply. With the most recent review, the Library of Congress declared that jailbreaking an Apple device is exempt from the DMCA. This ruling does not force Apple to cover jailbroken devices under the manufacturer's warranty; it simply means that individuals who may decide to modify their device in this manner will not be criminally prosecuted. In addition, any software downloaded on the device must be legally acquired; therefore, pirated software is still illegal under this act (Moren, 2010).

While this book will not delve into the process of jailbreaking any type of Apple device, it should be pointed out that there are methods available for just about any model and firmware version on the market. The Apple hacking community is continually developing new tools and techniques that allow users to have a better control over their device. In fact, recent apps have been released that allow even the Apple TV to be jailbroken. Using this method, an individual can even run applications such as the XBox Media Center on their Apple TV.

As an investigator, working with a jailbroken device for testing purposes can be a highly educational experience. There are applications available, such as Mobile Terminal and OpenSSH, that allow an individual to remotely connect to the device using commonly known commands such as "ssh" or "ftp." Once connected, the examiner has the capability to browse through the entire file system and understand the variety of files contained on the device. The directory structure is similar to what would be seen in a resulting disk image file after performing a physical acquisition; however, the structure is not exactly the same. Individual files or even the entire file system can be copied from the device to a forensic workstation using these same methods. Chapter 5 guides the examiner through an acquisition of the iPhone's raw disk image using a jailbroken device. Unfortunately, however, hard disk encryption is an issue when trying to acquire the raw disk image through this method on the 3G(s) and iPhone 4.

Forensics with Linux

While many of the commercial tools have been developed for Windows or Mac environments, the Linux platform deserves its own section, as it contains extremely powerful tools that can assist in a forensic investigation. Throughout the book, various hands-on exercises are performed to demonstrate to the user how a certain program or process is run. For example, forensic acquisitions are performed as well as various forensic tools run through a command prompt. Some tools make sense to run on a Mac workstation, while others are better performed on a Linux machine. Depending on the exercise, we will be jumping back and forth between operating systems, so be sure to note which platform is being used prior to following along. If you do not have a Linux or Macintosh workstation available, consider using a virtual machine to simulate the environment (building a Linux virtual machine is covered later in this section).

Introduction to Linux

In order to understand the Linux tools that will be used in Chapter 6, it is important to have an understanding of the Linux operating system as well as some of the basic commands. Linux was originally created by Linus Torvalds, a young student from Finland. The first version of the Linux Kernel (v1.0) was released in 1994, with the latest running version being 2.6. One of the more interesting aspects of the Linux kernel is that it was developed under the GNU General Public License. This means that the source code is freely distributed and available to the general public for use.

In Linux, all files are part of the same file structure, as opposed to a Windows environment, which has separate drives (C:/ - hard disk, D:/ - CD-ROM, etc.). If a user connects a hard drive and a USB drive to a Linux workstation, they will all be part of the same folder structure as shown in the following text:

```
kstrzempka@linux-001:/$ tree -L 1 /
/
├── bin
├── boot
├── cdrom
├── dev
├── etc
├── home
├── lib
├── lib32
├── lib64 -> /lib
├── lost+found
├── media
├── mnt
├── opt
├── proc
├── root
├── sbin
├── selinux
├── srv
├── sys
├── tmp
├── usr
├── var
```

In the above code, the "/" signifies the root of the file system. The following describes some of the folders in the root directories and the types of files they might contain:

- /etc: Configuration files for software that was downloaded and installed on the system.
- /home/<users>: Within the home directory, there will be a folder for each of the users on the system. Each user's files will then be stored within his or her particular folder.
- /dev: External devices that have been connected to the machine are listed here. Any SATA/SCSI devices connected over USB or firewire are listed as "/dev/sda," "/dev/sdb," etc. They are assigned letters in the order in which they are connected to the machine.
- /var: System log files are stored here.

For each folder or file on a Linux workstation, file permissions are shown for three different types of users: the owner, a group, and the world (others). They are listed as either "r" (read), "w" (write), or "x" (execute). In the following example, the user has read and write permissions, while the group and other have read-only. The "-" at the very beginning of each line signifies that the object is a file. If it were a directory, there would be a "d" in place of the hyphen, or an "l" if it were a link to another file or directory.

```
kstrzempka@linux-001:~/Desktop/book-screenshots$ ls -l
total 84
-rw-r--r-- 1 kstrzempka kstrzempka 24655 2010-12-15 17:38
iPhone-connected-DFU.png
-rw-r--r-- 1 kstrzempka kstrzempka 26203 2010-12-15 17:37
linux-iphone-normal.png
-rw-r--r-- 1 kstrzempka kstrzempka 27311 2010-12-17 15:15
nano-hosts-file.png
```

Various commands can be used to modify permissions on a file or folder. To change permissions, it is important to understand the numerical (or "octal") value for read, write, and execute assignments. Permissions are calculated based on the following values:

- Read = 4
- Write = 2
- Execute = 1

So, if a user, group, or other is assigned a "7," they would have read, write, and execute permissions. The command to modify permissions as well as a few examples are shown in the "Basic Linux commands" section.

Basic Linux commands

The following sections provide a breakdown of some of the common Linux commands including a description of the command, its general usage, and one or more examples of how the command can be applied. For a reference guide, see Appendix X: Linux Cheat Sheet.

- ***man** Description*: Pulls up online manuals for the requested command in the terminal window. Within the manual will be a detailed description of the command as well as its usage (including all of the options or "flags" for that command).

```
$ man [-][-k keywords] commands
```

In the following examples, the first command lists information on the "mount" command, while the second searches all manuals containing the characters "zip":

```
$ man mount
MOUNT(8)            Linux Programmer's Manual            MOUNT(8)

NAME
       mount - mount a filesystem
```

SYNOPSIS
    mount [-lhV]

    mount -a [-fFnrsvw] [-t vfstype] [-O optlist]

    mount [-fnrsvw] [-o option[,option]...] device|dir

    mount [-fnrsvw] [-t vfstype] [-o options] device dir

DESCRIPTION
    All files accessible in a Unix system are arranged in one big tree,
    the file hierarchy, rooted at /. These files can be spread out over
    seva eral devices. The mount command serves to attach the filesystem
    found on some device to the big file tree. Conversely, the umount(8)
    command will detach it again.

    The standard form of the mount command is
<snip>

$ man -k zip

Archive::Any::Plugin::Zip (3pm) - Archive::Any wrapper around
Archive::Zip
Archive::Zip (3pm)   - Provide an interface to ZIP archive files.
Archive::Zip::FAQ (3pm) - Answers to a few frequently asked questions
about Archive::Zip
Archive::Zip::MemberRead (3pm) - A wrapper that lets you read Zip
archive members as if they were files.
Archive::Zip::Tree (3pm) - (DEPRECATED) methods for adding/extract-
ing trees using Archive::Zip
bunzip2 (1)   - a block-sorting file compressor, v1.0.4
bzcmp (1)   - compare bzip2 compressed files
bzdiff (1)   - compare bzip2 compressed files
bzegrep (1)   - search possibly bzip2 compressed files for a regular expression
bzfgrep (1)   - search possibly bzip2 compressed files for a regular expression
bzgrep (1)   - search possibly bzip2 compressed files for a
regular expression
bzip2 (1)   - a block-sorting file compressor, v1.0.4
bzip2recover (1)   - recovers data from damaged bzip2 files
bzless (1)   - file perusal filter for crt viewing of bzip2
compressed text
bzmore (1)   - file perusal filter for crt viewing of bzip2
compressed text
funzip (1)   - filter for extracting from a ZIP archive in a pipe
gpg-zip (1)   - encrypt or sign files into an archive
gunzip (1)   - compress or expand files
gzip (1)   - compress or expand files
Image::ExifTool::ZIP (3pm) - Read ZIP archive meta information
lz (1)   - gunzips and shows a listing of a gzip'd tar'd
archive

```
mzip (1)              - change protection mode and eject disk on Zip/Jaz
drive
prezip-bin (1)        - prefix zip delta word list compressor/
decompressor
tgz (1)               - makes a gzip'd tar archive
unzip (1)             - list, test and extract compressed files in a ZIP
archive
unzipsfx (1)          - self-extracting stub for prepending to ZIP
archives
uz (1)                - gunzips and extracts a gzip'd tar'd archive
zforce (1)            - force a '.gz' extension on all gzip files
zip (1)               - package and compress (archive) files
zipcloak (1)          - encrypt entries in a zipfile
zipgrep (1)           - search files in a ZIP archive for lines matching a
pattern
zipinfo (1)           - list detailed information about a ZIP archive
zipnote (1)           - write the comments in zipfile to stdout, edit
comments and rename files in zipfile
zipsplit (1)          - split a zipfile into smaller zipfiles
```

- **help** *Description*: Displays information on the requested command, including usage and examples, similar to "man." Some commands use the - -help notation, while others simply use -h or -help.

```
$ mount --help

Usage: mount -V              : print version
       mount -h              : print this help
       mount                 : list mounted filesystems
       mount -l              : idem, including volume labels
So far the informational part. Next the mounting.
The command is 'mount [-t fstype] something somewhere'.
Details found in /etc/fstab may be omitted.
       mount -a [-t|-O]...   : mount all stuff from /etc/fstab
       mount device          : mount device at the known place
       mount directory       : mount known device here
       mount -t type dev dir : ordinary mount command
Note that one does not really mount a device, one mounts a filesystem
(of the given type) found on the device.
One can also mount an already visible directory tree elsewhere:
       mount --bind olddir newdir
or move a subtree:
       mount --move olddir newdir
One can change the type of mount containing the directory dir:
       mount --make-shared dir
       mount --make-slave dir
       mount --make-private dir
       mount --make-unbindable dir
One can change the type of all the mounts in a mount subtree
```

```
containing the directory dir:
     mount --make-rshared dir
     mount --make-rslave dir
     mount --make-rprivate dir
     mount --make-runbindable dir
A device can be given by name, say /dev/hda1 or /dev/cdrom, or by label,
using -L label or by uuid, using -U uuid.
Other options: [-nfFrsvw] [-o options] [-p passwdfd].
For many more details, say man 8 mount .
```

- ***cd*** *Description*: This command is used to change into another directory. In Linux, the special character "~" is used to represent the current user's home directory. For example, the user kstrzempka has a home directory on a Linux system at /home/ kstrzempka. From anywhere in the file system, you can use ~ to refer to /home/ kstrzempka. This works well for documentation, so throughout this book we refer to ~ and, even if you have set up a different user name, the command will still function as expected.

```
$ cd ~                    (changes into the user's home directory
from anywhere)
$ cd                      (changes into the user's home directory
from anywhere)
$ cd ~/Desktop/Projects  (changes into the "Projects" folder
located on the user's Desktop)
$ cd ..                   (changes directories up 1 level (back into
"Desktop")
$ cd ../../               (changes directories up 2 levels)
$ cd /                    (changes into the root file system folder
from anywhere)
```

- ***mkdir*** *Description*: Creates a directory in the current location, unless otherwise specified.

```
$ mkdir iPhone           (creates the "iPhone" folder in the cur-
rent directory)
$ mkdir -p ~/iPhone/Forensics/Book (creates the full path of
directories even if top levels do not exist)
```

- ***rmdir/rm*** *Description*: Removes existing directories or files based on the flags specified. The "rmdir" command will only remove empty folders. If there are files within the directory, these will first need to be removed prior to running the "rmdir" command. The "rm" command can be used to remove both files and folders and will prompt the user prior to removing. You can override the prompt with the -f option, but use with caution.

```
$ rmdir Linux                        (removes only an empty folder)
$ rmdir -p /Linux/Forensics/Book  (removes each folder within the
specified path)
$ rm -r Linux                        (removes the specified folder
and all of its contents)
```

```
$ rm -rf Linux                    (removes the specified folder
and all of its contents without prompting)
$ rm test.txt                     (deletes the specified file)
$ rm *.txt                        (deletes all .txt files within
the current directory)
$ rm *                            (deletes all files within the
current directory)
```

- *pico/nano Description*: Both pico and nano are CLI text editors that allow the creation and modification of text files. These commands must be run within the directory in which the user wishes to save the file. Pico will be used for this example, but nano is run the same way. To create a file, simply type the command.

```
$ pico
```

Typing "pico" will open the text editor within the CLI, allowing the user to enter whatever text he or she wishes (see Figure 1.7).

When the text has been entered, pressing "Ctrl+X" will "exit" the text editor and allow the user to save. As shown in Figure 1.7, this particular file was saved as "Test" and, upon hitting enter, was saved in the user's current directory.

To modify an already existing file, simply follow the command with the file name or full path and file name if the file is in a different directory:

```
$ pico existing-file.txt
```

FIGURE 1.7

Create File using "pico."

- *ls Description*: Lists files and folders. The "ls" command without any options specified will list the file/folder names only in the current directory. Adding the "-lh" options will provide a long listing with more details on the file, including permissions, ownership, size, and date and timestamps.

```
kstrzempka@linux-001:~/Desktop/book-screenshots$ ls
iPhone-connected-DFU.png  linux-iphone-normal.png  nano-hosts-
file.png

kstrzempka@linux-001:~/Desktop/book-screenshots$ ls -lh
total 84K
-rw-r--r-- 1 kstrzempka kstrzempka 25K 2010-12-15 17:38
iPhone-connected-DFU.png
-rw-r--r-- 1 kstrzempka kstrzempka 26K 2010-12-15 17:37
linux-iphone-normal.png
-rw-r--r-- 1 kstrzempka kstrzempka 27K 2010-12-17 15:15
nano-hosts-file.png
```

- *tree Description*: Shows the hierarchy of folders for the directory specified. If no parameters are specified, the current directory will be used. In Linux, the current directory is referred to as a single "." while one directory up is a double period "..". In the following output, the current directory is used, which happens to be the current user's home directory. The user can specify how many directory levels he or she wishes to view with the "-L" flag. In the first example, one level is shown, whereas in the second example, two levels of the source directory and files are shown. One must not forget that all the details of a command can be learnt by examining the man page (man tree) or specifying the command's help parameter (tree --help).

```
kstrzempka@linux-001:~$ tree -L 1
.
├── Desktop
├── Documents
├── Downloads
├── mnt
├── Music
├── Pictures
├── Public
├── sleuthkit-3.1.2
├── Templates
├── Ubuntu One
└── Videos

kstrzempka@linux-001:~$ tree -L 2 Desktop/
Desktop/
├── AutomatedTools
│   ├── Linux
│   ├── OSX
│   ├── README
│   └── README.Multiplatform
```

```
├── book-screenshots
│   ├── iPhone-connected-DFU.png
│   ├── linux-iphone-normal.png
│   └── nano-hosts-file.png
├── Directions for viewing recovered iPhone data.pdf
├── command-output
│   ├── 19691231.1910
│   ├── 19691231.1920
│   ├── 19700105.1955
│   ├── 20100817.1145
│   ├── 20100817.1149
│   ├── 20100903.1146
│   ├── 20100907.1118
│   ├── 20100907.1126
│   ├── 20100909.1034
│   └── 20100919.1031
├── iPhoneapp-mount
├── keychain.png
├── Photos.sqlite
├── plutil.pl
├── python-var-int.png
└── WXP-PRO-OEM.iso
```

- ***less*** Description: Displays specified text one page at a time. This command is commonly used in conjunction with other commands to show output one page at a time. The following command will display the contents of "large-document.pdf" one screen at a time within the terminal window:

  ```
  $ less large-document.pdf
  ```

Once you are in the less utility, there are a few key commands to remember.

- h: access help menu
- q: quit help menu
- spacebar: display one screen/page down
- b: display one screen/page up
- /: search for a pattern
- Enter: move one line down
- y: move one line up

There are many more commands and tricks to this powerful utility, so read the help screens, man page, or simply search the Internet for more helpful tips.

- ***cat*** Description: Outputs the contents of a file to the screen or to a new file if specified (without retaining the format of the file).

  ```
  kstrzempka@linux-001:~/Desktop$ cat textfile.txt
  iphone forensics is so much fun.

  This file contains unnecessary information used to display the
  workings of the "cat" command.
  ```

The "cat" command can be used in conjunction with "less" in order to display the contents of a file one page at a time.

This command can also be used to combine files into one (i.e., for split forensic images). This is often referred to as concatenating files.

```
$ cat file1.txt file2.txt file3.txt > final.txt
```

- *find Description*: Used to search for files in a directory hierarchy. The following command will list all of the files, including the full path, contained on the specified user's desktop:

```
$ find /home/kstrzempka/Desktop
```

The find command can also be used in combination with another command. For example, the following will run the "md5sum" command on the files from the "find" command:

```
$ find . -type f -exec md5sum {} \; > ~/md5.txt
```

In this example, the command instructs the computer to find a regular file (-type f) in the current directory (".") and execute (-exec) the strings command on all files found ({}). The "\;" signifies the end of the -exec command. It then takes that output and redirects it (>) to "md5.txt" in the user's home directory (Grundy, 2008).

If one runs a command against the results of a large number of files, one can run into issues. In those cases, one should research piping the output of the file command to a utility called xargs.

- *chmod Description*: Short for "change mode," this command changes file or folder permissions, as described in the previous section. Many examples are provided in the following text. Note that these commands must either be run in the directory in which "textfile.txt" is stored, or the full path to the file must be provided.

```
*Provides details on the file permissions for "textfile.txt"
kstrzempka@linux-001:~/Desktop$ ls -l textfile.txt
-rw-r--r-- 1 kstrzempka kstrzempka 264 2011-03-01 12:17 text-
file.txt
```

```
*Gives read, write, and execute permissions for the owner, and read
and execute permissions for group and world.
kstrzempka@linux-001:~/Desktop$ chmod 755 textfile.txt

kstrzempka@linux-001:~/Desktop$ ls -l textfile.txt
-rwxr-xr-x 1 kstrzempka kstrzempka 264 2011-03-01 12:17 text-
file.txt
```

```
*Gives read, write and execute permissions for the owner, and exe-
cute permissions for group and world.
kstrzempka@linux-001:~/Desktop$ chmod 711 textfile.txt

kstrzempka@linux-001:~/Desktop$ ls -l textfile.txt
-rwx--x--x 1 kstrzempka kstrzempka 264 2011-03-01 12:17 text-
file.txt
```

```
*Gives read, write and execute permissions for the owner, and read-
only permissions for group and world.
    kstrzempka@linux-001:~/Desktop$ chmod 744 textfile.txt

    kstrzempka@linux-001:~/Desktop$ ls -l textfile.txt
    -rwxr--r-- 1 kstrzempka kstrzempka 264 2011-03-01 12:17 text-
    file.txt
```

The "chmod" command can also be run on a group of files or a folder.

```
$ chmod 755 *        (Changes permissions of all files in the current
directory)
$ chmod 444 Files/ (Changes permissions of the "Files" directory and
all of the files within it)
```

- **chown** *Description*: Changes the owner or group of a specified file. In the following example, the original owner and group of "textfile.txt" was kstrzempka. The chown command changed the owner to "root." This command required "sudo" (see description for sudo command).

```
    kstrzempka@linux-001:~/Desktop$ ls -l textfile.txt
    -rwxr--r-- 1 kstrzempka kstrzempka 264 2011-03-01 12:17 textfile.txt

    kstrzempka@linux-001:~/Desktop$ sudo chown root textfile.txt
    [sudo] password for kstrzempka:

    kstrzempka@linux-001:~/Desktop$ ls -l textfile.txt
     rwxr--r-- 1 root kstrzempka 264 2011-03-01 12:17 textfile.txt
```

- **sudo** *Description*: Running a command with "sudo" in front of it gives the user elevated permissions, allowing him or her to run a command as a super user or another user. Sudo is required to run certain commands such as apt-get (to install software), chown (to change ownership), and many other commands depending on the files it must access. To use sudo, it is simply added at the beginning of a command and it requires the user to enter his/her password.

```
    $ sudo apt-get install hexedit
    [sudo] password for viaForensics:
```

- **apt-get** *Description*: The "apt" part of the apt-get command stands for Advanced Packaging Tool (APT) and allows the user to install and uninstall software, upgrade existing software, or even perform system updates. To successfully run this command, sudo is required.

```
    $ sudo apt-get install scalpel          (Installs scalpel software
    package)
    [sudo] password for viaForensics:

    $ sudo apt-get remove scalpel           (Uninstalls scalpel
    software package)
    [sudo] password for viaForensics:
```

```
$ sudo apt-get update                (Updates the APT package
index, which stores packages available for download)
[sudo] password for viaForensics:

$ sudo apt-get upgrade               (Upgrades APT package
versions, including security updates; must be run AFTER update)
[sudo] password for viaForensics:
```

- *grep Description*: Searches through a file or a list of files and folders for a specified phrase. It is equivalent to opening a document and doing a "find" for a certain phrase. The search is case sensitive, so if the user is unsure of whether a letter should be capitalized or lower cased, he or she must specify the "-i" (case insensitive) flag. This option will take longer, depending on the size of the file that is being searched. The general usage is:

```
$ grep keyword file.doc
```

The following contains several examples of the usage of "grep:"

```
$ grep Forensics iPhoneBook.txt         (will search for "forensics"
in the specified file)
$ grep -i forensics iPhoneBook.txt      (will search for forensics,
case insensitive, in the specified file)
$ grep "Katie Strzempka" iPhoneBook.txt  (will search the specified
file for "Katie Strzempka", case sensitive)
```

The next command searches the contents of all files on the user's desktop for the word "unnecessary." The results shown indicate that this word was found in "textfile.txt," and there are matches for this word in "WXP-PRO-OEM.iso" also. Because this is a binary file, further techniques will need to be used to make the content viewable.

```
kstrzempka@linux-wks-001:~/Desktop$ grep unnecessary *
textfile.txt:This file contains unnecessary information used to
display the workings of the "cat" command.
Binary file WXP-PRO-OEM.iso matches
```

- *Piping and redirecting files (| and >) Description*: The pipe character "|" (located above the "Enter" key on most keyboards) allows the output of one command to be sent to another for further processing. Output can also be redirected into another file using ">".

The following command takes the results of "cat file.txt" and pipes it to the "less" command, allowing the user to view the contents one page at a time.

```
$ cat file.txt|less
```

The next searches for "iPhone" in "book.txt" (using the grep command), then it takes the results and searches again for "iOS." The final results are then piped through "less" to be displayed one page at a time.

```
$ grep iPhone book.txt|grep iOS|less
```

Redirecting output from a command can also be helpful. The following command takes the output of book.txt (using the cat command) and copies the output into a file called "newdocument.txt" on the user's desktop:

```
cat book.txt > ~/Desktop/newdocument.txt
```

Redirection can be very helpful when running the "strings" command on a particular file, or an entire disk image. This very example is shown in detail in Chapter 6 – Data and Application Analysis ("Strings" section).

- ***xxd*** *Description*: This tool generates a hex dump of a provided file or disk image. It allows an examiner to view these files in hex format, jump to a specific offset, or even search the file for data. There are other hex editors that can also be used for this purpose; however, xxd is standard within a Linux build. The general usage is as follows:

```
$ xxd diskimage.dmg
$ xxd sms.db
$ xxd calendar.sqlitedb
```

The following command displays the Photos.sqlite file from an iPhone file system using xxd. When using xxd, it is better to either pipe it through "less" and view one page at a time, or redirect the output to another file for viewing, as there is a significant amount of data when using this command.

```
kstrzempka@linux-wks-001:~$ xxd ~/Desktop/Photos.sqlite|less
0000000: 5351 4c69 7465 2066 6f72 6d61 7420 3300  SQLite format 3.
0000010: 1000 0101 0040 2020 0000 003f 0000 0000  .....@...?....
0000020: 0000 0028 0000 0002 0000 000c 0000 0001  ...(.........
0000030: 0000 0000 0000 0000 0000 0001 0000 0000  .............
0000040: 0000 0000 0000 0000 0000 0000 0000 0000  .............
0000050: 0000 0000 0000 0000 0000 0000 0000 0000  .............
0000060: 0000 0000 0d00 0000 0d07 f400 0f12 0ec0  .............
0000070: 0dfa 0d5c 0cc7 0b7f 0b17 0a64 09cc 0945  ...\.......d...E
0000080: 08d6 085b 07f4 0000 0000 0000 0000 0000  ...[.........
```

At the beginning of a disk image, database, or other type of file, there are oftentimes a lot of zeros (in other words, no data). The "-a," or autoskip option, will jump straight to the section of the file that contains actual data:

```
kstrzempka@linux-wks-001:~$ xxd -a ~/Desktop/Photos.sqlite|less

0000000: 5351 4c69 7465 2066 6f72 6d61 7420 3300  SQLite format 3.
0000010: 1000 0101 0040 2020 0000 003f 0000 0000  .....@...?....
0000020: 0000 0028 0000 0002 0000 000c 0000 0001  ...(.........
0000030: 0000 0000 0000 0000 0000 0001 0000 0000  .............
0000040: 0000 0000 0000 0000 0000 0000 0000 0000  .............
0000050: 0000 0000 0000 0000 0000 0000 0000 0000  .............
0000060: 0000 0000 0d00 0000 0d07 f400 0f12 0ec0  .............
0000070: 0dfa 0d5c 0cc7 0b7f 0b17 0a64 09cc 0945  ...\.......d...E
```

```
0000080: 08d6 085b 07f4 0000 0000 0000 0000 0000  ...[..........
0000090: 0000 0000 0000 0000 0000 0000 0000 0000  ..............
*
00007f0: 0000 0000 650d 0717 391b 0181 0369 6e64 ....e...9....ind
0000800: 6578 476c 6f62 616c 7349 6465 6e74 6966 exGlobalsIdentif
0000810: 6965 7249 6e64 6578 476c 6f62 616c 730e ierIndexGlobals.
0000820: 4352 4541 5445 2049 4e44 4558 2047 6c6f CREATE INDEX Glo
0000830: 6261 6c73 4964 656e 7469 6669 6572 496e balsIdentifierIn
```

If you really want to get crazy, you can also use the "-b" option to view the image in binary!

```
kstrzempka@linux-wks-001:~$ xxd -b iPhone.dmg|less

05843f4: 00000000 01100001 00000000 01110000 00000000 01110000  .a.p.p
05843fa: 00000000 01101100 00000000 01100101 00000000 00101110  .l.e..
0584400: 00000000 01101101 00000000 01101111 00000000 01100010  .m.o.b
0584406: 00000000 01101001 00000000 01101100 00000000 01100101 .i.l.e
058440c: 00000000 01101001 00000000 01110000 00000000 01101111 .i.p.o
```

Having the ability to view a file or, better yet, a disk image, gives the examiner a significant amount of power. This option is further explored in Chapter 6 within the "Advanced Forensic Analysis" section.

Setting up a Linux virtual machine

In order to install and run the tools listed in the previous section, an examiner must have access to a Linux workstation. It is realized that access to this type of physical machine is not always available. For this reason, it is important to point out that Linux can be run in a virtual environment. In this section, the process of setting up a Linux virtual machine (VM) will be covered.

For this example, VirtualBox is going to be used. VirtualBox is now owned by Oracle and has a free license for academic and personal use. If you are using Virtual-Box for commercial work, please ensure you follow all licensing guidelines.

VirtualBox can be downloaded for many operating systems including Microsoft Windows, Mac OS X, and Linux (2.4 and 2.6) at http://www.virtualbox.org/. After VirtualBox has been installed, one will see the Oracle VM VirtualBox manager shown in Figure 1.8, where one can create and manage new virtual machines.

When creating the new VM, one must make sure that one has enough hard drive space (at least 20 GB is recommended) and as much RAM as can be spared.

Using the VirtualBox Manager GUI to create the new VM is straightforward. However, if one has access to an Ubuntu Linux 64-bit workstation or server but not the ability to run desktop applications, here are the steps one can follow to set up, configure, and run the new VM (Virtual Box 3.2.10).

From an SSH session, it is best to use the program screen so that if connection to the server is lost, one's VM remains active. Then, these steps are to be followed:

```
mkdir -p ~/vbox
cd ~/vbox
```

```
wget    http://ubuntu.mirrors.pair.com/releases/maverick/ubuntu-
10.10-desktop-amd64.iso

VBoxManage createvm -name iphone-book-vm -ostype Ubuntu -register

VBoxManage modifyvm iphone-book-vm --memory 1536 --acpi on --boot1 dvd \
--nic1 bridged --usb on --usbehci on --vrdp on --vrdpport 3392 \
--clipboard bidirectional --pae on --hwvirtex on --hwvirtexexcl
on --vtxvpid on \
--nestedpaging on --largepages on

VBoxManage modifyvm iphone-book-vm --bridgeadapter1 eth0

VBoxManage storagectl iphone-book-vm --name "IDE Controller" -add ide

VBoxManage createvdi --filename ~/vbox/iphone-book-vm.vdi \
--size 20000 --register

VBoxManage storageattach iphone-book-vm --storagectl "IDE Controller" \
--port 0 --device 0 --type hdd --medium ~/vbox/iphone-book-vm.vdi

VBoxManage storageattach iphone-book-vm --storagectl "IDE
Controller" \
--port 1 --device 0 --type dvddrive --medium ~/vbox/ubuntu-10.10-
desktop-i386.iso

VBoxHeadless -startvm iphone-book-vm -p 3392 &
```

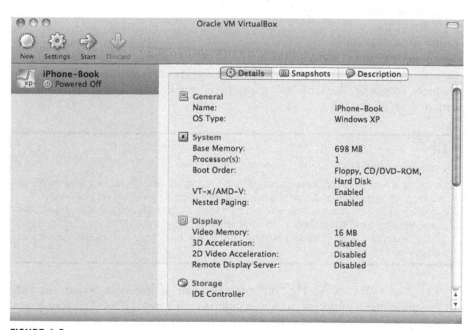

FIGURE 1.8

Oracle VM VirtualBox.

```
#need to eject DVD, the restart
VBoxManage storageattach iphone-book-vm --storagectl "IDE
Controller" --port 1 \
--device 0 --type dvddrive --medium none

#restart the virtual machine
VBoxHeadless -startvm iphone-book-vm -p 3392
```

At this point, the VM will start up and one can access the install using any remote desktop protocol (RDP) viewer such as Remote Desktop Connection on Windows, rdesktop on Linux, or Microsoft's Remote Desktop Connection Client for Mac. To access the above session, one would have to connect to <host server's IP:3392>. From there, the install is followed until it is time to reboot.

If you shutdown or the reboot ends the VBoxHeadless session, you can simply issue the command again to start the server backup. Then, RDP back into the machine and install openssh-server, so we can use ssh instead of the less efficient RDP:

```
sudo apt-get install openssh-server
```

Now, the VM's IP address can be found by running ifconfig and looking at the "inet addr" for eth0. One can use one's favorite ssh program (if on Windows, Putty can be tried for a great, free client) and ssh into the virtual machine. At this point, one can download and install any of the forensic tools listed in the previous section. Details on how to install and compile some of these programs, such as scalpel or time-line, can be found in Chapter 6.

Linux forensics tools
There are a number of free, open-source Linux tools that can be used during the forensic examination process. Most of these tools are covered in more detail in later chapters, including Chapter 5 on "Acquisitions" and Chapter 6 on "Data and Application Analysis."

TIP

Linux Forensics Tools

The use of advanced Linux forensic analysis tools can help an examiner locate crucial evidence in a more efficient manner. Some of these tools are extremely powerful and provide the capability to quickly index, search, and extract certain types of files. The Linux Leo website (http://linuxleo.com/) was created as an introduction to Linux for law enforcement officers and forensic examiners. It provides details on the use of the forensic tools discussed in this book as well as many others.

• *Creating a disk image*: The "dd" command can be used on a device where the examiner has root access, such as a jailbroken iPhone or iPad. This tool is generally used in forensics to acquire a full disk image of a hard drive, SD card, USB flash drive, or other device. Usage of the dd program on a jailbroken iPhone is described in Chapter 5.

- *Image verification*: In digital forensics, examinations are performed on the original media only if absolutely necessary. In most cases, a forensic copy is made of the device, and the examiner will analyze that image, so as to not modify the original media. In order to show that the working copy contains the same data as the original, it has become a best practice to create a unique signature for both the original and the copy by using a hash algorithm. If the values match, this technique shows that the forensic image is in fact a copy of the original. Most commercial tools will report either an MD5 or SHA1 hash value, two different algorithms, both of which are used for the same purpose. Linux commands can also be used to determine either of these values on an image or file.

- *Mounting and unmounting a disk image*: In order to view the contents of a file system on a mobile device, the image must be "mounted." Mounting a file system tells the operating system where in the directory tree the files on the device should appear. If a USB drive or other external device is connected to a computer, more often than not the computer will automatically mount the file system on these drives in order to allow the user to navigate through the files. In forensics, examiners are typically dealing with a disk image file rather than a physical device. Depending on the operating system used on the forensic workstation, various methods can be used to mount this image and view the files. Details relevant to mounting an iOS device image are covered in Chapter 6.

- *File carving*: This process scans an entire disk for specified file signatures in order to recover files or file fragments from the disk. Using this method, both deleted and undeleted files can be recovered since the process focuses on the content of the files rather than its metadata. This is a popular technique used in forensic examinations, as it has been largely successful in recovering deleted photos, e-mails, text messages, and other important data. File carving techniques are built into some forensic analysis tools; however, there are open-source Linux tools available that will perform this action as well. These tools can be run via command line against an iPhone, iPad, or other iOS device image in order to recover valuable files.

- *Creating a timeline of events*: There are a couple of tools available that are run against a disk image and will list out each and every file within the file system, both allocated and unallocated. From this list, the tool creates a timeline of events that have occurred on the device. This process is typically run against a hard drive, but can also be used on an iPhone, iPad, or another iOS's image file. The resulting timeline will show the file name, whether it was created, modified, or accessed, the date and time this event occurred, and other pieces of information that might be significant to an investigation. There are thousands, and sometimes hundreds of thousands of files on these devices, so having the ability to sort by time is an important step in this process. Timelines are typically the most useful when an investigator has a specific time frame to narrow down the choices. A couple of tools capable of creating the original file listing include The Sleuth Kit's "fls" tool by Brian Carrier and log2timeline by Kristinn Gudjonsson. Another tool within The Sleuth Kit, "mactime," then takes this file listing and creates a timeline from it.

- *Searching a disk image*: Once a physical image of a device is acquired, there are various tools that can be used to further analyze that image and search for specific keywords or other data. One of these methods involves the use of the Linux "strings" command. When run against a file (or even a full disk image), strings will extract printable characters that are at least four characters long. This command can be used against individual database files to potentially view and recover deleted data. Another method that allows the examiner to search for data is the use of a hex editor. By viewing a disk image within a hex editor, the examiner has the ability to jump to a specific area within the image. For example, if a particular e-mail address is of unique interest in a case, this address can be searched across the entire dmg. The examiner can then analyze the surrounding content.

In addition to the tools listed above, one of the most popular physical acquisition tools used on the iPhone, developed by Jonathan Zdziarski, offers the examiner command-line Automated Tools to use on either a Mac workstation or a Linux machine. The Linux-based tools are demonstrated in Chapter 5, and the Linux VM discussed in the previous section can be used to run these tools.

This list barely skims the surface of the variety of forensic methods that are available using a Linux environment. An excellent resource to assist examiners who may wish to incorporate Linux into their investigations is http://linuxleo.com/. The site contains documents, guides, files, and other items which may help introduce individuals to the Linux environment and how it can be used in forensics (Grundy, 2008).

SUMMARY

This chapter was intended to briefly introduce the various iPhone models, Apple's strategy leading up to the development of the iPhone, and the most common resources available for developers as well as mobile examiners interested in new tools and techniques. Some background information was provided on distinguishing between the various iPhone devices that are currently available. Many of the significant hardware components were also discussed, pointing out the type of baseband, processor, NAND Flash memory, and other modules contained within the device.

The next chapter focused more on the acquisition of an iPhone, tools that are capable of performing these acquisitions, and a classification system that groups these tools according to their capabilities. In addition to extracting data through an iTunes backup file, logical acquisition, or physical acquisition, some nontraditional methods were also covered, such as jailbreaking and unlocking an Apple device.

Finally, the integration of Linux within a forensic environment was covered to demonstrate the power of some of these tools. Basic Linux commands as well as the setting up of an Ubuntu VM were covered, concluding with an overview of some of the analysis tools that would be used throughout the remainder of the book.

References

Android Passes iPhone in US Market Share – Slashdot. (2011, January 8). Slashdot: News for nerds, stuff that matters. Retrieved January 14, 2011, from http://mobile.slashdot.org/article.pl?sid=11/01/09/0039211

Apple Inc. (2010). Mac OS X Lion Sneak Peek. Mac OS X Lion. Retrieved December 17, 2010, from www.apple.com/macosx/lion

Brothers, S. (2007). iPhone tool classification. The Apple examiner. Retrieved January 14, 2011, from http://www.appleexaminer.com/iPhoneiPad/ToolClassification/ToolClassification.html

CBS. (2010, February 15). Number of cell phones worldwide hits 4.6B. Breaking news headlines: Business, entertainment & world news. Retrieved January 19, 2011, from http://www.cbsnews.com/stories/2010/02/15/business/main6209772.shtml

Costello, S. (n.d.). iPhone features comparison. iPod – Apple iPhone & iPhone Apps. Retrieved January 19, 2011, from http://ipod.about.com/od/decidingwhichipodtobuy/a/iphone_chart.htm

Grundy, B. J. (2008, December). The law enforcement and forensic examiner's introduction to Linux. Linux LEO. Retrieved February 9, 2011, from http://linuxleo.com/Docs/linuxintro-LEFE-3.78.pdf

McGlaun, S. (2010, February 23). iPhone takes 3rd in smartphone sales for 2009 – SlashGear. SlashGear – Feeding your gadget and tech obsessions. Retrieved January 14, 2011, from http://www.slashgear.com/iphone-takes-3rd-in-smartphone-sales-for-2009–2375312

Moren, D. (2010, July 26). Jailbreaking officially granted DMCA exemption. Macworld. Retrieved January 17, 2011, from http://www.macworld.com/article/152935/2010/07/jailbreak_exemption.html

National Institute of Standards and Technology (NIST). (2010, November). Mobile devices. NIST Computer Forensic Tool Testing Program: Project overview. Retrieved January 10, 2011, from http://www.cftt.nist.gov/project_overview.htm

Semiconductor Insights. (n.d.). Teardowns. TechInsights. Retrieved January 20, 2011, from www.ubmtechinsights.com/reports-and-subscriptions/teardowns/

United States Copyright Office. (1998, December). The Digital Millennium Copyright Act of 1998. Retrieved January 17, 2011, from http://www.copyright.gov/legislation/

Wired. (2008, July 3). iPhone timeline highlights the handset through the ages. Wired.com. Retrieved January 19, 2011, from http://www.wired.com/gadgetlab/2008/07/iphone-timeline/

Device features and functions

INTRODUCTION

In order to forensically examine a mobile device, it is important to understand the inner workings of that device. There are various Apple devices capable of storing an individual's personal data. On top of that, each of these models contains unique features, which are important to understand prior to investigating the data within.

Being aware of the available devices running iOS as well as the settings and options within them can be a key aspect in an iPhone investigation. The configuration of the iPhone or iPad settings can affect the manner in which the data is acquired. In addition to understanding the physical device, iTunes also plays an important role in an iPhone investigation. This chapter will cover the functions of an iOS device as well as how these devices interact with iTunes to send, receive, and store user data.

APPLE DEVICE OVERVIEW

While this book focuses mainly on the iPhone and forensic techniques associated with it, it is also important to note that most of these forensic methods may be applied to other Apple devices as well. For this reason, a brief overview of some of the more popular iOS devices will be covered.

In April 2010, Apple released the iPad, its version of a tablet computer. Used mainly for audio and video capabilities, the iPad originally arrived running iOS version 3.2.2. In November 2010, version 4.2.1 of the operating system was released. Similar to the iPhone, the iPad offers touch-screen functionality as well as many of the same applications. Apps on the iPad are downloaded in a similar fashion through the iTunes App Store. The iPad can also be synced with iTunes and even has the capability of placing and receiving phone calls using voice over IP through Wi-Fi or the 3G network.

Apple TV was originally released on January 9, 2007. The original model contained a 40 GB hard disk drive, which was replaced months later with a newer model storing 160 GB. This device connects with the user's high-definition (HD) television using an HDMI (High-Definition Multimedia Interface) cable and provides the capability to stream audio and video from YouTube, Netflix – a computer running iTunes – or any iOS device. A second version of Apple TV was released in October 2010, which was much less expensive but lacked the hard drive storage. Instead of downloading videos and other files to be stored on the device, with the second-generation Apple TV, everything is streamed over wireless using an A4 processing chip, decreasing the overall size and cost. In addition, 8 GB of Flash storage is also available for caching, to allow seamless play.

The iPod, a portable media player, is another popular Apple product that is synchronized with iTunes in order to store music, videos, photos, and more, depending on the model. There are various flavors of the iPod, including the iPod Classic, iPod Shuffle, iPod Nano, and iPod Touch. Each has varying storage space and functions.

- *iPod Classic*: The original iPod was first released in 2001. There have since been six generations of this device, ranging from 5 to 160 GB. The iPod Classic most commonly supports music, videos, TV shows, games, and photos.
- *iPod Shuffle*: This member of the iPod family is much smaller in size and does not have a display. It was originally intended to be a simple, cost-effective way of allowing the user to listen to songs at random or on "shuffle." The first-generation iPod Shuffle arrived in early 2005, and as of December 2010 the fourth-generation model was available. Without a display screen, the shuffle strictly supports audio files, including music, podcasts, or even audio books. Also incorporated is the "Voiceover" feature, which announces the name of an artist or play list (Apple Inc., n.d.).
- *iPod Nano*: Since 2005, six generations of the iPod Nano have been in development. A slim version of the iPod Classic, the nano supports several audio types and has a small display in which the user can navigate through play lists, albums, and songs. The more recent models have added extra features such as the ability to "shake" the device to shuffle to the next song, an on-board video camera, FM radio, and as of the sixth generation, a touch-screen display (Apple Inc., n.d.).
- *iPod Touch*: The iPod Touch is a combination of a personal data assistant (PDA) and portable media player. There are four generations of this device, with the first released in 2007. The iPod Touch offers greater functionality than the other iPod models, including a camera, HD video recorder, FaceTime, voice control, gaming, and more. It can be compared with the iPhone, but lacking cellular network access (Apple Inc., n.d.).

With the release of the Mac OS X Lion in summer 2011, the Mac is even now becoming more "iOS-like" than ever before. A Mac App Store has been released, which will allow easy browsing and downloading of apps, similar to the App Store for the iPhone or iPad. Apps will also be displayed on the desktop, and referred to as the "Launchpad." Click an app on the Launchpad, and it is opened full screen, minimizing any other open applications or tools. Finally, "Mission Control" takes all the applications running on your Mac and consolidates them into one area for the user to view. This includes any open programs, various Spaces, the Dashboard, and more. Selecting one of these items will minimize Mission Control and launch that particular program (Apple Inc., 2010).

OPERATING MODES

The above devices are capable of running in various operating modes, including Normal, Recovery, or Device Failsafe Utility (DFU) modes. These will be referenced often throughout the remaining chapters since certain modes are required in order to perform a particular function on the device. For example, to perform an upgrade or system recovery, the device must be placed in Recovery mode.

Normal mode

When the device is powered on in a typical fashion, this is known as normal mode. Most activities performed on an iPhone will be run in normal mode, unless otherwise specified.

Recovery mode

For Recovery mode, the user or examiner will boot the device into iBoot, bypassing the loading of the operating system. iBoot is Apple's stage 2 bootloader, and is where Recovery mode resides. This operating mode is required to perform certain functions such as activating a device, upgrading or downgrading the iPhone, or sometimes to perform a forensic physical acquisition.

To enter Recovery mode, power off the device (by holding down the button on the top of the phone until you see "slide to power off" appear on the device). Next, hold down the "Home" button, and then connect the device to a computer via a USB connector while continuing to press the "Home" button. Continue to hold until "Connect to iTunes" appears (as shown in Figure 2.1), and then release.

By connecting the cable, you are giving power to the device. An alternative option would be to first connect the device to a computer, power off the device, and then hold the "Home" button down while at the same time pressing the power button.

DFU mode

DFU mode is also required to initiate various actions on the iPhone, most commonly to perform a physical acquisition. It is referred to by some as "Device Firmware Upgrade."

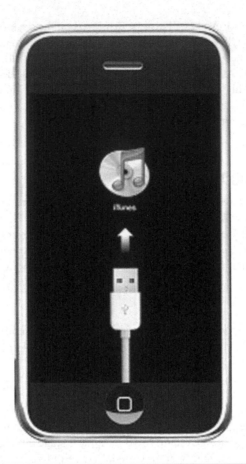

FIGURE 2.1

iPhone in Recovery Mode.

To enter DFU mode, make sure the iPhone is connected to the computer. iTunes should *not* be running at this time. If iTunes starts when the device is connected, be sure to exit by selecting "iTunes > Quit iTunes" at the top left corner of the Mac (or on Windows, simply "X" out of the program). With the device either powered on or off, hold down the "Home" button and the "Power" button together for 10 seconds, then release the power button (while continuing to press "Home") for 10 more seconds. It is important to hold for exactly 10 seconds. When successfully in DFU mode, the screen will be black. If you see the Apple logo or other signs that the device is booting, the process was done incorrectly.

To verify whether the device is in DFU mode on a Mac, System Profiler can be run. Once launched, select the "USB" option, and you should see a device similar to what is shown in Figure 2.2. A "USB DFU Device" will be displayed if done correctly, otherwise just an Apple iPhone device will appear.

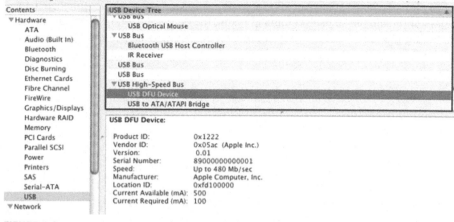

FIGURE 2.2

System Profiler – USB DFU Device.

System Profiler can also be searched using a Terminal window. First, enter the following command to launch System Profiler:

```
$ system_profiler | less
```

From there, enter the following command to search for a device in DFU mode (the results for this command are shown in Figure 2.3):

```
/DFU
```

Some of the newer tools used to get a physical image on an iPhone require Linux. To verify the device is in DFU mode on a Linux workstation, a similar process can be used. Connect the device to the Linux box, and enter the "lsusb" command in a Terminal window to display information about all USB devices connected to that

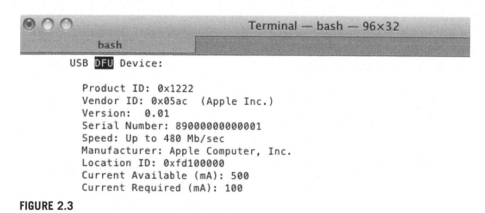

FIGURE 2.3

System Profiler via Terminal Window.

particular machine. When an iPhone running in normal mode is connected to a workstation and the "lsusb" command is run, the output will show an Apple device, including the model number, serial number, and other details about that particular device:

```
kstrzempka@linux-wks-001:~$ lsusb -v | less

Bus 002 Device 015: ID 05ac:1294 Apple, Inc. iPhone 3GS
Device Descriptor:
    bLength                 18
    bDescriptorType          1
    bcdUSB                2.00
    bDeviceClass             0 (Defined at Interface level)
    bDeviceSubClass          0
    bDeviceProtocol          0
    bMaxPacketSize0         64
    idVendor            0x05ac Apple, Inc.
    idProduct           0x1294 iPhone 3GS
    bcdDevice             0.01
    iManufacturer            1 Apple Inc.
    iProduct                 2 iPhone
    iSerial                  3 036b901d79efd9f7894baf444dca4e08ab9f8008
    bNumConfigurations       4
    Configuration Descriptor:
        bLength              9
        bDescriptorType      2
        wTotalLength        39
        bNumInterfaces       1
        bConfigurationValue  1
```

When an iPhone running in DFU mode is connected to a workstation and the "lsusb" command is run, the output will be similar, but will also show that the iPhone is a "DFU" device.

```
kstrzempka@linux-wks-001:~$ lsusb -v | less

Bus 002 Device 016: ID 05ac:1227 Apple, Inc.
Device Descriptor:
    bLength                 18
    bDescriptorType          1
    bcdUSB                2.00
    bDeviceClass             0 (Defined at Interface level)
    bDeviceSubClass          0
    bDeviceProtocol          0
    bMaxPacketSize0         64
    idVendor            0x05ac Apple, Inc.
    idProduct           0x1227
    bcdDevice             0.00
    iManufacturer            1 Apple Inc.
```

```
iProduct              2 Apple Mobile Device (DFU Mode)
iSerial               3
bNumConfigurations    1
Configuration Descriptor:
```

Notice that both the Product ID and the serial number are different depending on the operating mode. When a firmware upgrade is performed, it is necessary to modify the "idProduct" field to ensure that only the DFU driver is loaded (Microcontroller Division Applications, 2003). It can also help an examiner determine whether a device is in DFU mode (i.e., if the serial number is displayed, it is most likely in "Normal" mode).

Exiting Recovery/DFU mode

Whether in Recovery or DFU mode, the same process can be used to return back to Normal mode. Press the power and home buttons at the same time until the Apple logo appears, and the device will reboot. More often than not, this key sequence will successfully load the phone back into normal operating mode.

There is the possibility of the device entering what is referred to as a "Recovery Mode Loop," where the iPhone will constantly reboot into recovery mode. This can occur during the jailbreaking or unlocking process. If this occurs, there are several open source tools available to assist the user in exiting out of a Recovery Mode Loop, such as RecBoot or iRecovery. Both tools are free and available for download on Windows and Mac environments, with iRecovery also available on Linux. These tools communicate with the stage 2 bootloader (iBoot/iBSS) over a USB connection in order to exit Recovery Mode Loop.

Installing iRecovery on Linux and Mac involves one easy step of downloading the source files. Windows users must also install libusb to allow access to USB devices. To use iRecovery, the user runs the program by entering the following in a Terminal window:

```
$ ./iRecovery -s
```

Next, the following commands are executed:

```
$ setenv auto-boot true
$ saveenv
$ /exit
```

Finally, the user can initiate a reboot, and the device should start up in normal mode. The process is a bit more complex using iRecovery since this tool offers other functions as well, such as uploading files (iRecovery, 2009). Jonathan Zdziarski's physical acquisition tool utilizes iRecovery to automatically reboot the iPhone when necessary. This tool will also be discussed later as it can play an important role in the acquisition process.

RecBoot is much more straightforward for the purposes of exiting a Recovery Mode Loop. It has two purposes: enter recovery mode or exit recovery mode (refer to Figure 2.4 for RecBoot user interface). For this reason, the interface is

FIGURE 2.4

RecBoot Exit Recovery Mode.

much more user friendly. The user simply clicks the button and the device is automatically rebooted into normal operating mode.

The various operating modes are most often used during the forensic imaging process and are discussed further in Chapter 5.

SECURITY

Various iPhone settings allow the user to protect unauthorized access to their device and data. Some of these configurations are not set by default. Additionally, certain functions or custom applications are not as secure as they might appear, leading the user to have a false sense of security.

Device settings

An iPhone user has the option to set a PIN on their device in order to prevent unauthorized access. By default, the PIN is a four-digit, numeric code, but by modifying the "Simple Passcode," setting can be set to a variable length. Upon entering the passcode incorrectly 10 times, the user also has the option to set the device to automatically erase all content. Another unique option that is offered involves Apple's MobileMe membership. Among other elements, MobileMe allows the user to remotely set a passcode in the event that a device is stolen.

On certain devices running iOS version 4.0 or higher, hardware encryption is also possible through a feature referred to as "Data Protection." When a passcode is set, the device settings will show "Data Protection is Enabled" (see Figure 2.5). Enabling this feature creates an encryption key, activating an added layer of security for e-mail messages and attachments. This encryption makes forensic recovery of these devices much more complex. The iOS devices that contain hardware encryption, and therefore offer Data Protection, include the iPhone 4, iPhone 3G(s), iPod Touch, and iPads (Apple Inc., December 2010).

Another optional configuration is to set the device to automatically lock after a set amount of time. A user might consider this option as an effort to increase battery life or prevent unauthorized access to the device if it is left unattended. Upon seizing an iOS device, if it is not already "locked," a best practice might be to immediately go into the

FIGURE 2.5

iPhone – Data Protection.

device settings and set the auto-lock to "Never." This will prevent the device from locking out and require the examiner to enter a passcode to access the device. If the device model and operating system supports a physical acquisition, then the passcode will not be an issue; however, in the event that only a logical acquisition can be performed, this step of removing the auto-lock is crucial. Of course, this also drains the battery much more quickly, so be sure to get that device to a charger as soon as possible.

Finally, restrictions on various applications can be enabled, which allows the user to control access to particular apps. A passcode can be set to prevent unauthorized access to Safari, YouTube, iTunes, and other applications on the phone. This feature is ideal for parents who may want to restrict their child's access to certain functions on the iPhone.

Secure erase

There are several ways in which an iPhone can be wiped. Within the device itself is the option to either "Reset All Settings" or "Erase All Content and Settings." The latter is a full secure erase and, depending on the amount of data on the phone, can take anywhere from a few minutes to over an hour to complete. Internal testing has proven that this method truly does wipe the device, leaving no valuable data to be recovered (refer to Chapter 4 – "iPhone and iPad Data Security" for details on the methods used for testing).

Another option is to perform a remote wipe. This method can be completed through an e-mail account synced with the device, a MobileMe account, or through a downloaded application. A remote wipe would come in handy in the event that the device was lost or stolen and the owner wanted to prevent access to their data. Chapter 4 covers some of the research and testing performed on these devices to determine whether a remote wipe does a thorough job. In some cases, data can still be recovered through forensic techniques.

While both the previous methods have been forensically tested to ensure they are effective, the "erase data after ten failed passcode attempts" technique has not.

App security

iPhone users have a high expectation that their personal information is secure. But mobile phones are drastically different from traditional computers and represent a new and unique threat to customer data. It is assumed that customized mobile applications are secure and avoid exposure of confidential user data and credentials, but that is not always the case.

Various internal testing procedures have been performed to evaluate the data exposure and security of multiple mobile applications by using forensic techniques. To test the app, it is installed and used the way a typical user would. The data is then examined to determine whether sensitive information is left on the device or transmitted over the network unencrypted. The findings resulted in many of these apps storing user names, passwords, or other related application data on the device or even confidential data in transit across a wireless network.

It is important for consumers to understand the risks involved in using these applications, especially when sensitive data is involved, such as with financial applications. The overview, methodology, and results of these findings can be found at http://viaforensics.com/appwatchdog/. Many of the forensic techniques used to perform app analysis on these devices are discussed in later chapters, and application security is specifically covered in Chapter 4.

iTUNES INTERACTION

iTunes offers various functions, allowing the user to manage files, apps, software versions, and more on their iPhone device. The following sections discuss the main features.

Device synchronization

Once an iPhone is connected to iTunes, the user can initiate synchronization between the software and the device. This process will load all the applications, music, videos, pictures, etc. that are stored in iTunes onto the device, based on user-defined settings. When a sync is performed, the data within iTunes takes precedence and any differences will be removed from the device. iTunes can be configured to perform an automatic sync each time the device is connected, or a manual sync which must be initiated by the user. Custom apps, such as those developed by corporations, can be installed onto the device using this synchronization method; however, they must first be approved by Apple. MobileMe can also be used in conjunction with iTunes to sync calendar, contacts, mail accounts, and more.

iPhone backups

The user also has the option to create a backup of the iPhone once connected to the computer. An automated backup is initiated during the sync process or when an update or restore is performed. The backup files are stored in a certain location, depending on the type of operating system running on the user's machine.

- Windows XP: C:\Documents and Settings\<user name>\Application Data \Apple Computer\MobileSync\Backup\
- Windows Vista/Windows 7: C:\Users\<user name>\AppData\Roaming\Apple Computer\MobileSync\Backup\
- Macintosh: Users/<user name>/Library/Application Support/MobileSync/ Backup/

Each backup folder contains several files. Status.plist provides the status of the last sync/backup. Info.plist contains information about the device in general, including device name, build version, IMEI (International Mobile Equipment Identity), phone number, etc. Manifest.plist includes a list of all the backed up files, their modification time, and hash value. The remainder of the files will include several *.mddata and *. mdinfo files (for iTunes versions prior to 8.x, these will appear as *.mdbackup files). For all of these backup files, the file name is SHA1 hash value of that particular file. These are the actual backup files of the iPhone's applications and settings. Opening these files as is will not be legible, as they are what Apple refers to as Binary plists. In order to view the content of the backups, these files need to be either viewed using specialized software or converted in another manner.

iTunes also allows the user to initiate an encrypted backup by entering in a password prior to syncing the backup files. Encrypted backups add a significant level of difficulty to the data recovery process – even to the point of impossibility with a complex enough password. However, it is important to note that this option is not required, prompted, or set as the default, and as a result it is reasonable to assume that few users would choose this option.

The analysis of both encrypted and unencrypted backups will be covered in later chapters.

With the release of iOS version 4, if a backup is not passcode protected, the keychain file (containing user name and password data) is encrypted using hardware keys stored on the iPhone. If the keychain database file is opened, certain information can be viewed, but passwords are encrypted.

If a backup is password-protected, the keychain file is now encrypted using software keys generated from the backup password. What this means is that, as long as the backup passcode is known, it is possible to get to the keychain file's encrypted data.

iPhone restore

There are two different restore options: to restore the iPhone from a pre-existing backup file or to restore a device back to factory settings. Restoring from a backup will pull all settings and application data from that backup and sync that data to the device. Performing a full software restore removes the active file system from the device and restores it back to the default factory settings. Both restore methods can be performed in iTunes, and it is important to understand the difference between the two in order to prevent loss of data.

Once a factory restore is performed, the user will have to re-activate the device by connecting it to iTunes (as prompted on the display). Once the iPhone is activated, data can then be restored from a backup file or setup as a brand new device.

iPhone iOS updates

Apple will occasionally release iPhone iOS version updates which may introduce new features, fix bugs from previous versions, or increase security. The user has the option to remain on the current operating system or upgrade to the most recent. Upgrades are done through iTunes and are fairly simple to do.

Upgrade

Once the phone is connected to a computer running iTunes, the user simply clicks the "Update" button (see Figure 2.6) and the latest software is updated onto the device.

The iPhone contains two disk partitions, which will later be discussed in more detail. The partition containing the user data is separate from that containing the firmware. When a firmware upgrade is initiated, the latest operating system software

Version

Update	A newer version of the iPhone software is available (version 4.2). To update your iPhone with the latest software, click Update.
Restore	If you are experiencing problems with your iPhone, you can restore its original settings by clicking Restore.

FIGURE 2.6

iTunes Update and Restore.

is installed within that firmware partition. This process is forensically sound since the user data is in a separate container and, therefore, not modified by the update.

Downgrade

For one reason or another, a user may wish to go back to a previous iOS version. Perhaps after upgrading, it was determined that additional security holes were revealed. Also, some 3G users found that updating their device to iOS v4.x caused their devices to decrease in speed and efficiency. From a forensic examiner's stand-point, downgrading a device could be crucial in recovering data from a device. The available forensic tools will run only on certain supported versions. If the model and/ or firmware version are not supported, the device may need to be downgraded in order to be acquired. Regardless of the reason, there is the option to downgrade to a previous iOS version. This process varies per device, and is also not supported for certain devices and operating systems.

To downgrade, a similar process is used. The first step, however, is to download a copy of the old .ipsw (iPhone software) file that the user wishes to downgrade. These .ipsw files can be found on various websites, such as www.iclarified.com. Apple does not provide these files, as their goal is to ensure all users are running the latest firmware updates. Once the iPhone software file is downloaded and saved onto the user's workstation, the phone should then be connected to the workstation running iTunes. To update to a firmware version other than the latest available, the user would right-click on update and navigate to that particular .ipsw file. This process is typically successful for the earlier models, prior to 3G(s). The downgrade only effects the firmware partition, so the user data slice should not be affected. This has been the case with the phones that have been internally tested by the authors; however, downgrading or modifying the phone in any way is still a risky process to perform on a piece of evidence.

For later models, this downgrade process is not possible without performing advanced technical steps. Some of these models, including iPhone 4 and certain 3GS models depending on when they were shipped, contain the new bootrom. Apple decided to start signing the firmware versions, requiring iTunes to "get permission" before upgrading/downgrading to a different firmware version. Presumably, the reason for this is that Apple wants to keep its customers running the latest software versions. In any case, if an attempt is made to downgrade on one of these devices, iTunes will display an error and prevent the update.

In order for Apple to sign-off on a restore file, it first checks the SHSH blobs against its servers. SHSH blobs, also known as ECID SHSHs, are unique signatures on a device. This signature is checked against Apple's servers, and if that particular signature does not correspond with the most recent iOS firmware, Apple will not verify that file, preventing iTunes from performing a restore (Asad, April 2010). The hacking community has come up with workarounds for each version to get past this obstacle, but it can be a complex process if you are not accustomed to it.

The basis behind this downgrade process is to trick iTunes into thinking that the SHSH signature has been verified. Depending on the iOS version and model, the exact steps may vary slightly; however, the overall process remains the same. The following steps provide a high-level overview of this process:

1. Save SHSH blobs from current device and iOS version.
2. Modify the "hosts" file to communicate with an alternative server other than Apple's.
3. Perform an iTunes Restore and select an old .ipsw file.
4. Use iRecovery, RecBoot, or another tool to exit out of Recovery mode if needed.

These steps will now be covered in greater detail; however, we will be using a specific model and version for this example. To view a complete step-by-step guide on this and other versions, refer to www.redmondpie.com (Asad, July 2010).

Save SHSH blobs

The key to performing a successful downgrade is to first save the SHSH blobs that are unique to your device and iOS version. The signature for an iPhone 3GS running iOS 3.1.2 will be different from the signature of the same device running iOS 3.1.3. So prior to upgrading, be sure to always save the SHSH blobs on your workstation or a remote server. They can later be used to downgrade back to that version. If the files are not saved and the device is upgraded, there is no way to revert back to a previous firmware version.

There are various open source tools available that can be used for this purpose, including AutoSSH and Tiny Umbrella. For this scenario, we will be using Tiny Umbrella on a Macintosh to save the SHSH files from a 3GS running firmware version 4.0 (this particular software is also available for Windows or Linux).

Once the software is downloaded and running, the iPhone should be connected to the workstation in normal mode. For this particular device model and iOS version, an iTunes version later than 9.0 should be running. Make sure you are using the iTunes version that supports your device. If, after connecting your device to the computer, the "Save My SHSH" button in Tiny Umbrella is grayed out, you are most likely running the wrong version of iTunes. Once the device is successfully connected, you should see the name, model, and firmware version of your device displayed in the drop-down box. After verifying that it is the correct device, select the "Save My SHSH" button (see Figure 2.7).

To verify that the correct files were saved, select the "Display SHSHs" button within the application. You should see your device model, firmware version, and serial number displayed as shown in Figure 2.8.

Modify hosts file

In this step, we are going to modify the hosts file on our workstation by changing the IP address for Apple's verification servers to the IP address for Cydia's server.

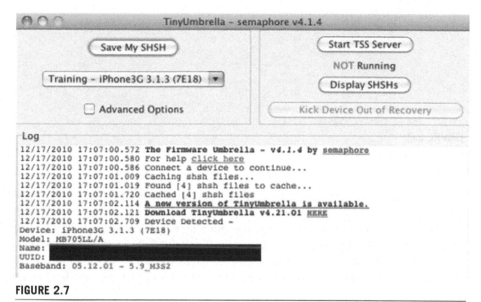

FIGURE 2.7

Tiny Umbrella – Save My SHSH.

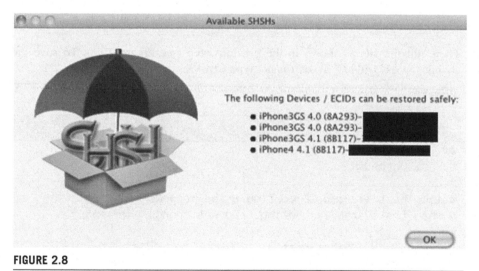

FIGURE 2.8

Tiny Umbrella – Available SHSHs.

On a Mac, the hosts file can be found by selecting "Go" then "Go to Folder" from the Finder (refer to Figure 2.9). Type in "/etc/" (full path is /private/etc and is a hidden folder), and once that folder opens, the hosts file should be viewable.

In Windows, the hosts file is located at C:\Windows\System32\drivers\etc\hosts.

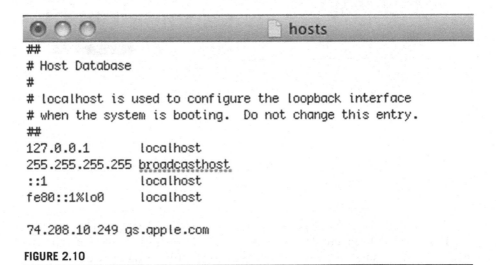

FIGURE 2.9

Locating "Hosts" File.

On a Linux workstation, the hosts file is located in the root directory under the /etc folder.

Depending on the privileges of the user running on your machine, you may not have access to directly modify this file. A best practice is to make a copy of it on your desktop, modify, then save it back to its original location. Open the hosts file using a text editor, and add the following line (see Figure 2.10): 74.208.105.171 gs. apple.com

On Linux, this update can be done via command line by entering the following in a Terminal:

```
$ cd /etc
$ nano hosts
```

Then edit the file as shown in the previous step (see Figure 2.11). To save the changes, press Ctrl+O. To exit nano, type Ctrl+X.

```
 ⊙ ○ ○                                        📄 hosts
##
# Host Database
#
# localhost is used to configure the loopback interface
# when the system is booting.  Do not change this entry.
##
127.0.0.1         localhost
255.255.255.255 broadcasthost
::1               localhost
fe80::1%lo0       localhost

74.208.10.249 gs.apple.com
```

FIGURE 2.10

Modified "Hosts" File.

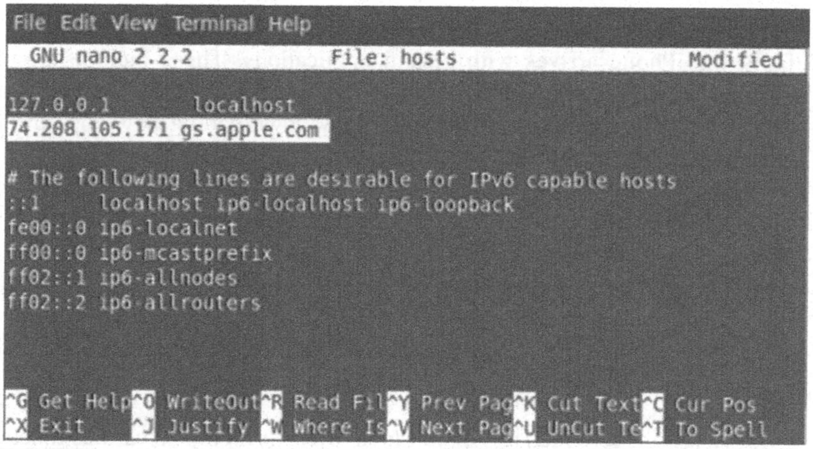

FIGURE 2.11

Modified "Hosts" File – Linux.

It is this line that is going to make iTunes think it is contacting Apple's server to verify the device signature when in fact it is being verified by the Cydia server. Once this verification process is complete, iTunes will allow us to complete the downgrade process.

NOTE

Modifying Hosts File

The system "hosts" file can be modified to assist in a firmware downgrade by redirecting traffic intended for Apple's server to an external server. Do not forget to either comment out or completely remove the redirection entry once the process is complete.

Restore .ipsw file

At this point, you should have saved the SHSH blobs, modified the "hosts" file, and downloaded the .ipsw file for the firmware version that you wish to downgrade to. Start iTunes, making sure that you are running the supported version, and connect the device to your workstation. Right-click "Restore" (on a Mac, hold down alt/option then click) and browse to the .ipsw file that was downloaded to your machine to initiate the downgrade.

Exit Recovery mode

Once the process is complete, the device will be in Recovery mode. To exit, you should be able to use the standard process of holding down the "Home" and "Power" buttons simultaneously until the Apple logo appears. If by chance the device became stuck in the Recovery Mode Loop, RecBoot or iRecovery will do the trick.

The App Store

By default, the iPhone arrives with certain applications. These include the most common apps, such as Messages, Calendar, Photos, Weather, and more. A user can customize the applications on their phone by downloading new apps through the iTunes App Store (which arrives on the iPhone by default).

The App Store contains iPhone applications including categories such as Games, Music, Productivity, and Travel. In order to login to the App Store, the user has to first create a login or use their existing iTunes user ID and password. Apps are easily installed on the device, and notifications are even sent to the user when new versions of those apps are available.

MobileMe

MobileMe is a service provided by Apple which offers its members various functions. Mentioned above was the ability to sync e-mail, contacts, and calendar with Apple devices. MobileMe stores all of the user's data, and automatically pushes it out to sync with multiple devices. Users can also store photos, videos, and other files using both the "Gallery" and "iDisk" features. iDisk provides up to 20 GB of remote data storage, allowing access from any computer, iPhone, iPad, or iPod Touch.

Another tool available through MobileMe is the ability for a user to locate a lost or stolen iPhone. Using the "Find My iPhone" feature, a user can sign-in to their MobileMe account and display the approximate global positioning system (GPS) location of the missing device. This option works as long as "Find My iPhone" has been enabled in the device settings. In addition to GPS location, a message can also be sent to the device to let someone know how to get in contact with the owner. Additionally, a user can remotely set a passcode or initiate a remote wipe in the event the device has been stolen.

All of these features can be accessed in one location at me.com.

SUMMARY

In order to forensically examine an iPhone, it is important to understand the options available on the device. This chapter covered various iOS devices and some of their most common features. The numerous security functions should be considered prior to performing a forensic analysis. If the device supports Data Protection and the passcode is enabled, there is the possibility that some or all of the data will be encrypted.

The correlation between the iPhone and iTunes was also discussed in detail. This software plays an important role in what data is loaded on the iPhone. In addition, backups of the device are also pulled down when the device is synced, providing the examiner with an alternative method of acquiring data. Firmware upgrades, downgrades, and device restores are also performed through iTunes.

Many of these functions will play a significant role in the acquisition and analysis of the iPhone.

References

Apple Inc. (n.d.). Apple – Play music and more on iPod.. Apple. Retrieved December 17, 2010, from http://www.apple.com/ipod/

Apple Inc. (2010, December 1). iOS 4: Understanding data protection. Apple – Support. Retrieved December 17, 2010, from http://support.apple.com/kb/HT4175

Apple Inc. (2010). Mac OS X Lion Sneak Peek. Mac OS X Lion. Retrieved December 17, 2010, from www.apple.com/macosx/lion

Asad, T. (2010, April 30). Save SHSH Blobs (ECID SHSH) of iPhone 3.1.3 and iPad 3.2 | Redmond Pie. Redmond Pie. Retrieved December 17, 2010, from http://www.redmondpie.com/save-shsh-blobs-ecid-shsh-iphone-3.1.3-ipad-3.2-9140709/

Asad, T. (2010, July 15). Downgrade iOS 4.1 to iOS 4.0/3.1.3/3.1.2 iPhone 4, 3GS, 3G and iPod Touch [How to Guide] | Redmond Pie. Redmond Pie. Retrieved December 17, 2010, from http://www.redmondpie.com/downgrade-ios-4.1-to-ios-4–3.1.3–3.1.2-how-to-guide/

Microcontroller Division Applications. (2003). Device Firmware Upgrade (DFU) implementation in ST7 USB devices. STMicroelectronics. Retrieved March 7, 2011, from www.st.com/internet/com/search/search.jsp?q=device%20firmware%20upgrade&entqr=3&entsp=a&output=xml_no_dtd&sort=date:D:L:d1&client=ST_COM_PlanA_frontend&ud=1&oe=UTF-8&ie=UTF-8&proxystylesheet=ST_COM_PlanA_frontend&site=ST_COM

iRecovery: Get Out iPhone from Recovery Mode Loop on Restart | iPhone. (2009, July 18). iHackintosh | iPhone Jailbreak, Unlock and Mods. Retrieved December 17, 2010, from http://www.ihackintosh.com/2009/07/irecovery-iphone-recovery-mode-loop-restart/

File system and data storage

3

INFORMATION IN THIS CHAPTER:

- iPhone Data Storage
- File System

INTRODUCTION

A key aspect of a mobile forensic analysis is understanding what data can be recovered, where the data is stored, and more importantly, how to access that data. Certain mobile devices contain alternative storage locations in addition to the Flash memory on the device, such as external or embedded SD cards. This chapter covers the type of data that can be stored on an iPhone, where one must look for this data, and how the data is being stored behind the scenes.

WHAT DATA IS STORED

It is reasonable to assume that any information that can be viewed on an iPhone will be permanently stored on the device until it becomes overwritten. Most of this data is stored as part of an application installed on the device. There are various types of applications, including those that ship with the iPhone, those that are installed by the manufacturer, those installed by the wireless carrier, and those installed by the user through the iTunes App Store (or those installed on a jailbroken phone through other sources).

Chapter 6, which covers Data and Application Analysis, explores in detail the files and data stored for individual applications; in brief, some of the general information that can be recovered from an iPhone is as follows:

- Default application data (Calendar, Call Logs, Voicemail, Text and Multimedia Messages, Photos, Videos, YouTube, Google Maps, Voice Memos, Notes, Contacts, Web History, and Bookmarks);
- Geographical location information (global positioning system (GPS) coordinates for photos and videos taken from the device and applications that store location data);
- Synchronized data (videos, songs, and pictures synced via iTunes; e-mail accounts and content setup through the mail application on the device);
- General device settings (Wi-Fi and Bluetooth information; firmware and software versions on the device);

- Downloaded application data (any application that was downloaded through the iTunes app store or an alternative source typically stores data relevant to that application);
- User names, e-mail addresses, and some passwords.

WHERE DATA IS STORED

The iPhone has a standard directory structure in which various files are stored (refer to Appendix C for a full listing of the folders and files recovered from an iPhone). Because it does not contain an external storage slot, all data are stored internally on the device (as opposed to other mobile devices that contain external SD cards or emulated SD cards). To display the iPhone's hierarchy, a jailbroken phone is remotely connected through Wi-Fi, using the same techniques as described in Chapter 5 – Imaging a Jail-broken Device. From a Macintosh computer, the phone is connected through SSH in order to navigate through the file system. Immediately upon logging in to the device, the "ls" command is used to list the directory contents.

```
3GS-40:/ root# ls -l
total 58
lrwxr-xr-x 1 root admin      23 Sep 17 12:11 Applications -> /var/stash/
Applications/
drwxrwxr-x 2 root admin      68 May 31 2010 Developer/
drwxrwxr-x 14 root admin    680 Sep 17 12:11 Library/
drwxr-xr-x 3 root wheel     102 Jul 30 2010 System/
lrwxr-xr-x 1 root admin      11 Mar  4 10:20 User -> /var/mobile/
drwxr-xr-x 2 root wheel    2108 Sep 28 11:28 bin/
drwxr-xr-x 2 root wheel      68 Oct 28 2006 boot/
drwxrwxr-t 2 root admin      68 May 19 2010 cores/
dr-xr-xr-x 3 root wheel    1555 Mar  4 10:20 dev/
lrwxr-xr-x 1 root wheel      12 Sep 17 12:11 etc -> private/etc//
drwxr-xr-x 2 root wheel      68 Oct 28 2006 lib/
drwxr-xr-x 2 root wheel      68 Oct 28 2006 mnt/
drwxr-xr-x 4 root wheel     136 Feb 25 11:57 private/
-rw-r--r-- 1 root admin   15290 Sep 16 17:43 restore.log
drwxr-xr-x 2 root wheel    1326 Sep 17 12:11 sbin/
lrwxr-xr-x 1 root wheel      16 Sep 17 12:11 tmp -> private/var/tmp//
drwxr-xr-x 6 root wheel     306 Sep 17 12:12 usr/
lrwxr-xr-x 1 root wheel      12 Sep 17 12:12 var -> private/var//
```

Most of the data that an examiner would be interested in is stored in the "private/var/mobile/" path (on an iPhone disk image, the "mobile" folder will be at the root of the mounted image); however, valuable forensic evidence can also be found in other locations. Within the Mobile directory, there are three subfolders: Applications, Library, and Media. Any downloaded apps will be stored in the Applications folder in a format similar to that shown in Figure 3.1. Each downloaded application has an

▼ 🗀 mobile	Jan 11, 2011 3:00 PM
▼ 📁 Applications	Jan 28, 2011 4:44 PM
▶ 📁 3CD749AD-701F-...1A-AC9C51D426FF	Jan 18, 2011 10:29 AM
▶ 📁 A80398AA-1B36-...3C5-90EE31F3BA3C	Jan 20, 2011 11:30 AM
▶ 📁 C86D1767-9EAC-...BD-BF018AED024F	Jan 28, 2011 4:31 PM
▶ 📁 C9636536-582E-4...5-3C9C05ABF812	Jan 28, 2011 4:44 PM
▶ 📁 FA06A4AA-0EC9-...47-9CAA16698F19	Jan 12, 2011 2:48 PM

FIGURE 3.1

Applications Directory.

application identifier, which becomes the folder name and is the same across all devices, as shown in Figure 3.1.

The contents of each application folder are generally the same among all apps. Some standard folders and files include the following:

- A Documents folder containing relevant files for that particular app, such as plists, text documents, or images;
- A Library folder containing Cached data, Cookies, Preferences, and if applicable, WebKit data. "Preferences" is where user login data is commonly stored if that is required for the application being used;
- The application bundle, which can be extracted to view individual files containing code and other files on which the application is dependent;
- A "tmp" folder, which is empty in most cases.

In the following listing, the contents of the Yahoo! iPhone application are displayed, with some file names (such as logos and icons) removed for simplicity. This structure represents a standard application directory. Looking at the top-level directories, one can see the Documents, Library, and tmp folders, as well as the Yahoo! app folder outlined above. The "iTunes Artwork" and "iTunesMetadata.plist" files are standard files found in all downloads installed through the iTunes App Store. The actual application bundle can be extracted to view more details on the development of that particular application. In this example, the "Info.plist" may contain application version numbers, release dates, or perhaps user login data. Depending on the application, varying configuration files will be found. This is a popular area to look for stored application data.

```
kstrzempka@linux-wks-001:~/Desktop/iPhoneapp-mount/mobile/
Applications$ tree FA06A4AA-0EC9-4E0C-B947-9CAA16698F19/
FA06A4AA-0EC9-4E0C-B947-9CAA16698F19/
├── Documents
│   ├── last_location.txt
│   └── OKURLCache
│       ├── Dictionary.plist
│       ├── E8117953-62EF-454C-8FC6-6EE60E8FCA31
│       ├── EC699560-327D-45DE-8B6C-4D5544095B99
│       └── F2A80C4D-5859-4C2F-A9DB-BCD1527B6BCE
```

```
├─ iTunesArtwork
├─ iTunesMetadata.plist
├─ Library
│   ├─ Caches
│   ├─ Cookies
│   │   └─ Cookies.plist
│   ├─ Preferences
│   │   ├─ com.apple.PeoplePicker.plist  ->  /private/var/mobile/
Library/Preferences/com.apple.PeoplePicker.plist
│   │   └─ com.yahoo.frontpage.plist
│   └─ WebKit
│       ├─ Databases [error opening dir]
│       └─ LocalStorage
│           └─ http_m.mg.mail.yahoo.com_0.localstorage
├─ tmp
└─ Yahoo!.app
    ├─ blueprint.xsd
    ├─ bpResourcesVoice.bundle
    │   └─ Info.plist
    ├─ CodeResources -> _CodeSignature/CodeResources
    ├─ _CodeSignature
    │   └─ CodeResources
    ├─ config.xml
    ├─ config.xsd
    ├─ Default.png
    ├─ de.lproj
    ├─ en.lproj
    ├─ Entitlements.plist
    ├─ es.lproj
    ├─ fr.lproj
    ├─ Icon.png
    ├─ Info.plist
    ├─ it.lproj
    ├─ oneKit
    ├─ PkgInfo
    ├─ pt.lproj
    ├─ ResourceRules.plist
    ├─ SC_Info
    ├─ Settings.bundle
    │   ├─ en.lproj
    │   │   └─ Root.strings
    │   └─ Root.plist
    ├─ SettingsGenericSelectionView.nib
    ├─ SettingsGenericTextView.nib
    ├─ SettingsView.nib
    ├─ Sounds
    ├─ Yahoo!
    └─ zh_tw.lproj
```

Outside of the downloaded applications, the more common data is typically stored in either the "Library" or "Media" folder within specific subfolders. For example, text messages are stored under Library > SMS, in a file named "sms. db." The iPhone file system is structured in an intuitive manner for most of the data.

There are, however, other files on the root of the device which have required a bit more research to understand the data within them. One example of this involves GPS location information stored on the device. Many different applications often ask the user if they wish to enable GPS for that particular app, including the on-board camera and video camera. For this reason, GPS data can often be found for pictures or videos that were taken from the device. When iOS 4.0 was released, changes were made to part of the iPhone's file system layout. One of the major transformations involved a file called "consolidated.db." This database contains a wide array of GPS data and includes latitude and longitude coordinates, time stamps, cell tower locations, and Wi-Fi/ Bluetooth connections from that device. There is only one instance of this file and it is not stored within an individual application folder, despite the fact that this database may contain information about individual applications. More details on recovering GPS data from consolidated.db and other locations can be found in Chapter 6.

HOW DATA IS STORED

Data on the iPhone is stored in a number of ways. In the following sections, each form of data storage is covered in order to provide examiners with an understanding of how potential evidence can be located or recovered.

1. Internal storage
2. SQLite database files
3. Property lists
4. Network
5. Other

Internal storage

Unlike many of the code division multiple access (CDMA) devices, which have an SD card slot, the iPhone does not contain any form of external storage (other than a SIM card). All data is stored in the internal NAND Flash memory. In the "iPhone Disk Partitions" section later in this chapter, slice 2 (or "rdisk0s2") is where all the user data files are stored. It is this partition that is imaged during a physical acquisition of the device. A listing of the top-level files and directories in which much of the user data is stored is listed below. A significant portion of Chapter 6 focuses on these main directories, as well as other portions of the file system.

```
├── Applications
│   ├── 3CD749AD-701F-46E2-951A-AC9C51D426FF
│   ├── A80398AA-1B36-4810-A3C5-90EE31F3BA3C
│   ├── C86D1767-9EAC-43CE-99BD-BF018AED024F
```

```
|   |── C9636536-582E-43EF-AEA5-3C9C05ABF812
|   └── FA06A4AA-0EC9-4E0C-B947-9CAA16698F19
|── Library
|   |── AddressBook
|   |── Caches
|   |── Calendar
|   |── CallHistory
|   |── Carrier Bundle.bundle -> /System/Library/Carrier Bundles/
310410
|   |── com.apple.iTunesStore
|   |── com.apple.itunesstored
|   |── ConfigurationProfiles
|   |── Cookies
|   |── Keyboard
|   |── Logs
|   |── Mail
|   |── Maps
|   |── MobileInstallation
|   |── Operator Bundle.bundle -> /System/Library/Carrier Bundles/
310410
|   |── Preferences
|   |── RemoteNotification
|   |── Safari
|   |── SMS
|   |── Voicemail
|   |── WebClips
|   └── WebKit
└── Media
    |── com.apple.itdbprep.postprocess.lock
    |── com.apple.itunes.lock_sync
    |── DCIM
    |── Downloads
    |── iTunes_Control
    |── Photos
    |── Podcasts
    |── Purchases
    |── Recordings
    └── Safari
```

As all data are stored on the internal device, having the ability to image the iPhone in a way that pulls off both allocated and unallocated data can be crucial in an investigation. Deleted text messages, photos, or videos can often make or break a case, thus making a physical acquisition of the user data partition (rdisk0s2) ideal.

SQLite database files

One of the more common types of data storage used by many mobile application developers is the use of a SQLite database. Databases are used for structured data storage and SQLite is a popular database format that appears in many mobile systems as well as traditional operating systems.

SQLite is popular for many reasons. Notably, the entire code base is high quality, open source, and released to the public domain. The file format and the program itself is very compact and contains significant functionality in less than a few hundred kilobytes. Unlike more traditional relational database management systems (RDBMS), such as Oracle, MySQL, and Microsoft's SQL Server, with SQLite the entire database is contained in a single cross-platform file.

Applications need to be able to store and retrieve data in an efficient manner. Developers have commonly created their own individual file formats for this purpose; however, many are now turning to SQLite because it is free, open-source, high quality, and efficient. Even after a system crash, SQLite transactions are still available.

Apple developers have leveraged SQLite databases for data storage within the iPhone. Many of the popular default applications are stored in this format such as the Address Book, Calendar, Notes, Text Messages, Photos, Voicemails, and more. Data within these files is broken up into tables, which contain the actual data. Figure 3.2 displays the SMS SQLite database structure within SQLite Database Browser on a Mac. A listing of all the tables is shown, with the "Message" table actually selected.

Information on SQLite files can also be retrieved through command line. On a Linux Ubuntu workstation, a database file can be viewed and modified. The following command opens the SMS.db file using SQLite version 3:

```
kstrzempka@linux-001:~/sqlite$ ./sqlite3 sms.db
SQLite version 3.7.4
Enter ".help" for instructions
Enter SQL statements terminated with a ';'
sqlite>
```

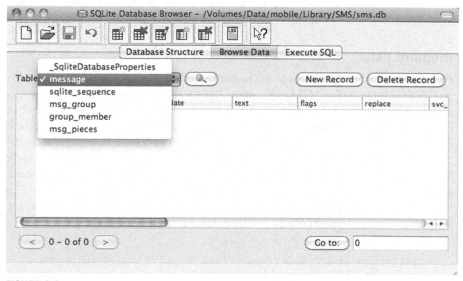

FIGURE 3.2

SMS Database Structure.

Once open, various commands can be run in order to retrieve data. For example, the following lists all tables in the database:

```
sqlite> .tables
_SqliteDatabaseProperties    msg_group
group_member                 msg_pieces
message
```

The next command describes the structure of the message table, referred to as the "schema." The schema describes the way in which the database will be organized in its own special language.

```
sqlite> .schema messages
CREATE TABLE message (ROWID INTEGER PRIMARY KEY AUTOINCREMENT,
address TEXT, date INTEGER, text TEXT,
flags INTEGER, replace INTEGER, svc_center TEXT, group_id INTEGER,
association_id INTEGER, height INTEGER,
UIFlags INTEGER, version INTEGER, subject TEXT, country TEXT, headers
BLOB, recipients BLOB, read INTEGER);
```

Looking at the schema of the messages table is just another way of understanding the different fields within that table as well as all data types associated with that field. Another way of looking at this information is through the SQLite Database Browser that was used earlier. This software is a free, open-source tool used to create, design, and edit database files that support SQLite. SQLite Database Browser is available for Mac, Linux, and Windows platforms, and can be downloaded at http://sqlitebrowser. sourceforge.net. Other SQLite database viewing options are also available at http:// www.sqlite.org/cvstrac/wiki?p=ManagementTools

Since such a significant amount of iPhone data can be found within SQLite files, an examiner should make it a priority to understand how these databases are leveraged. Details on recovering information from these files will be covered in Chapter 6.

Property lists

Property lists are used by applications to store, organize, and access various data types on iOS devices as well as Mac OS X. More commonly referred to as "plists," these files are made up of a hierarchy of three classes, all bundled up into one "list." These three classes consist of the Cocoa Foundation, Core Foundation, and XML. When a plist is created in XML format, an application is then able to read from it, while at the same time converting the XML properties into their appropriate objects to be used in both the Cocoa and Core Foundations (Apple Inc., 2010). A property list in XML format, opened on a Mac using TextWrangler, looks similar to the text displayed below. This is a portion of the "com.apple.Maps.plist" file. In it, latitude and longitude coordinates, and other data (not necessarily shown here) can be easily identified.

```
<?xml version="1.0" encoding="UTF-8"?>
<!DOCTYPE plist PUBLIC "-//Apple//DTD PLIST 1.0//EN" "http://www
. apple.com/DTDs/PropertyList-1.0.dtd">
```

```
<plist version="1.0">
<dict>
    <key>DirectionsMode</key>
    <integer>2</integer>
    <key>DirectionsRouteStartStepIsActive</key>
    <false/>
    <key>DirectionsStepIndex</key>
    <integer>-1</integer>
    <key>DirectionsViewType</key>
    <integer>0</integer>
    <key>LastViewMode</key>
    <integer>0</integer>
    <key>LastViewedLatitude</key>
    <real>41.871318817138672</real>
    <key>LastViewedLongitude</key>
    <real>-87.721084594726562</real>
    <key>LastViewedZoomScale</key>
    <real>13.778828620910645</real>
    <key>RouteEndStringIsAtom</key>
    <false/>
    <key>RouteStartStringIsAtom</key>
    <false/>
    <key>SearchMode</key>
    <integer>1</integer>
    <key>SearchStringIsAtom</key>
    <false/>
    <key>SelectedEndSearchResult</key>
    <integer>0</integer>
    <key>SelectedSearchResultType</key>
    <integer>0</integer>
    <key>SelectedStartSearchResult</key>
    <integer>0</integer>
    <key>TrafficEnabled</key>
    <false/>
```

A property list can be stored in either XML format or binary format (which is used by the Cocoa Class OS layer). Apple began storing certain preference files in binary format in order to reduce the file size and make application access more efficient. As an example, repeated values within a file need to be stored only once and can be referenced when needed later in the file. Also, data can be stored in bytes rather than in a string. These are just a few examples of how binary plists (or bplists) can reduce the file size of a property list (Caithness, 2010).

If a property list is formatted as XML, the file can be viewed using any standard text editor. If stored in binary format, which is essentially a more compact version of the XML plist, the file must be opened by an application that can convert it to ASCII. Plutil, which stands for "property list utility" is one of these applications. This tool converts plist files between binary and text formats when run against a property list file. It also has the capability to scan a property list file and check it for proper XML syntax. Plutil is purely command-line driven and can be run on Windows, Linux, or Mac OS X (PERL, 2008). By default, plutil is installed on a Mac in the directory /usr/bin/plutil, and is available for download on the Internet for Windows and Linux. Prior to conversion, a binary plist is unreadable and shows something like "bplist00" followed by any number of unrecognizable characters.

To convert this file to ASCII format, the following command can be run using plutil:

```
$ /usr/bin/plutil -convert xml1 Bookmarks.plist
```

To convert from XML to binary format, run the following:

```
$ /usr/bin/plutil -convert binary1 Bookmarks.plist
```

No output will be shown, but when the user attempts to open the file, the format will have been converted to either binary or XML, depending on the command that was run. Another helpful option that can be run against a property list file is the "-lint" option. When incorporating this option into the command, the utility will let the user know whether the plist contains syntax errors:

```
$ /usr/bin/plutil -lint Bookmarks.plist
Bookmarks.plist: OK
```

Data within a property list can be of various types, including strings, numbers, binary data, dates, and Boolean values. Because a property list consists of three classes of data, this data must be represented in three different ways. The various data types as well as the ways in which they are represented to each class are demonstrated in Table 3.1 (Apple Inc., 2010).

Table 3.1 Property List Data Types

Data Type	XML Element	Cocoa Class	Core Foundation Type
array	<array>	NSArray	CFArray (CFArrayRef)
dictionary	<dict>	NSDictionary	CFDictionary (CFDictionaryRef)
string	<string>	NSString	CFString (CFStringRef)
data	<data>	NSData	CFData (CFDataRef)
date	<date>	NSDate	CFDate (CFDateRef)
number-integer	<integer>	NSNumber (intValue)	CFNumber (CFNumberRef, integer value)
number-floating point	<real>	NSNumber(floatValue)	CFNumber (CFNumberRef, floating-point value)
Boolean	<true/> or <false/>	NSNumber (boolValue==YES or boolValue==NO)	CFBoolean (CFBooleanRef; kCFBooleanTrue or kCFBooleanFalse)

On the iPhone in particular, property lists are commonly used by applications on the device in order to present options to the user. In particular, Safari web history and bookmarks, YouTube data, Favorites, and many other preference files are stored within property lists. Property list use has simplified mobile application development. Programmers can use these configuration files in order to modify features and functions within the application. Changes can be made to an application by simply modifying the plist and updating this file on the device.

For more details on binary and ASCII plists, refer to CCL Forensics presentation on "Property Lists in Digital Forensics." This document contains the history of property lists, the structure of both XML and binary format, the algorithm used to convert between the two formats, and how to carve and parse property list files and content.

Network

Another option that developers have is storing data in the cloud rather than on the device itself. Initially, very few applications took advantage of the network as a storage option; however, as devices and applications mature, network storage is gaining leverage. There are many applications available on the iTunes store that allow file sharing and network access. Some examples of these include My Network Folders, Air Sharing, QMobile, and Dropbox. These applications operate in several ways. One method allows the device to upload or download stored files through a web browser. Another option involves connecting the device to a computer, mounting it as a drive, and then copying files to and from the device. As an example of a file sharing app, Dropbox has become a widely popular file sharing website, which has mobile applications for iOS, Blackberry, and Android devices. The current application, version 1.3, was updated on November 10, 2010 and has over 1100 mostly positive ratings. After it is installed and used, all user activity is stored within the "Applications" folder. More details on the analysis of this particular application is reviewed in Chapter 6.

MEMORY TYPES

iPhone devices have two primary types of memory, volatile (RAM) and nonvolatile (NAND Flash) memory. Each provides a different insight into the device's data.

RAM

RAM is used by the system to load, execute, and manipulate key parts of the operating system, applications, or data, and is not saved on reboot. Like traditional computers, RAM can contain very important information which applications use to process data. Some examples include:

- passwords,
- encryption keys,
- user names,
- app data, and
- data from system processes and services.

The ability to acquire RAM from a device can be crucial in an investigation; however, it is important to get this information prior to the device being shut down or rebooted. While examining memory from a standard Windows hard drive, Linux workstation, or even Android device is possible, there is currently no method to recover memory from a live iPhone device. Up until early 2011, RAM acquisition of Mac OS X could be accomplished to some extent by recovering the "sleepimage" file, located in /private/var/vm/sleepimage. The purpose of this file is to store what the Mac had in its memory when the system went to sleep. When the computer is "woken," the information contained in the sleepimage file is re-distributed to memory in order to allow the Mac to return to its original state prior to sleeping (Sleepimage, 2010).

In early 2011, Mac Memory Reader was released. This is a command line utility that performs a memory dump on a Mac OS device and outputs the results onto an external device (Valenzuela, 2011). Unfortunately, Mac Memory Reader does not apply to iOS devices yet.

NAND Flash

Unlike RAM, NAND Flash is nonvolatile and thus data is preserved even when the device is without power or it is rebooted. The NAND Flash is used to store not only system files but significant portions of the user's data as well.

NAND Flash memory has characteristics very different from the magnetic media found in modern hard drives. These properties make NAND Flash ideal storage for mobile devices, while at the same time presenting a number of challenges for programmers and opportunities for forensic analysts.

First, NAND Flash has no mechanical moving parts like the spinning platters and arms found in traditional magnetic hard drives. This improves the durability and reduces both the size and power consumption of the device. The memory is distributed as one or multiple chips, which often integrate both NAND Flash and RAM and are directly integrated into the circuit board of the device.

NAND Flash also has very high density and is cost effective to the manufacturer. This, of course, makes it very popular with manufacturers. One side effect of the manufacturing process and technology in general is that NAND Flash literally ships with bad blocks directly from the manufacturer. The manufacturer will generally test the memory as part of the manufacturing process and mark bad blocks in a specific structure on the NAND, which is described in their documentation. Software that then directly interacts with the NAND Flash can read the manufacturer's bad block markers and will often implement a bad block table that can logically track the bad blocks on the system and remove them from operation. This greatly speeds up bad block detection and management. So, while NAND Flash is more physically durable than spinning platters, its error rate is much higher and must be accounted for in development and use.

Another significant limitation of NAND Flash is that it has a very limited write/ erase lifespan before the block is no longer capable of storing data. The lifespan varies by device and is largely impacted by the amount of data stored per NAND Flash cell, the central building block for storing the 1 or 0 bit(s). If the cell stores only a single bit (single-level cell or SLC), then the NAND Flash supports around 100,000 write/erase cycles for a 1-year data retention. However, NAND Flash rarely uses SLC, as manufacturers (and consumers) demand more data storage in devices that are of similar size or smaller. The technology has moved to multilevel cells (MLCs), where a cell can store 2, 3, or even more bits per cell. However, this not only complicates the manufacturing process and slows down the write/erase cycle but also significantly reduces the endurance of the device. A typical MLC NAND Flash storing 2 bits per cell experiences a 10-fold reduction in endurance (measured as a 1-year data retention) with a value of approximately 10,000 write/erase cycles. As the bit density per cell increases, the endurance continues to drop, which must obviously be addressed by the controlling device.

Unlike RAM and NOR Flash (which also has Flash memory and is typically used in systems such as a computer's basic input output system or BIOS), NAND Flash cannot be accessed randomly. Instead, access to data is achieved via an allocation unit, called a page, which is typically between 512 and 2048 bytes, but generally increases as the overall size of NAND Flash increases. As an example, on one 32 GB iPhone 4 device, there were shown to be 8192 bytes per page. Even though NAND Flash does not provide the fast random access like RAM, access time is still quite fast since it does not require the mechanical platter and arm movements used in traditional spinning hard drives. The pages are then organized into a larger logical unit called a block, which is typically much larger than a traditional 512 GB hard drive sector. When a block is allocated for writing, the pages inside the block are written sequentially.

Within the iPhone's file system, there is a file called "ADDataStore.sqlitedb" that contains specific details related to the NAND Flash contained within that device. With some of the earlier models, this database was empty. However, when populated, the "Scalar" table will contain information similar to the following:

```
        key = com.apple.NANDInfo.NumVirtualBlocks
daysSince1970 = 15008
        value = 1952

        key = com.apple.NANDInfo.PagesPerVirtualBlock
daysSince1970 = 15008
        value = 1024
```

```
        key = com.apple.NANDInfo.BytesPerPage
daysSince1970 = 15008
        value = 8192

        key = com.apple.NANDInfo.NumLogicalReads
daysSince1970 = 15008
        value = 6224374

        key = com.apple.NANDInfo.NumLogicalWrites
daysSince1970 = 15008
        value = 9026722

        key = com.apple.NANDInfo.NumFreeVirtualBlocks
daysSince1970 = 15008
        value = 1804

        key = com.apple.NANDInfo.NumWearLevelOps
daysSince1970 = 15008
        value = 726518

        key = com.apple.NANDInfo.NumPhysicalReads
daysSince1970 = 15008
        value = 6420028

        key = com.apple.NANDInfo.NumPhysicalWrites
daysSince1970 = 15008
        valuc = 10489657

        key = com.apple.NANDInfo.NumPhysicalErases
daysSince1970 = 15008
        value = 12266
```

Key characteristics of NAND Flash are the operations available for reading and writing:

- Read (page)
- Write (page)
- Erase (block)

While individual pages can be read or written, the erase operation only functions at the block level. When a block is erased, the entire block is written over with 1's (or 0xFF in hex). The erase operation is the only mechanism by which a 0 can be changed to a 1 in NAND Flash. This point is worth belaboring. In a traditional hard drive, if a value is changed from a 0 to a 1 (or vice versa), the program simply seeks the value on the hard drive and applies the appropriate voltage to change and store the new value. However, the fundamental architecture of NAND Flash provides only one mechanism to change a 0 to a 1 and that is via the erase function which is applied at the block level, not an individual page level. For this reason, a page can be written only once, and if the value of the page needs to be changed, the entire block must be erased and then the page rewritten.

Here is a specific example using a single byte for simplicity: Let us say this particular byte holds the decimal value 179 and we want to add 39 for a total value of 218. For those unfamiliar with converting numbers between base10, hex (base16), and binary (base2), the built-in calculator programs in Windows, Mac OS X, and Ubuntu Linux, all provide a programmer mode that will perform the conversions. For the numbers above, we have the conversions between numbering systems shown in Table 3.2.

So the value 179 contains three 0's and two of them need to change to 1's to present our new value of 218. However, NAND Flash cannot make that change without erasing the entire block. So, if this single byte were attempted without the erase, the result would be 146, not 218. Here is how this happens:

```
1011 0011 (original byte, 0xB3 or 179 decimal)
1101 1010 (new byte to write, 0xDA or 218 decimal)
---------
1001 0010 (resulting byte, 0x92 or 146 decimal)
```

As the byte does not contain all 1's (0xFF), the only portions of the write cycle that will succeed are 1's either remaining a 1 or changing to a 0. Whenever the write function encounters a 0 and is requested to change to a 1, it fails and simply retains the 0 value. The resulting byte is 0x92 or 146 base10 – clearly not the value intended. Another way to describe the write function is that it only changes the changed 1 values to a 0 when requested, the equivalent of the "logical and" of the two values.

In summary, a page can be written only once and, if it needs to be rewritten, the entire block must first be erased.

As one can tell, NAND Flash imposes various restrictions and limitations and thus developers and file systems must be Flash-aware to effectively work within the constraints. Two important techniques deployed are error-correcting code (ECC) and wear leveling. Both have significant implications for forensics and data recovery.

First, ECC is a technique in which an algorithm is used to detect data errors on read or write operations and correct some errors on the fly. Since NAND Flash degrades over time through usage, the system must be able to detect when a page or block is going bad and recover the data stored there. After a number of errors or failed operations is exceeded (typically three failed operations), the page or block will be marked bad and added to the bad block table.

The second important algorithm used to effectively manage NAND Flash on the iPhone is the wear-leveling code. Wear leveling spreads the writing of data across the

Table 3.2 Decimal, Hex, and Binary Representation of Integers		
Decimal (base10)	**Hex (base16)**	**Binary (base2)**
179	0xB3	1011 0011
218	0xDA	1101 1010

entire NAND Flash to avoid overutilization of a single area, which would wear those blocks out more quickly. It is built into HFS Plus (Hierarchical File System Plus) with the goal of reducing writes and deletes to the NAND so that the data is preserved as long as possible. Wear-leveling is also the reason why so much information can be recovered from the device. Old data copies are not deleted, but instead marked as "unallocated." For this reason, there are latent copies of sensitive iPhone data that can be analyzed for information but may have been deleted days, weeks, or months earlier. This analysis is discussed further in Chapter 6.

iPHONE OPERATING SYSTEM

iOS is the operating system that was developed specifically for the iPhone, but now it is also used to run applications on other Apple devices including the iPad, iPod Touch, and Apple TV. There are many similarities between iOS and Mac OS X though the former was developed specifically with mobile devices in mind (Apple Developer, 2010).

Apple's developer site dedicates an entire section to the iOS Dev Center. As mentioned in Chapter 1, the iOS software development kit (SDK) contains tools needed to create and test mobile applications within an iOS environment. These Xcode tools also allow developers to test their code within an iOS Simulator to ensure the app is functioning properly.

iOS layers

The iOS kernel is loosely based on the Mac OS X kernel, and contains several layers that are used to run applications. The layers include Core OS, Core Services, Media, Cocoa Touch, and Applications. The following is a description of each of the architecture layers within iOS (Apple Developer, 2010):

- *Core OS*: This layer sits directly on top of the device hardware and provides services including low-level networking, access to external accessories, and memory management/file system handling. The "Common Crypto" is an example of one of the dynamic libraries stored at this layer. It helps to create and manage certificates and is called upon by the Keychain Services (within the Core Services layer) in order to provide encryption/decryption functions for the Keychain files.
- *Core Services*: In conjunction with the Core OS, this layer provides the fundamental system services that all applications use. It contains fundamental interfaces, mostly C-based, in order to allow for file access and low-level data types. These interfaces include functions such as Core Foundation, CFNetwork, SQLite, and more. Security Services are found at this layer, including Keychain Services, which are used to implement data storage and cryptographic functions within the keychain database on the device.

- *Media*: The Media layer is where graphics, audio, and video technologies are contained.
- *Cocoa Touch*: The Cocoa Touch layer contains technologies that provide the infrastructure needed to implement the visual interface for applications. Here, most of the technologies use Objective-C.

FILE SYSTEM

The file system used by iPhones and other Apple devices, including Mac computers, is HFS Plus. Originally, HFS was used; however, many enhancements have been made for the HFS Plus volume format including disk space efficiency, international-friendly file names, future support for named forks, and the ability to boot on operating systems other than Mac OS. The information provided in Table 3.3 contains some of the differences between the original HFS file system and HFS Plus (Apple Developer, 2004).

HFS Plus contains allocation units referred to as "allocation blocks." A typical block size stores 4 KB of data; however, the block size will vary depending on the physical disk. If an allocation block is too large, there is the risk of wasting storage space. As an example, if a file is 9 KB in size (with allocation blocks of 4 KB), that particular file will use up three blocks, even though a significant portion of the third block will contain no data. No other files can store data on that third block because it is already being used (Kubasiak, Morris key, & Varsalone, 2009).

A tool known as fsstat was developed as part of Brian Carrier's Sleuth Kit. This particular tool displays details about a file system contained on an image file. In the following, the fsstat command is run against an iPhone disk image file. The output

Table 3.3 HFS versus HFS Plus

HFS	HFS Plus	Description
16 bits of allocation blocks	32 bits of allocation blocks	A larger number of files allocated per volume
File name encoding is in MacRoman	File name encoding is in Unicode	Unicode allows for international-friendly file names
System Folder ID startup support	Supports a dedicated startup file	Allows Operating Systems other than Mac OS to boot from HFS Plus volumes
512 byte catalog node	4 KB catalog node	Larger catalog improves efficiency
2^{31} byte maximum file size	2^{63} byte maximum file size	Increased user benefit

displays the type of file system, name of the volume, and other information about that image, such as when it was created and modified (Carrier, n.d.).

```
Katie-Strzempkas-MacBook:fstools kstrzemp$ fsstat iPhone-3G-313.dmg
FILE SYSTEM INFORMATION
--------------------------------------------
File System Type: HFSX
File System Version: HFSX

Volume Name: Data
Volume Identifier: 79d2d6f99b3ca938

Last Mounted By: fsck_hfs
Volume Unmounted Improperly
Mount Count: 79534

Creation Date:         Tue Jan 11 21:00:26 2011
Last Written Date:       Thu Feb 3 12:16:34 2011
Last Backup Date:      Wed Dec 31 18:00:00 1969
Last Checked Date:       Tue Jan 11 15:00:26 2011

METADATA INFORMATION
--------------------------------------------
Range: 2 - 16815
Bootable Folder ID: 0
Startup App ID: 0
Startup Open Folder ID: 0
Mac OS 8/9 Blessed System Folder ID: 0
Mac OS X Blessed System Folder ID: 0
Number of files: 1826
Number of folders: 408

CONTENT INFORMATION
--------------------------------------------
Block Range: 0 - 3836825
Total Range in Image: 0 - 3836824
Allocation Block Size: 4096
Number of Free Blocks: 3819106
```

Various arguments can be run with the fsstat command to retrieve specific information about the file system. One example of these arguments is the listing of the various file system types recognized by fsstat:

```
kstrzempka@linux-wks-001:/$ fsstat -f list
Supported file system types:
    ntfs (NTFS)
    fat (FAT (Auto Detection))
    ext (ExtX (Auto Detection))
    iso9660 (ISO9660 CD)
```

```
hfs (HFS+)
ufs (UFS (Auto Detection))
raw (Raw Data)
swap (Swap Space)
fat12 (FAT12)
fat16 (FAT16)
fat32 (FAT32)
ext2 (Ext2)
ext3 (Ext3)
ufs1 (UFS1)
ufs2 (UFS2)
```

The Disk Utility program on a Mac can also be used to obtain information about a hard disk or disk image. This program is commonly used to erase, format, partition, or repair a drive. It can also be used to mount disk images, such as an iPhone DMG file. Disk Utility is stored under /Applications/Utilities and can be run through a GUI (Graphical User Interface) or via command line. To simply get information about an iPhone disk image, the "diskutil" command can be run against a mounted image. The output of that command is shown below. Because the image was mounted on a Mac, some of the information is applicable to the workstation rather than the iPhone itself. For example, the Volume Name, Mount Location, etc. all relates to the Mac on which the iPhone image was mounted. The total and available size applies to the image of the iPhone.

```
Katie-Strzempkas-MacBook:Desktop kstrzemp$ diskutil info /Volumes/
Data/
    Device Identifier:        disk2
    Device Node:              /dev/disk2
    Part Of Whole:            disk2
    Device / Media Name:      Apple read/write Media

    Volume Name:              Data
    Escaped with Unicode:     Data

    Mounted:                  Yes
    Mount Point:              /Volumes/Data
    Escaped with Unicode:     /Volumes/Data

    File System:              Case-sensitive HFS+
    Type:                     hfs
    Name:                     Mac OS Extended (Case-sensitive)
    Owners:                   Disabled

    Partition Type:           None
    Bootable:                 Not bootable
    Media Type:               Generic
    Protocol:                 Disk Image
    SMART Status:             Not Supported
    Volume UUID:              292F1301-EDBD-3D2E-8721-5731386E9E6D
```

```
Total Size:              15.7 GB (15715635200 Bytes) (exactly
30694600 512-Byte-Blocks)
Volume Free Space:       15.6 GB (15642976256 Bytes) (exactly
30552688 512-Byte-Blocks)

Read-Only Media:         No
Read-Only Volume:        Yes
Ejectable:               Yes

Whole:                   Yes
Internal:                No
OS 9 Drivers:            No
Low Level Format:        Not Supported
```

Volumes

Each HFS Plus system is made up of volumes, which represent a portion of the physical disk. Each system can be made up of one or more volumes, with each volume consisting of a header, and alternate header, and five special files. Three out of the five special files contain a B-tree structure: Catalog File, Extents Overflow File, and Attributes File. A B-tree is a data structure that allows data to be efficiently searched, viewed, modified, or removed. It is made up of nodes that store key information, allowing for fast searches (Kubasiak et al., 2009).

- *Volume Header/Alternate Volume Header*: The header contains volume information, including allocation block size as well as which blocks are available for use. It also contains metadata about each of the five special files (Kubasiak et al., 2009).
- *Startup File*: Contains information required for booting the device (Kubasiak et al., 2009).
- *Allocation File*: This file is used to track used versus unused blocks. The format of this file consists of one bit for every allocation block. If the bit is set, the block is in use; if it is not set, the block is available for use.
- *Catalog File*: The catalog file contains file and folder information, which is used to locate any file and folder within the volume. It stores the hierarchy of directories and files, each having its own 32-bit catalog node ID (CNID). Apple has reserved certain CNIDs for certain files in an HFS Plus volume (Kubasiak et al., 2009).
- *Extents Overflow File*: This file contains data on fragmented files as well as those with bad blocks (Kubasiak et al., 2009).
- *Attributes File*: The attributes file allows the association of a data stream with a particular file or folder (Kubasiak et al., 2009).

Journaling

One attribute of the HFS Plus file system is that it allows the option of "journaling." When journaling is enabled, a log of changes is kept, which keeps track of the changes it plans to make prior to making them in the main file system. In the event of a system or hardware component failure, the journal is used to help restore the disk back to its original state prior to the failure. Instead of having to check the entire file system, the OS just looks at recent journal transactions, allowing for a fast recovery.

iPhone disk partitions

Two disk partitions exist on the NAND Flash. The first is the system, or firmware partition, which is where the OS as well as basic applications resides. When firmware upgrades are performed on the device, the system partition is updated. With few applications actually installed here, the system partition takes up only a small portion of storage space on the device. It is configured to be read-only by default, except while performing a software upgrade. During this process, the entire partition is formatted by iTunes, without affecting any of the user data.

The user data partition, also referred to as "Slice 2," takes up most of the space on the NAND. This is where most, if not all, evidentiary data can be found. Information on the default applications, those downloaded through the iTunes App Store, and other stored data can all be found on this partition. This image, after being forensically acquired, can be renamed as a ".dmg" file and mounted on a Mac for analysis (more on this in Chapter 6). While both slices can be imaged and analyzed, the user data, or "Media" partition, is what is typically acquired. This partition is mounted on the device at "/private/var."

Table 3.4 provides a breakdown of the two disk partitions and provides information on mount points, information stored, and more.

As a test iPhone that had previously been jailbroken was available, the device could be connected in order to view the mounted partitions. The phone was connected through SSH, and the "mount" command was run on the root of the device. The System partition is shown first as being mounted on "/" (or root) as well as the User Data partition mounted on /private/var. Both partitions show HFS as the file system, and the User Data partition even shows that journaling is enabled.

Table 3.4 iPhone Disk Partitions

	Partition 1 "System"	Partition 2 "User Data"
Referred to as	System or firmware partition; Slice 1	User Data or Media partition; Slice 2
Storage on device	0.93/8 GB; 1.4/16 GB; 2.7/32 GB	7.07/8 GB; 14.6/16 GB; 29.3/32 GB
Mount location on iPhone	"/" (root)	"/private/var"
Type of data stored	Operating system, basic applications, firmware upgrades	All user data (SMS, Call Logs, Photos, iTunes files, etc.)

```
3GS-40:~ root# mount
/dev/disk0s1 on / (hfs, local, noatime)
devfs on /dev (devfs, local, nobrowse)
/dev/disk0s2s1 on /private/var (hfs, local, journaled, noatime,
protect)
```

The above information showed block devices, while the following are the raw disk images on the iPhone. Rdisk0 is the entire disk, including all partitions. Rdisk0s1 is the firmware partition, or Slice 1 as described above, just as Rdisk0s2 is the User Data partition. On a 3GS device, "rdisk0s2s1" is also shown.

```
3GS-40:/dev root# ls -lh rdisk*
crw-r---- 1 root operator 14, 0 Feb 9 10:53 rdisk0
crw-r---- 1 root operator 14, 0 Feb 9 10:54 rdisk0s1
crw-r---- 1 root operator 14, 0 Feb 9 10:53 rdisk0s2
crw-r---- 1 root operator 14, 0 Feb 9 10:54 rdisk0s2s1
```

SUMMARY

Understanding where, and more importantly how, data is stored on a device can play an important role in recovering all potential data. This chapter has outlined the type of data that could potentially be stored as well as its location and the format in which it is saved on the device. While other mobile devices may contain external data storage in the form of SD cards, the iPhone stores all data to its internal NAND Flash memory. Here, data is stored in common file types such as SQLite databases and Property Lists. The NAND implements features such as wear-leveling, which spread writes and deletes out across the device in order to extend the lifespan.

While data recovery from the device at rest has several potential methods, there is no ideal way to recover volatile memory from an iPhone. A method of recovering RAM from a Mac OS workstation was recently developed, so it is possible that iPhone RAM recovery is not far behind.

The previous sections covered both the operating system and the file system used by Apple iOS devices. This file system, HFS Plus, added improvements to its original version in order to increase efficiency. Journaling is a feature within HFS Plus, which is used to log changes and allow the device to quickly recover from a system failure.

Finally, the disk partitions contained on the iPhone were discussed. The firmware partition is where the operating system and basic applications are located and also where firmware upgrades are performed. The User Data partition contains the rest of the data stored on the device. It is this second partition, or Slice 2, where data recovery is performed. The acquisition and analysis of this User Data partition are covered in Chapters 5 and Chapter 6, respectively.

References

Apple Developer. (2004, March 5). HFS Plus volume format. Mac OS X reference library: Technical Note TN1150. Retrieved February 5, 2011, from http://developer.apple.com/library/mac/#technotes/tn/tn1150.html

Apple Developer. (2010, July 8). iOS overview. iOS reference library. Retrieved February 21, 2011, from developer.apple.com/library/ios/#referencelibrary/GettingStarted/URL_iPhone_OS_Overview/index.html#//apple_ref/doc/uid/TP40007592

Apple Inc. (2010, March 24). Introduction to property lists. Apple developer. Retrieved February 3, 2011, from http://developer.apple.com/library/ios/#documentation/Cocoa/Conceptual/PropertyLists/Introduction/Introduction.html

Caithness, A. (2010, December). Property Lists in Digital Forensics. Computer forensics, digital forensics, computer analysis, evidence – CCL Forensics. Retrieved February 10, 2011, from http://www.ccl-forensics.com/pdf/property_lists_in_digital_forensics_web.pdf

Carrier, B. (n.d.). FSSTAT(1) manual page. The Sleuth Kit (TSK) & autopsy: Open source digital investigation tools. Retrieved February 7, 2011, from http://www.sleuthkit.org/sleuthkit/man/fsstat.html

Kubasiak, R. R., Morris key, S., & Varsalone, J. (2009). *Macintosh OS X, iPod, and iPhone forensic analysis DVD toolkit.* Burlington, MA: Syngress Pub.

PERL Implementation of OS/X Plutil (March 2008). Starlight computer wizardry home page. Retrieved January 10, 2011, from http://scw.us/iPhone/plutil/

Sleepimage – The Mac OS X sleepimage file explained (2010, October 11). OS X daily. Retrieved February 10, 2011, from http://osxdaily.com/2010/10/11/sleepimage-mac/

Valenzuela, I. (2011, January 28). Mac OS forensics how-to: Simple RAM acquisition and analysis with Mac memory reader. SANS – Computer forensics and incident response with Rob Lee. Retrieved February 10, 2011, from http://computer-forensics.sans.org/blog/2011/01/28/mac-os-forensics-howto-simple-ram-acquisition-analysis-mac-memory-reader-part-1

iPhone and iPad data security

INTRODUCTION

The integration of smart phone devices in corporations can greatly benefit both the business and the employees. The Blackberry, by Research in Motion (RIM), has been commonly used in business and is known as being one of the most secure mobile devices on the market. These devices have been used for some time now for the purpose of syncing business contacts and corporate e-mail via a Blackberry Enterprise Server (BES) hosted within the corporation. The BES server typically sits between the employee workstations or smart phone devices and the company's exchange or e-mail servers. With the increased popularity of iPhone devices and multiple varieties of Androids, the use of smart phones is continually increasing. These devices have the capability to connect with Microsoft Exchange, or other e-mail services, and provide the option of synchronizing corporate e-mail, contacts, and calendar events. Corporations have a difficult choice to make when deciding which of the available mobile devices is the most secure and will protect sensitive internal information from being accessed by the outside world.

In addition to mobile phones, tablet devices such as the iPad are also in high demand. The use of this device in particular is on the rise in corporations for various reasons. The large screen provides better visibility for reading e-mails or other business documents. In addition, employees no longer require a laptop to travel to meetings or other locations. The iPad is a portable device that can provide similar capabilities as an employee workstation, including easy access to e-mail, a web browser, calendar, and more. Finally, deploying these devices within a corporation has never been easier from a support standpoint. Virtual private network (VPN) and Wi-Fi access are readily available on this device as well as the iPhone. Connecting to a wireless access point can be done within seconds. In addition, ActiveSync is used to pull down data from the Microsoft Exchange Server, and requires only a one-time e-mail account setup to connect to the company's internal network.

DATA SECURITY AND TESTING

Both corporate and individual mobile device users expect their personal data to be either stored in a secure manner or not stored at all. With the wide range of tools available on the device, including banking and other financial applications, a significant amount of sensitive information is being stored and transmitted. In addition, some corporations allow their employees to connect their personally owned mobile devices to the company's internal network, mainly to send and receive e-mail through Microsoft Exchange via ActiveSync. When used in this manner, a wide range of internal information is potentially being stored on the device. For this reason alone, it is important to understand what type of data can be recovered from these devices as well as how simple it is to retrieve this data.

Apple devices are starting to become more widely known for their ability to protect user data. This, in combination with employee preference of iPhones and iPads, has led to corporations taking a closer look at whether these devices make the cut. Both the iPad and recent models of the iPhone (3G(s), iPhone 4, and iPod Touch) are said to provide hardware encryption for all data stored on the device as well as data transmitted over the network. On the iPad in particular, this encryption is enabled by default and cannot be removed by the user (Apple Inc., 2010). As it is possible to remotely wipe the devices in the event of its being lost or stolen, the belief exists that the user's data is protected.

Apple has dedicated an entire section of their website to the deployment of iPads in an organization. Many of these resources contain detailed instructional guidelines on incorporating the use of the iPad throughout an organization. Technical guidelines are provided on Microsoft Exchange ActiveSync, VPN and wireless capabilities, device security, and use of certificates and encryption. As this chapter is not meant to be a how-to guide on deploying iPads or iPhones within an organization, the focus is going to be on device and application security, and whether Apple has truly earned its place as a leader in mobile device security in the corporate world.

Computer crime laws in the United States

There are several federal laws in the United States that deal with the security of data at rest and in transit on a digital device. In this section, a few of the most common laws on digital crime are outlined, with a brief description of each.

At the federal level, the U.S. Department of Justice (DOJ) divides computer crime into three distinct areas, two of which have broad application to the types of crimes involved when compromising a mobile device. The two areas are (Country, n.d.) the following:

- *Computer Fraud and Abuse Act (CFAA)*: The CFAA focuses on attacks against computers of government and financial institutions or computers involved in interstate or foreign commerce. The Act covers both narrow areas such as accessing computers without proper authorization to gain data related to national security issues and more broad sections such as accessing a computer without proper authorization to fraudulently gain something of value. The CFAA was amended by the National Information Infrastructure Protection Act to cover new abuses and also those intending to commit the crimes.

- *Electronic Communications Privacy Act (ECPA)*: The ECPA is another law covering computer crimes, which makes it illegal to intercept stored or transmitted electronic communication without authorization. The ECPA contains several key areas:
  - Communication in transit including oral, wire, or electronic communications (Wiretap);
  - Data at rest (Stored Communication Act), which protects data stored on non-volatile memory;
  - Collecting communication metadata such as phone numbers, IP addresses, and other data used to route communication (but not the message itself). This is called the "pen registers and trap and trace devices," which refers to the actual devices and techniques used to capture the information.
- *Cyber Security Enhancement Act (CSEA)*: Passed along with the Homeland Security Act in 2002, the CSEA permits an Internet service provider (ISP) to disclose customer information to a government agent if there is reason to believe that the information is related to a serious crime. This way, law enforcement officers can gain access to this information without having to wait for a warrant as previously required by the ECPA (SANS Institute, 2004).
- *Digital Millennium Copyright Act (DMCA)*: Enacted in 1998, the DMCA includes a section on "Circumvention of Technological Protection Measures." This portion of the document prohibits the circumvention of copyrighted technology. The act is reviewed every three years to determine whether specific technologies remain applicable (SANS Institute, 2004). As it relates to the iPhone, the DMCA originally prohibited users from jailbreaking an Apple device, as the process involves bypassing and modifying the standard firmware partition. In 2010, it was determined that jailbreaking a device was exempt from the DMCA.

In addition to federal and state laws which criminalize computer crimes, a host of regulatory bodies govern corporations who operate in industries that deal with sensitive data. Many of the regulations provide not only specific guidelines and requirements the firms must follow but also civil and criminal statutes with both financial penalties and, in the most serious cases, incarceration. A list of the better-known regulations includes the following:

- Payment Card Industry Data Security Standard (PCI)
- Health Insurance Portability and Accountability Act (HIPAA)
- HITECH Act Enforcement Interim Final Rule (additions to HIPAA)
- Federal Information Security Management Act (FISMA)
- Family Education Rights and Privacy Act of 1974 (FERPA)
- Gramm–Leach–Bliley Financial Services Modernization Act of 1999 (GLBA)
- Sarbanes Oxley (SOX)

This section covered only briefly the laws related to computer crimes. However, it should be clear that there are laws designed to protect data both in transit and at rest.

Data protection in the hands of the administrators

In Chapter 2, the general guidelines were briefly discussed, suggesting ways of providing additional layers of data protection. One of the methods discussed was the option within the device settings to apply a passcode. If enabled, the user creates a four-digit PIN (personal identification number) on the device, which is required to access any of the data or applications within. To add complexity, the user also has the option to modify the default "Simple Passcode" configuration in order to create a more complex passcode. If the firmware version of the iPhone or iPad is prior to iOS 4.0, this option is not available and only the four-digit PIN can be enabled. When either of these devices is deployed in an organization, however, there are a variety of passcode policies available. Administrators have the option to enforce not only the creation of a passcode for all employees but also the specification of other security enhancements such as a minimum length, a specified number of complex characters, and alphanumeric requirements; in addition, forced password changes can also be customized to meet the needs of the organization (Apple Inc., 2010). Figure 4.1 provides details related to the passcode requirement options that are available.

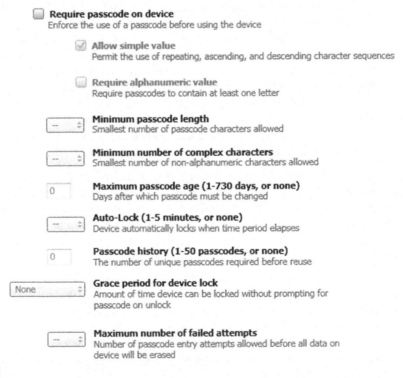

FIGURE 4.1

Passcode Policy Configurations.

Security policies such as those discussed above are controlled through Configuration Profiles, which allow the device to communicate with the company's internal network. These profiles are XML (Extensible Markup Language) files that contain various specifications for device security or other modifiable settings contained on the iPhone or iPad. VPN and Wi-Fi settings can be set within a Configuration Profile as well as e-mail accounts and login credentials. Once this particular profile template is created for an organization, it can be administered on all corporate devices through various methods. Devices can be synced with a version of iTunes in which the profile has been loaded. The most popular form of Configuration Profile deployment is through the iPhone Configuration Utility, shown in Figure 4.2. This piece of software is a simple way to manage many devices. In addition to installing Configuration Profiles on an Apple device, this utility can also be used to manage the installation of Provisioning Profiles and custom-developed applications (these are discussed further in the "Application Security" section).

Also controlled through Configuration Profiles or Over-The-Air (OTA) updates are settings that restrict access to specified applications. Common restrictions might include default applications on the device such as YouTube, the iPod feature, or Safari, but control can be extended to many other features contained on the device (refer to Figure 4.3 for available restrictions). For example, if a corporation wishes to prevent users from installation of custom applications through the iTunes App Store, this particular process can be restricted. A corporation also has the option to control

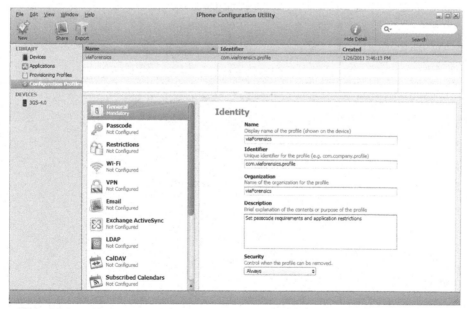

FIGURE 4.2

iPhone Configuration Utility – Creating a Profile.

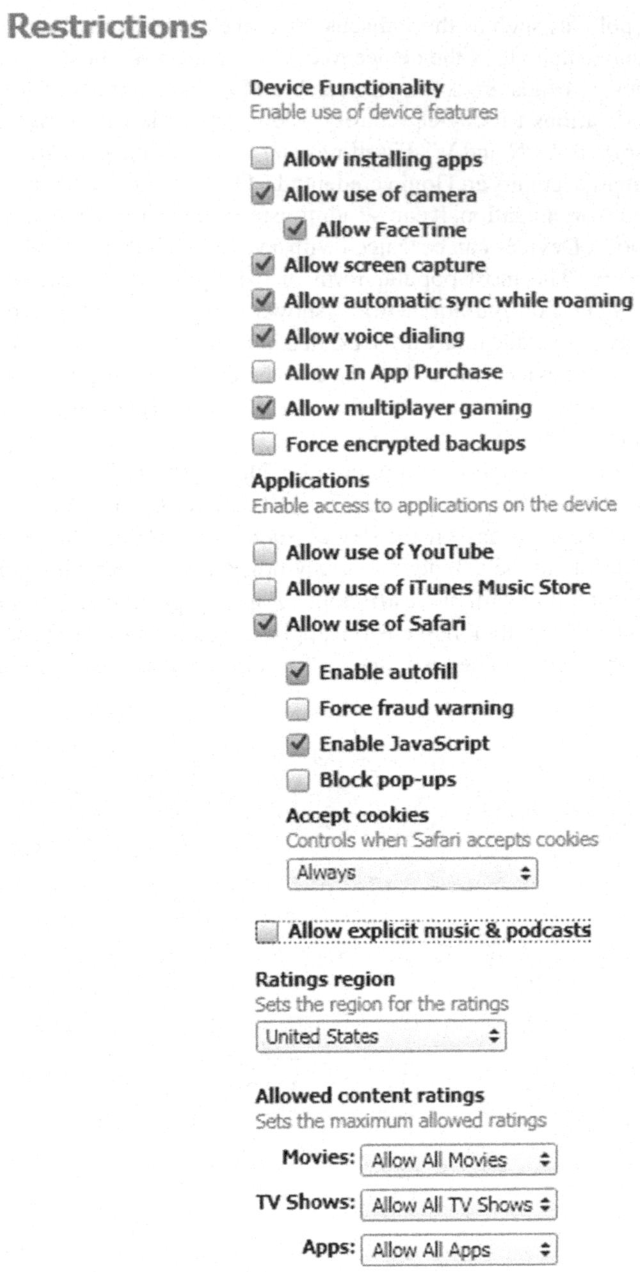

Restrictions

Device Functionality
Enable use of device features

- ☐ **Allow installing apps**
- ☑ **Allow use of camera**
  - ☑ **Allow FaceTime**
- ☑ **Allow screen capture**
- ☑ **Allow automatic sync while roaming**
- ☑ **Allow voice dialing**
- ☐ **Allow In App Purchase**
- ☑ **Allow multiplayer gaming**
- ☐ **Force encrypted backups**

Applications
Enable access to applications on the device

- ☐ **Allow use of YouTube**
- ☐ **Allow use of iTunes Music Store**
- ☑ **Allow use of Safari**

  - ☑ **Enable autofill**
  - ☐ **Force fraud warning**
  - ☑ **Enable JavaScript**
  - ☐ **Block pop-ups**
  - **Accept cookies**
    Controls when Safari accepts cookies

    | Always | ⇕ |

- ☐ **Allow explicit music & podcasts**

Ratings region
Sets the region for the ratings

| United States | ⇕ |

Allowed content ratings
Sets the maximum allowed ratings

Movies: | Allow All Movies | ⇕ |

TV Shows: | Allow All TV Shows | ⇕ |

Apps: | Allow All Apps | ⇕ |

FIGURE 4.3

iPhone Configuration Utility – Restrictions.

iTunes usage within the organization. Some features cannot be restricted, and tasks such as software updates fall within this realm (Apple Inc., 2010).

Configuration Profiles can be signed, encrypted, and locked, preventing individual users from modifying device settings. "Signing" a profile prevents any alteration of the settings within, and encrypting the profile prevents the contents from being viewable. All these features will ensure that each device on the network is configured in a way that falls within the security standards set forth by the organization (Apple Inc., 2010).

Security testing procedure

From a forensic examiner's standpoint, one might wonder if these security measures are sufficient. Even with the required alphanumeric passcode and access restrictions to certain applications, the fact remains that sensitive data is still stored on the device somewhere. The question is where it is being stored, and how easily it can be acquired. Extensive testing and analysis has been performed on various mobile devices to determine those that are the most secure versus those that insecurely store internal data, such as company e-mail, passwords, or other application data. As part of this process, the iPhone 3G(s) (running iOS 3.1.3) and iPhone 4 (running iOS 4.0) were among the devices tested. Research and analysis of each phone was performed to determine how secure the device was and how easy it would be for an individual to recover sensitive data. The following steps were included in this process, each of them discussed in greater detail in subsequent sections:

- The device was connected to an Exchange account via ActiveSync to test e-mail account and content storage.
- The remainder of the device was populated with simulated test data, including SMS, Contacts, Calendar, and other commonly used applications while simultaneously capturing wireless traffic.
- When testing was complete, the device was forensically imaged. An acquisition of the backup files as well as a logical and physical acquisition was performed to determine the difficulty level in acquiring various pieces of data.
- Network transmissions were analyzed for any signs of unsecured data, such as exposure of credentials or other unencrypted information.
- A similar analysis was performed after the device had been remotely wiped, and then again after a secure wipe using the device settings. This process would determine the effectiveness of the erasing methods.

Data population

Prior to loading any data on the devices themselves, test e-mail accounts were set up for both Microsoft Exchange (Outlook) and Gmail. Each of these accounts was populated with a set of test data prior to being synchronized with any device. Specific contacts were set up within these accounts, as well as calendar events/appointments. Finally, e-mails with unique key words were sent to and from each of the accounts and thoroughly documented. Recording these procedures in detail would later assist in the process of determining what data still remained on the device, if any.

Once the accounts were set up, the process of simulating "typical user activity" began. Each device was populated within call history, text messages, photos, web history, and other commonly used applications contained on the device. The test data population was similar across devices when possible. Table 4.1 contains a detailed description of the steps that were followed for this data population scenario.

Table 4.1 Device Population Scenario

Function	Description
Activation	If necessary activate phone with wireless carrier
Wi-Fi	Connect the device to viaForensics Wi-Fi access point
Contacts	Sync device with exchange account and verify sync. Set to at least 30-day sync period
Call Logs	Place 25 outgoing calls
Camera	Take 10 pictures with the device at random; Sync device with 20 pictures from PC; Delete three of the on-board camera pictures; Delete picture1, picture2, picture3, picture4 from synced photos
Video	Take two videos using the on-board video camera (or using the iCamcorder application); Sync the device with two additional videos from PC; Delete one on-board video; Delete one synced video
Exchange Mail	Verify whether the mailbox contains the mail that synchronized with Exchange; Open message having three attachments and open each attachment; Forward a received message to viaforensics. test@gmail.com, then delete it from the inbox; Delete received message from vtest@viaforensics.com; Create and save new draft; Create and save second new draft, delete draft; Create and send message to corresponding Gmail account
Gmail	Sync e-mail from Gmail account, last 30 days or more if possible; Open message and photo attachment, forward message; Open the message received from corresponding Exchange account, delete it; Create a new message and save as a draft; Create and send a new message with photo from device attached; Create and send an email message to viaForensics
Text (SMS/MMS)	Send text/mms messages to multiple recipients: Recipient 1: Create and send four SMS, one MMS containing photo from on-board camera. Save one draft unsent; Recipient 2: Send four SMS and two MMS containing photos from on-board camera. Delete two sent SMS and one sent MMS; Recipient 3: Send four SMS. Save one draft unsent; Recipient 4: Send four SMS. Delete all sent messages (entire thread)
Exchange Calendar	Verify calendar items sync from Exchange. Make changes to the calendar using local calendar app: Add one appointment for 8/2/2010 at 13:00; Delete one appointment from 8/4/2010

Table 4.1 Device Population Scenario—cont'd

Function	Description
Gmail Calendar	Verify Gmail calendar synced if applicable. Make changes to the calendar using local calendar app: Create and save appointment for 8/30/2010 at 07:00; Delete the added appointment
Notes	Create three total notes. Delete third note
Songs	Sync device with six songs from PC
Web History	Create web history – manually type various web addresses into the address bar and follow links. Create a history including Gmail, EBay, viaForensics.com, Monster.com, Engaget.com, ChicagoCubs.com, CNet.com and Craigslist. Additional details: Sign into Gmail via web; Create four Bookmarks (Favorites); Search in EBay, Monster and Craigslist; On viaforensics.com, select appWatchdog > Findings; Delete monster.com Internet history
Google Searches	Use the Google home page or search bar to search for 10 specified search terms
Applications	Install and use applications as available for device. Log in using test accounts. Facebook; eBay; Pandora Radio; Zillow; YouTube; Other utilities as needed for testing
Google Maps	Open map and find current location; Use driving directions feature to generate directions
Voice mail	Set up and use visual Voice mail if available; Place three calls to the device to populate the visual Voice mail; Delete the third VM
Voice Memo	Create two voice memos; delete the second memo

Forensic imaging

Once the devices were populated with the above information, they were ready to be forensically imaged. For those readers who may have skipped straight to Chapter 4, forensic imaging refers to the acquisition of disk and memory contents from a device. The purpose of forensic imaging is to make a copy of the electronic evidence, which will later be used for analysis. This prevents data from being modified on the device itself, and keeps the evidence "pristine." Once the disk and memory contents are extracted from the device, this data is copied into an external file that can be stored as read-only on a forensic workstation and later examined using a variety of forensic tools. The intent is to have the ability to search across the entire disk image for specific data that was on the device. Logical imaging acquires only the active file system, while a physical acquisition refers to a copy of an entire disk or device partition. For complete details on logical and physical forensic imaging, refer to Chapter 5.

The goal of this assessment was also to image and analyze the iPhones after various wiping techniques were performed in order to verify the success or failure of both the remote wipe and the full reset. For this reason, each device was imaged four times:

1. After initial device population
2. After removing the ActiveSync connection
3. After performing a remote wipe using ActiveSync
4. After performing a full reset using the settings on the device.

For each of these steps, the same acquisition process was utilized.

First, the iPhone was connected to iTunes in order to perform a backup of the device (see Chapter 2 for instructions on how to perform an iTunes backup). Both an unencrypted backup and an encrypted backup were performed in order to determine whether data could be extracted from each. Forensic tools would later be used to convert the backup files into readable ASCII characters and attempt to recover data from them.

Next, a logical acquisition was performed on the device using Lantern, one of the available iPhone Forensics commercial tools. The version utilized in this assessment was 1.0.6.0. Through this process, similar data files are recovered as from the backup files. However, many forensic tools, including Lantern, will extract some of the common data from the raw files and incorporate them into a reporting tool, making it easier to view the results.

Finally, a physical image of the iPhone was performed utilizing one of the two techniques currently available. This method extracts a copy of the entire user partition over a USB (universal series bus) connection. A bit-by-bit image of this disk partition is extracted and later analyzed for data. The resulting disk image file was marked as read-only in order to prevent any changes to the data.

Data security assessment and methodology

During the device activation and data population process, the device was connected to a wireless router from which network traffic was being captured. This allowed us to determine whether Secure Socket Layers (SSLs) were being used for exchange synchronization as well as any exposure of credentials or other sensitive data. The remainder of the data was analyzed using the data files acquired from the forensic imaging process.

Analysis of data at rest

Data at rest refers to data that is stored on nonvolatile memory, as against data stored in RAM or in transit across the network. This type of data is acquired through a forensic acquisition (see Chapter 5) and the resulting image is then analyzed for data.

Depending on the type of mobile user, a wide range of data can be recovered from data at rest. Many chapters in this book discuss the array of information and data files that can potentially be stored on an iOS device, including default application data such as text messages, call logs, contacts, voice mails, pictures, videos, web history, and more. In a corporate environment, not only can this basic data be found but business users will typically sync their device with their corporate e-mail account as well. On top of that, there is also the possibility of data storage involving attachments, voice mails, and faxes containing sensitive internal information.

One example to highlight the significance of accessing data at rest involves the iPhone's built-in e-mail application. Assuming a user's Microsoft Exchange e-mail account was synced to the device, data related to this account was stored in a central location, namely user names, Exchange Servers, and the protocol and port over which the account was synced. Passwords are also stored in the database, but in an encrypted format. On devices running iOS 4, these passwords can be recovered quite easily (see Chapter 5, section on "Backup Acquisition," for more details on how this password can be recovered). Researchers in Germany were also successful in performing an attack on the iPhone, which accessed and decrypted passwords contained in the Keychain database on the device. Here, e-mail passwords were recovered, as well as voice mail, VPN, Wi-Fi, and certain application passwords as long as they leveraged the Keychain file for storing credentials (International Data Group, 2011).

There are two primary techniques that can be used by either a forensic examiner, or potentially an attacker, in the event of a device being stolen. The first technique, typically used by examiners, requires physical access to the actual device. With this method, a forensic acquisition and analysis is performed using one of the various tools available. The remaining chapters in this book go into this technique in great detail, with Chapter 5 covering Forensic Acquisitions and Chapter 6 covering Application and Data Analysis. Chapter 7 walks the reader through the use of many of the commercially available forensic tools. While physical access to a device is not necessarily easy to achieve for a potential attacker, possible scenarios include lost or stolen phones, as well as phones that are replaced with newer models but not securely wiped. In addition, people who travel internationally, especially executives at corporations, may find that their phones are temporarily confiscated and examined by customs officials as they enter a country. In this scenario, the officials have physical access to the device.

The other technique, more commonly used by attackers, is accessing data at rest through remote exploits, vulnerabilities, and malicious software. One exploit involved the ability to spoof web pages even when traffic was running over an encrypted SSL connection. In this attack, a configuration file is modified and, as long as the user accepts the changes (which appear to be coming from a valid source), the attacker has the ability to modify a variety of settings. The Safari web browser could be disabled or other applications on the device affected, depending on the particular change made in that configuration file (Goodin, 2010). Another example occurred in August 2010. This attack allowed a jailbroken iPhone to be remotely connected to using a PDF exploit. Days later, Apple did release a patch for this vulnerability (USA Today, 2010). Given these examples, the possibility of remotely exploiting an Apple device is real, and protective measures are necessary to prevent such attacks.

Analysis of data in transit

Data in transit describes data that is sent over a network (cellular, Wi-Fi, or other networks) or is located in the RAM. At some point, data that was recovered from the device (or data at rest) was also sent over the network. An example of this includes sending a text message to another user, or web browsing over a wireless connection.

Several well-known techniques are used by attackers to compromise data in transit and the list of new techniques either discovered by security researchers themselves or by practitioners is growing by the day. Some of the well-known techniques include the following:

- Man-In-The-Middle (MITM) attack
- MITM SSL attack
- Domain Name System (DNS) spoofing attacks (including /etc/hosts)
- Baseband Attack

The baseband attack is a recent development that focuses on the cellular modem baseband firmware. Ralf-Philipp Weinmann discovered security holes in Qualcomm and Infineon firmware for GSM baseband processors, which allow the phone to be turned into a spying device. Weinmann was able to successfully hack a non-jailbroken iPhone and gain access to the text messages on the device. The exploit allowed him to run as the "mobile" user on the device, enabling privileged access to the device. An additional exploit involved the TMSI overflow attack, which causes a heap overflow in the GSM baseband stack of Apple iOS devices prior to 4.2. This attack can lead to remote code execution on the baseband processor (Sinful iPhone, 2011).

While the baseband attacks are more recent, the MITM attacks have been around for a long time and are therefore well understood. This attack intercepts traffic and presents a spoofed certificate to the client to impersonate the server. When successful, the MITM attack can induce the client to disclose login credentials (user name/password) to the false server, or even read all communication between the client and the server. If an attacker is able to position his or her computer between the iPhone (or other Apple device) and the ultimate destination, he or she can launch the attack. Many users reuse user names and passwords. Once the attacker has one user name and password, he or she can begin to research more about the consumer and generally will be able to quickly find additional systems that can be accessed.

The HTTPS protocol uses TLS/SSL (Transport Layer Security/Secure Sockets Layer) to provide critical data protection during Internet transmission. With the proper use of this protocol, all data submitted or received by the application is encrypted and cannot be read by a third party. If a mobile application does not implement SSL, as is mostly the case, it will connect, authenticate, and transmit data over the network in clear text. A standard MITM attack would be able to recover this data. However, if an application does implement SSL but does not properly verify the SSL certificate, this app would be susceptible to a MITM SSL attack.

The final technique listed above is a DNS spoofing attack. A DNS entry tells a computer or other device how to associate a hostname with an IP address. With DNS spoofing, the device is tricked into thinking that a hostname is associated with a certain IP address, when in fact it is not. One example of DNS spoofing involves the "hosts" file on a computer (the location of the hosts file on various operating systems can be found in Table 4.2).

The purpose of this file is to map hostnames to IP addresses, overriding external DNS resolution (see below for the standard content within a hosts file). This example is from a hosts file on a Microsoft Windows XP system.

Table 4.2 Hosts File Locations	
Operating System	**Location**
Windows 2000/XP/Vista	C:\WINDOWS\system32\drivers\etc\hosts
Mac OS X 10.2 and newer	/private/etc/hosts
Linux	/etc/inet/hosts or /etc/hosts
iOS	/etc/hosts
Android	/system/etc/hosts

```
# Copyright (c) 1993-1999 Microsoft Corp.
#
# This is a sample HOSTS file used by Microsoft TCP/IP for Windows.
#
# This file contains the mappings of IP addresses to host names. Each
# entry should be kept on an individual line. The IP address should
# be placed in the first column followed by the corresponding host name.
# The IP address and the host name should be separated by at least one
# space.
#
# Additionally, comments (such as these) may be inserted on individual
# lines or following the machine name denoted by a '#' symbol.
#
# For example:
#
#      102.54.94.97      rhino.acme.com      # source server
#      38.25.63.10       x.acme.com          # x client host

127.0.0.1  localhost
```

If an iPhone application is improperly designed, an application would connect to any host responding to the desired hostname, leading to client login credentials being sent to the false host. For example, the hosts file could be modified to redirect secure. nameofyourapp.com to an internally controlled IP address and server. When the hosts file is updated to the device, the application will then redirect all traffic to the internal server, allowing an attacker or investigator to view sensitive application data. If the app is designed appropriately, it will fail as soon as the hosts file is updated.

Findings
The recovered data was analyzed at various steps in the process in order to determine how effective the various wiping procedures were. The device was imaged and analyzed after the data population process, removal of ActiveSync, remote wipe via ActiveSync, and full reset on the device itself.

A large amount of data could be recovered after the device was initially populated. From the backup files alone, common application data was acquired including contacts, call logs, photos, videos, and Exchange and Gmail account information. From the encrypted backup, a password recovery tool was able to easily crack the encrypted backup password and recover even more data than was possible with the unencrypted backup files. In addition to the typical data recovery, the password recovery tool also allowed the extraction of all account user names and passwords that leveraged Apple's keychain database. This included Microsoft Exchange and Gmail passwords. While the e-mail content was not physically recovered through either the backup files or logical acquisition, the ability to recover the user name and password would allow a malicious user to log in to that particular e-mail account.

Through the physical acquisition, much more data was recoverable, specifically content that was originally on the device but had at some point been deleted. E-mail content, including deleted e-mails, was extracted as well as all other application data that was placed on the device during the data population phase.

While network data exposure was not necessarily high, some data was transmitted over the network unencrypted. Certain websites that were visited during the testing process required a user name and password for access. In some instances, these login credentials could be seen within the captured traffic. Random web browser and YouTube search terms were also uncovered, as well as some data remnants from downloaded applications.

The next step involved removing the ActiveSync connection, which in turn removed Microsoft Exchange from the iPhone. While this is not a form of "wiping" the device, it is assumed that some users may expect that simply removing the e-mail client would also remove their personal e-mail account information and messages. As part of the removal process, calendar events and contacts were also unsynced. When complete, the device was again imaged in the same manner as the previous step.

While a backup and logical acquisition would not show any data related to the Exchange e-mail client, the physical acquisition revealed a large amount of data. All contacts including phone numbers and e-mail addresses were still found, as well as calendar appointments, the user's e-mail account information, and the e-mail content itself. This process showed that the simple removal of an e-mail client does not actually delete any of this data from the device.

Following the removal of Microsoft Exchange, the e-mail client was once again synced with the device along with the same test data. In this step, a remote data wipe was initiated from the corporate end, and upon observing the device, it was automatically rebooted into Recovery Mode when the process was finished. The phone displayed a message showing that it needed to be connected to iTunes in order to be activated. Instead of reactivating the phone, a physical image was immediately taken of the device.

The physical image was analyzed and showed a lack of user data. Further forensic analysis techniques were used in order to ensure that user data was in fact wiped from the device. While some standard database and configuration files were recovered, no user data was actually found.

After the previous remote data wipe, the device was populated with a few more data items. From there, a factory reset was performed through the settings on the device. The user interface spells out clearly what will be erased and what will remain after the reset. The "Erase all Content and Settings" option was selected. When complete, the phone rebooted into recovery mode where the user is instructed to connect to iTunes to reactivate the device.

The phone was reimaged to perform a post-wipe investigation, looking for data that might still be existing on the device. Similar analysis techniques were performed as in the previous step, and once again no data could be found. In summary, a factory reset does a thorough job of wiping the data from the device.

APPLICATION SECURITY

The ability to acquire custom applications is one of the primary reasons for the popularity of these devices. There have been over 10 billion application downloads on the iOS App Store since its development (Evansville, 2011). In the business category alone, users have a wide range of applications to choose from. Specifically for the iPad, Apple advertises certain "business apps" to appeal to their corporate consumers. Office documents can easily be viewed and edited within the iPad, including word documents, spreadsheets, presentations, and PDFs. Applications used for these types of files include Pages, Keynote, QuickOffice Connect, Numbers, and more. While these common applications would suffice for most corporate users, there are apps available for just about any type of business out there. For airline pilots, there is an app that allows viewing airport diagrams and manuals. Applications are available that allow the user to build floor plans, track inventory, and provide visual reports and charts for financial data. From the information technology standpoint, there are mobile apps available that allow an administrator to remotely connect to other devices, manage systems on the network, or even send and receive files from another device.

Now imagine if you are the Chief Security Officer at an organization, and your employees are downloading various applications such as those mentioned above. While they may be helpful to assist the user with daily work activities, there is no guarantee that the content is securely stored on the device. Consider the amount of sensitive company information that is potentially being stored within these applications. Certain application developers take their work seriously and put forth a strong effort to encrypt the data that is being stored by their application. There are also many developers out there who are simply doing this because they have an interest in it. In other words, not all application developers take data security into consideration throughout the application development process.

The development of secure third-party applications also makes claims to help protect data on the iPhone. Applications such as "Good for Enterprise" by Good Technology, Inc. are intended to provide secure access to Exchange and Lotus Domino e-mail as well as calendar and contacts (Mobiledia, 2011). Additional applications are available to help prevent the device from being stolen. Specifically, one application will set off an alarm if an attempt is made to steal the device. Other applications might track the GPS location of the device and send e-mail notifications on the steps taken. For example, if a certain website was visited, this information would be sent to the owner's e-mail address. Finally, some applications will go so far as to encrypt all data on the device. However, in order to guarantee that these applications are actually doing what they are set out to do, the device itself would need to be examined by an individual with sufficient technical knowledge.

The Colorado Information Analysis Center (CIAC) was created in response to the September 11 attacks to protect the citizens and infrastructure of Colorado. In November 2010, this group released an Intelligence Bulletin that discussed the security risks associated with smart phones. This bulletin covers the vulnerabilities associated with smart phones in general as well as the threats specific to Apple devices and software. The CIAC points out that one of the most significant vulnerabilities on smart phones right now is the fact that employees use these devices to connect to their work e-mail and other internal documents. For this reason, data theft has now expanded from a loss of personal data to a loss of sensitive business data as well. Specifically mentioned as a risk on Apple's platform is the use of the iPhone by "more than 70% of Fortune 100 companies" (Colorado Information Analysis Center, 2010).

Both corporate and individual consumers need a way to determine whether an application is secure prior to installing it on their device, and, more importantly, placing personal or company-sensitive information within the app. Every time people use their mobile devices to check bank accounts, update their status on social networking sites, or do online shopping or other online activities, there is a chance that personal information is saved to the mobile device. Users typically carry their mobile devices with them, which puts the device and its personal information at greater risk of loss or theft. In general, developers want to provide secure applications; however, the rapid development and release of mobile applications in response to consumer demand has resulted in less rigorous security testing.

Corporate or individual mobile app consumers

To mitigate the risks, a mobile security audit can be performed by a third party to understand what type of corporate data might be stored on a device and where that data might end up (e.g., on a user's home computer in a backup file), and to test the effectiveness/capability of remote wiping. This way, if a device is lost or stolen, the risk of corporate data loss can be lessened.

After discovering numerous mobile application security vulnerabilities in the course of performing forensic work, the authors and colleagues at viaForensics began auditing the security of data in popular applications and disclosed their findings publicly on their website. The goal of the free public service, called appWatchdog, is to improve mobile app data security and protect consumers. As consumer awareness of the data security risks rises, developers will be encouraged to thoroughly review their apps prior to release and achieve a higher level of security. The findings can be viewed at http://viaforensics.com/appwatchdog/. viaForensics plans to release a mobile app that will check the installed apps on an Android device and provide appWatchdog results for those already audited. It will allow consumers to suggest an app for review as well as contact the app developer if they have any concerns.

The appWatchdog service uses forensic techniques to determine whether user names, passwords, credit card numbers, or other application data are being insecurely stored or transmitted on the device. The process involves installing the application and using it just as a typical user would. The device is then forensically imaged and analyzed for personal information and application data. The findings are first communicated to the app developer and then publicly disclosed in order to provide this information directly to consumers. Users can then make an informed decision on whether they wish to continue using that application, or perhaps wait for the developer to release a more secure version.

Each application is reviewed on the basis of certain criteria, depending on the application being analyzed. For example, with a mobile payment app, the app would be analyzed for user name, password, application data, and credit card numbers. However, for other applications, credit card numbers may not be relevant. The following criteria are explained in further detail, with the top three being the most applicable to most applications:

- *Securely stores passwords?* If any type of password is being stored unencrypted on the device, the application would get a "Fail."
- *Securely stores user names?* Application data are examined to determine whether user names are being stored unencrypted on the device.
- *Securely stores application data on the device?* Each application is analyzed for app-related data. For example, financial apps are searched for account numbers, balances, and transfer information. Other applications might store additional personal user data, such as e-mail address, phone number, or address.
- *Securely stores credit card information?* For applications handling credit card information, data was examined to determine whether the full credit card number is stored unencrypted on the device as well as any supporting data associated with it, such as address on the account, expiration date, or security number on the back of the card.
- *Additional security tests.* These tests might include capturing wireless data sent from the mobile device and examining that traffic for user names, passwords, PINs, and any other relevant application data. Additional security tests are typically more time consuming and therefore only performed for an in-depth application security review.

Since this service is intended to inform mobile application users, individuals are also able to suggest certain apps that they wish to be reviewed. The suggested application is added to a queue for later processing.

Another way for users to protect their data in the event of a lost or stolen device is through Apple's MobileMe account. Discussed in detail in Chapter 2, this is an annual membership that allows its members to synchronize their iPhone data with their MobileMe account on the Internet. This way, if the device is stolen, they can initiate a remote wipe (also offered through this server) and still have all their data stored within their MobileMe account.

The CIAC bulletin suggests ways in which some of the security vulnerabilities on a smart phone can be mitigated (CIAC, 2010). Just a few of these examples are given as follows:

- Keep device and desktop software up-to-date.
- Disable remote connectivity for features such as Bluetooth when they are not in use.
- Encrypt files that contain corporate or personal information using a strong encryption password.
- Be suspicious of URLs sent in e-mails or text messages.
- Do not leave smart phones unattended.
- Enable security software already installed on smart phones.
- Clear smart phone memory before disposing of it.

These are just a few ways in which people can protect both personal and corporate data stored on their devices. Additional recommendations for device and data security are provided later in this chapter.

Corporate or individual mobile app developers

While the testing discussed in the last section only touches on the criteria mentioned above and looks at things from a user perspective, analysis can also be done from a mobile application developer's point of view. Instead of simply looking at the files in which user data is commonly stored, application-related files can also be parsed and thoroughly analyzed. By looking at things from this angle, examiners can gain a better understanding of how the application works including the configuration files it relies upon.

A thorough application security audit leverages both advanced forensics and security tests to uncover security flaws, protecting both developers and users. viaForensics provides these testing services and a certification, called appSecure. This service leverages advanced mobile forensic techniques in order to provide an in-depth analysis of that particular application. The items listed below are just a few of the criteria evaluated to determine whether a mobile application is secure.

- How does the application handle web history and caching?
- Does the application securely transmit login data?
- Does the application avoid MITM attacks?
- Does the application securely transmit sensitive data?
- Is the application protected from session hijacking?
- Is the application able to permanently delete data and prevent storage on the device?

- Does the application securely handle interruptions?
- Does the application properly secure data in backups?

A similar testing methodology can be effectively applied by internal forensics and security teams provided they have the tools and expertise, as well as the budget and time, to execute the tests.

Application security strategies for developers

The results of appWatchdog and appSecure have led to some general guidelines mobile app developers should consider while designing, developing, and testing their apps. This list, as with others, is not comprehensive but provides some noteworthy concepts for consideration.

User names

Avoid storing user names in plain text on the device. For obvious usability issues, you may decide to cache the user name on the device and so the consumer does not have to type it in every time. However, consider masking a portion of the user name, which would provide enough information for the consumer to identify his or her user name but not enough for an attacker to have the entire user name. The user name is obviously one component needed to log in to an account, and if attackers know little about it, they will not be very effective.

For example, let us suppose that an application that accesses sensitive health information requires a user name and the consumer has created one called "kstrzempka." However, after the initial log, if the application only stores "kstr******" and then displays that back to the user, it would be clear that they are logging into the correct account. However, an attacker would only know the first four characters. Furthermore, if the mask (using "*" in this case but could be presented in other ways) does not give away the overall length of the user name, it makes it even more difficult for the attacker to guess.

Finally, more online services are requiring more complex user names which must be of a certain length and alphanumeric. So, while a user name of "kstrzempka" might be fairly easy to guess, KatieStrzempka1027 would be far more difficult. Some sites may even place further restrictions on the user name where it cannot contain any portion of your basic profile information such as your name.

Passwords

Perhaps far more vulnerable are applications that store the password in plain text. There are several strategies to avoid this serious problem. First, as discussed in the previous section, the users could simply be forced to type their password in when running the app. If you think about logging in to a banking website from your home computer, you must log in every time. While you stay logged in for your current session, once a certain period of inactivity has passed (or you log out), you can no longer access the protected website without reentering your user name and password.

Another approach to consider is the use of security tokens to avoid storing the real password on the mobile device. If a user securely authenticates to a protected resource on the Internet, a security token can be generated that not only expires after a certain period of time but is also unique to that device. While someone with physical access to the phone could access the protected resource, it would only last until the token's expiry, at which point they would need the user name and password again. Furthermore, if the security token was specific to the device and was compromised remotely, the token would not provide access to the restricted resource. Methodologies that use the security token approach would also not place any other resource on the Internet at risk even if the account holder used the same user name and password, which is quite common.

Implementing a token-based authentication scheme is more complicated than a simple user name and password, and it is a methodology that is not as widely used or understood by developers. However, a number of APIs (Application Programming Interfaces) providing this functionality are available and maturing.

There are many different schemes and techniques that can be used to securely authenticate users which would not require a mobile app to store the user name and password in plain text on the mobile device. Over time, app developers must begin to utilize these more secure methodologies to better protect their customers.

Credit card data

Most people in the security industry are familiar with the Payment Card Industry (PCI) Data Security Standard (DSS), which provides standards for protecting credit card data. Prior to the formation of the PCI Security Standards Council (SSC), the major credit card vendors had their own individual standards for protecting card data. In 2006, the PCI SSC was launched by the following payment brands:

- American Express
- Discover Financial Services
- JCB International
- MasterCard Worldwide
- Visa Inc.

These brands have a vested interest in reducing fraud in the payment card industry. In the version 2.0 document "Requirements and Security Assessment Procedures" published in October 2010, the specific requirements of the PCI DSS are listed. Below is a small sample of requirements that would cover situations where credit card data is used in a mobile app (Documents Library, n.d.).

- 3.2 Do not store sensitive authentication data after authorization (even if encrypted). Sensitive authentication data includes the data as cited in the following requirements 3.2.1 through 3.2.3.
- 3.2.1 Do not store the full contents of any track (from the magnetic stripe located on the back of a card, equivalent data contained on a chip, or elsewhere). This data is alternatively called full track, track, track 1, track 2, and magnetic-stripe data.

- 3.2.2 Do not store the card verification code or value (three-digit or four-digit number printed on the front or back of a payment card) used to verify card-not-present transactions.
- 3.2.3 Do not store the PIN or the encrypted PIN block.
- 3.3 Mask PAN (primary account number) when displayed (the first six and last four digits are the maximum number of digits to be displayed).
- 3.4.1 If disk encryption is used (rather than file- or column-level database encryption), logical access must be managed independently of native operating system access control mechanisms (e.g., by not using local user account databases). Decryption keys must not be tied to user accounts.

The PCI DSS, while not without criticism, is a fairly mature standard with the goal of protecting a staggeringly large volume of financial transactions. It is interesting to compare some of the standards the PCI DSS have developed over time such as requiring encryption, limiting the storage of sensitive information, and masking sensitive information when displayed to screen.

It should really go without saying that storing the credit card in plain text on a mobile device would not only violate every PCI DSS standard but would also place the card owner at great risk if the device was compromised. Perhaps not surprising, the appWatchdog service described above checks for credit card data stored in plain text and unfortunately uncovers this information in some applications.

If an app requires payment processing, it would be advisable to integrate with a mature online service such as PayPal or Google Checkout, or work with a payment provider to implement a secure payment application. Be advised that this is a significant undertaking from a development and testing perspective as well as for ongoing security procedures that must be in place.

Sensitive application data

Many mobile apps contain sensitive data the consumers would not want out of their control. There are various levels to the data, and below is a simplistic list designed to illustrate the levels:

1. Contains no sensitive user data – for example, a calculator app would not contain any sensitive user data;
2. Contains no sensitive user data but has some potential meta data – for example, an application would not contain any sensitive user data but might contain the GPS coordinates and date/time stamp when it was run;
3. Contains user data that is not sensitive – some applications are intended for public consumption such as messages people share on Twitter. If users were informed that all of their Twitter messages could be read by the world, most (except those that add privacy protection to their messages) would not be concerned;
4. Contains sensitive user data – many applications fall into this category and contain sensitive user data such as one's full e-mail messages, SMS and MMS messages, voice mail, call logs, and more;

5. Contains highly sensitive user data – this is a special level that covers apps that contain financial information, health care information, password vaults, and other apps which place the consumer at great risk if their security is compromised.

It is helpful to differentiate the sensitivity of data an app contains in order to provide appropriate levels of security. If a calculator app required two-factor authentication and AES-256 encryption, users would obviously be annoyed and might try to calculate the 15% tip on paper (which once written down would place it at risk for a number of physical and social engineering attacks).

However, the appWatchdog service regularly uncovers apps containing sensitive data of levels 4 and 5, which are stored in plain text on the NAND Flash. If you develop an application with sensitive data at this level, you should protect the data with some level of security. Some of the options include the following:

- *Do not store the data* – This is the simplest approach and mitigates any attack against the device that gains access to the NAND Flash. As discussed previously, the cryptographic algorithms used to protect data in transit are far more effective than any approach to securing data at rest (at least on a mobile device). Most mobile devices are highly connected to the Internet and thus caching the data is not necessary. Of course, there are advantages to caching the data, which include providing access even if the device is offline as well as improving the application's responsiveness.
- *Encrypt the data* – As discussed previously, encrypting data at rest on a mobile device requires that the keys are also stored on the device, and as such it cannot provide perfect security. However, if the keys are sufficiently difficult to locate, it provides a higher level of protection than plain text. Also, as remote attacks against mobile devices increase, they may gain access to the NAND Flash but not other areas where the encryption keys are stored, such as in nonvolatile memory. If the data was in plain text, it would be at risk. However, if the data is encrypted, the consumer would be protected in this instance.

Securing sensitive app data is critical to protecting consumers, and over time the industry must mature and consider this a requirement for apps.

Secure Socket Layer

One final area to discuss is the implementation of SSL, which protects data in transit. It is critical that app developers properly implement SSL including a full validation of the digital certificates to prevent MITM attacks. While SSL is effective in protecting data in transit, without proper implementation it leaves the users highly vulnerable to an attack. While testing apps for the appWatchdog service, a test attacking machine would regularly display the user name and password for apps not in scope as they would automatically execute (i.e., some apps log in on a schedule to check to new messages) and fall victim to the compromise. Developers must fully and securely implement SSL in their apps to protect consumers.

Besides properly implementing and validating SSL in the mobile app, it is necessary to securely configure SSL on the server. SSL has been available since the 1990s to secure data transmission on untrusted networks. Earlier implementations of SSL contained security flaws that had to be addressed to ensure secure transmission. Over time, the algorithms were improved to reduce the risk of a brute-force attack.

One common problem is that the people responsible for implementing SSL on the server are not necessarily security engineers and so they tend to focus on server infrastructure. They might implement and test SSL and it would appear to be secure; however, there are vulnerabilities. For example, MD5 is a common encryption algorithm that has been widely used for more than 10 years. While still considered useful for applications such as file integrity checking, authorities have designated it for retirement from use in securing communications. The U.S. Department of Homeland Security CERT group states in Vulnerability Note #836068, "Software developers, Certification Authorities, website owners, and users should avoid using the MD5 algorithm in any capacity. As previous research has demonstrated, it should be considered cryptographically broken and unsuitable for further use" (US-CERT, 2009).

Real-time cracking of this encryption remains impractical, but stronger encryption is supported by all major web browsers and mobile devices. TLSv1, more than 10 years old, was found to be vulnerable to a "renegotiation attack" in 2009. In this attack, the server treats the client's initial TLS handshake as a renegotiation and thus believes that the initial data transmitted by the attacker is from the same entity as the subsequent client data (US-CERT, 2010).

Thierry Zoller, a security consultant, has provided a well-written summary with visual depictions of the steps involved. While many different attacks are explained, Figure 4.4 is the first example provided in this summary that helps illustrate the attack.

Most servers using TLSv1 have been patched to close this vulnerability; however, the TLSv1 protocol has been updated and a more current TLSv1.2 offers the latest technology and stronger encryption ciphers available.

Securing the transmission of sensitive data from a mobile device requires coordination, diligence, and a thorough understanding of SSL/TLS from not only the app developer but also the team that maintains the server participating in the secure communication. While SSL has been available for some time and may be taken for granted, it is important that a thorough implementation and testing of the security implementation occurs.

RECOMMENDATIONS FOR DEVICE AND APPLICATION SECURITY

Both the iPhone 3G(s) and iPhone 4 represented risk of data exposure as learned from this research and testing. Unless the device has been fully wiped, there is always potential for the recovery of sensitive data including email contents and user credentials. Even after enabling the passcode on the device and providing alternative security measures, the data still remains.

What causes more concern is perhaps Apple's implementation of data encryption, which is the primary reason for many entities upgrading to the new device.

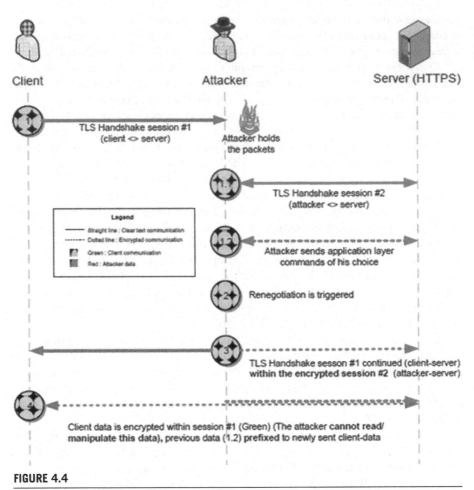

FIGURE 4.4

Generic TLS Renegotiation Vulnerability.

However, with proper forensic techniques, the encryption is rendered completely ineffective and provides a misleading sense of security to its users. In particular, the data contents within encrypted backup files can be unencrypted and viewed with the use of inexpensive software. This software not only makes the data legible but it also provides additional information including keychain user names and passwords.

The good news for users with devices running iOS 4.0 or higher is that the hardware encryption mechanism has not been fully cracked. While the allocated files within the file system are still recovered (in other words, data that has not been deleted), unallocated files are not yet able to be acquired. A significant amount of data can still be recovered; however, measures to protect the device should still be administered.

Regardless of the model or firmware running on the device, a large amount of data is at risk for exposure. There are a few general recommendations for how a user can be proactive by securing the information on their device.

- *Passcode*: The passcode on the device should not only be enabled, but, when available, it should also contain alphanumeric and special characters. The password should contain enough complexity to prevent a brute-force attack from easily cracking it. Within a corporation, using the Configuration Profile to enable strict password requirements is strongly recommended.
- *Restrict access to applications*: Using the iPhone Configuration Utility (or another program to modify Configuration Profiles) enables restrictions on the device to prevent access to various features. The specific security policies will need to be determined by each organization; however, some suggested settings would disable YouTube and force encrypted backups.
- *Microsoft Exchange (Outlook) e-mail setup*: It is understood that one of the most common uses of smart phones within a corporation is to synchronize e-mail with the internal network. When the e-mail client is initially set up and the account added, always select the "Use SSL" option in order to retrieve incoming mail. This configuration will encrypt the traffic, providing an added layer of security.
- *Know your apps*: A significant portion of sensitive data stored on these devices derives from custom applications that have been downloaded from the App Store. E-mail addresses, passwords, bank account numbers, and credit card numbers are just a few examples of the personally identifiable information that has been found through viaForensics' application testing. Before one uses an app, one must consider the information it is requesting, as well as the information one can acquire by using it. If you see it on the screen, there is a good chance that it can be recovered from the device.

These suggestions are extremely high-level, and in no way completely protect the data contained on a mobile device. Recommendations will vary from one iPhone model to the next and one iOS version to the next. A full mobile device audit would be recommended in order to fully understand all of the vulnerabilities available on the specific device that may be selected for an organization.

While there are several variations of models and iOS versions, there are significantly more unique applications on the market. Even two apps that may be similar (such as two unique banking apps) could be programmed with varying levels of security. For this reason, all applications should also be analyzed for vulnerabilities and insecure data storage prior to being released to consumers.

SUMMARY

Data protection on mobile devices is a top priority for any corporation intending to deploy smart phones to their employees. In order to prevent unauthorized users from accessing internal information or personal user data, it is necessary to understand the inner working of the device as well as what data can potentially be acquired from that device. This chapter covered in-depth research done on both the iPhone and the iPad. This research involved populating the devices with known data and later analyzing that device to determine what kind of information could be retrieved. Detailed steps of this process were discussed and the findings revealed.

Mobile applications make up a large part of smart phone use within a corporation. The iPhone's and iPad's internal "Mail" application is commonly used to synchronize the device with the company's Microsoft Exchange server in order to receive e-mails. Some businesses also develop their own custom mobile apps to be used by their employees, clients, or sometimes, the general public. Testing these applications to ensure that they do not insecurely store and transmit app data should be a requirement in the development process. This extra step will benefit both the application users and the developers.

To conclude, the chapter offers general recommendations to secure an iOS device, or applications installed on the device. First, guidelines are provided for mobile application developers to help them produce secure applications. These recommendations suggest ways to prevent sensitive user data from being stored in plain text on the device. Finally, both corporate and individual consumers are provided with options to proactively secure their mobile applications and mobile devices, in general.

References

Apple, Inc. (2010, November). iPad in business-resources. iPad security. Retrieved January 25, 2011, from http://images.apple.com/ipad/business/docs/iPad_Security.pdf

Colorado Information Analysis Center. (2010, November 23). Security risks associated with Smartphones. Colorado Information Analysis Center. Retrieved January 31, 2011, from http://info.publicintelligence.net/CIAC-SmartPhones.pdf

Country. (n.d.). Computer crime law: guide to computer crimes law – computer crime law info. Worldwide Legal Directories. Retrieved February 11, 2011, from http://www.hg.org/computer-crime.html

Documents Library. (n.d.). PCI security standards documents: PCI DSS, PA-DSS, PED standards, compliance guidelines and more. Retrieved February 12, 2011, from https://www.pcisecuritystandards.org/security_standards/documents.php?agreements=pcidss&association=PCI%20DSS

Evansville Courier and Press. (2011, January 28). New apps improve publication experiences for iPad. Evansville Courier & Press: Local Evansville, Indiana News Delivered Throughout the Day. Retrieved February 11, 2011, from http://www.courierpress.com/news/2011/jan/28/new-apps-improve-publication-experiences-for/

Goodin, D. (2010, February 2). iPhone vulnerable to remote attack on SSL. The register: Sci/Tech news for the world. Retrieved February 11, 2011, from http://www.theregister.co.uk/2010/02/02/iphone_malicious_config_attack/

International Data Group. (2011, February 10). iPhone attack reveals passwords in six minutes – Software, security, phones, operating systems, Mac OS, iPhone, Fraunhofer Institute for Secure Information Technology, Exploits/vulnerabilities, encryption, consumer electronics.

Techworld. Retrieved February 11, 2011, from http://www.techworld.com.au/article/376245/iphone_attack_reveals_passwords_six_minutes/

Mobiledia. (2011, January 25). iPhone use in business boosted by security apps. Mobiledia. Retrieved January 27, 2011, from http://www.mobiledia.com/news/80681.html

SANS Institute. (2004, June 1). Federal computer crime laws. SANS Institute InfoSec Reading Room. Retrieved February 11, 2011, from www.sans.org/reading_room/whitepapers/legal/federal-computer-crime-laws_1446

Sinful iPhone. (2011, January 18). New baseband hack at Pwn2Own, but no unlock (yet). Retrieved February 11, 2011, from www.sinfuliphone.com/showthread.php?t=59274

US-CERT Vulnerability Note VU#120541. (2010, June 2). CERT knowledgebase. Retrieved February 13, 2011, from http://www.kb.cert.org/vuls/id/120541

US-CERT Vulnerability Note VU#836068. (2009, January 21). CERT knowledgebase. Retrieved February 13, 2011, from http://www.kb.cert.org/vuls/id/836068

USA Today. (2010, August 9). Apple says it has patch for remote attack on iPhone, iPad. USA Today. Retrieved February 11, 2011, from http://www.usatoday.com/tech/products/software/2010–08–09-apple09_ST_N.htm

Acquisitions

5

INTRODUCTION

Before we dive into the actual iPhone forensic techniques, it is important to note that there are a number of considerations that influence the technique a forensic analyst should use. This section covers the different types of investigations as well as the various methods of data retrieval from an iOS device or its backup files.

iPHONE FORENSICS OVERVIEW

Forensic imaging refers to the acquisition of disk or memory contents from a device into an external file that can be stored and examined using forensic tools. The purpose of creating a forensic image of a device is to have a duplicate copy for analysis so that the original evidence remains pristine. In the digital world, we have the capability of running the analysis against a working copy so as not to modify the contents of the original device.

The "holy grail" of any forensic acquisition is the performance of a bit-by-bit copy of the original media and retention of proof that the two are identical by comparing the unique cryptographic signatures of the original and the copy to ensure they match. While the processes and procedures for this are well established in traditional hard drive-based computer forensics, the process for mobile forensic devices has proven to be quite a challenge. Unlike hard drives, which can be removed, or computers, which can start in special read-only forensic environments, cell phones have a very limited operating system and cannot boot into a forensic environment, and the memory is typically nonremovable. Logical copies are usually the only method of performing mobile forensics outside of imaging removed memory cards or reading SIM (subscriber identity module) card data.

Types of investigations

There are a variety of situations that might benefit from the results of an iPhone forensic investigation. While the application of forensics is common to all the situations, each individual situation may require different procedures, documentation, and overall focus.

The first situation people generally think of is investigations that will likely be adjudicated in a criminal or civil court of law. In these situations, there are a number of important considerations:

- Chain of custody
- Detailed contemptuous notes and final reporting
- Possible validation of results using different tools or investigators
- Fact- or opinion-based testimony

Another common scenario involves internal investigations within corporations. These investigations may end up as litigations in court but often they are used to determine the root cause of an issue (whether it is a system, external attack, or internal employee) and may result in disciplinary action against an employee. Internal corporate investigations can cover many areas but the most common include the following:

- Intellectual property or data theft
- Inappropriate use of company resources
- Attempted or successful attack against computer systems
- Employment-related investigations including discrimination, sexual harassment, etc.
- Security audit, random or targeted

There is also a need for forensics in cases involving family matters. The most common cases involve the following:

- Divorce
- Child custody
- Estate disputes

One other area where forensic investigation can be of significant value is the security and operation of a government. A government is usually the largest employer in a country and the United States is a good example. According to U.S. Census Bureau data, data from the 2009 Annual Survey of Public Employment and Payroll revealed that the Federal government across all functions had over 3.0 million employees while state and local governments had 16.6 million full-time equivalent employees (Government Employment & Payroll, n.d.).

Beyond employment-related matters, countries are also potential targets of attacks and intelligence gathering by foreign agencies. Forensics can play a key role in thwarting attacks against a country, investigating successful attacks and counter-intelligence scenarios, and providing valuable intelligence needed for the governing of the country.

Difference between logical and physical techniques

The forensic techniques used to recover data from an iPhone are either logical or physical in nature. A logical technique extracts allocated data and is typically achieved by accessing the file system. Allocated data simply means that the data is not deleted and is accessible on the file system.

Physical techniques, on the other hand, target the physical storage medium directly and these do not rely on the file system itself to access the data. There are advantages to this approach, the most significant being that physical techniques may provide access to deleted data. As discussed in Chapter 3 (File System and Data Storage), file systems often only mark data as deleted or obsolete and do not actually erase the storage medium unless needed. As the physical forensic techniques provide direct access to the storage medium, it is possible to recover not only the allocated data but also the unallocated (deleted or obsolete) data.

Of course, the analysis of an iPhone physical acquisition is generally far more difficult and time consuming. Also, the physical techniques are more difficult to execute and missteps could lead to the device becoming inaccessible.

Modification of the target device

One of the guiding principles of any forensic investigation is avoiding modification of the target device in any manner. In many cases, this is quite achievable. For example, let us assume you are handed a desktop computer that is not powered on. You are informed that it was seized from a suspect and you need to launch a forensic investigation. Because you can account for the computer only from the point that you take custody, the device is fairly easy to investigate without material changes to the data. A typical investigation would fully document the computer, remove the hard drive, connect it to a physical write blocker, and effect a bit-by-bit forensically sound acquisition of the hard drive. The investigation would then take place on copies of the forensic image and the original device would remain unchanged.

As the power and functionality of computers increased, this ideal situation became more and more difficult to achieve. First, let us assume you are called to the scene of an investigation and there is a desktop computer, but this time the computer is in operation. Any interaction with that computer, whether you simply move the device or even physically unplug the device, will modify it in some way. While many examiners advocate simply unplugging the computer, you certainly change the computer as the contents of RAM, open network connections, and more (all of which can be quite valuable in an investigation) are permanently lost.

On the other hand, if you decide to examine the device while it is running, any interaction might change the device. To further complicate an investigation, it is possible that the computer is leveraging encryption and, while the device is running, that data may be accessible. However, if the device is powered off and the examiner does not have the encryption key, he or she may permanently lose the ability to recover that data.

Servers that have their special hardware or complex setups, or simply cannot be powered down without significant impact to other systems or people are another complicating factor. In these cases, the examiner must interact directly with the device while it is running even though such actions will change the device.

Of course, mobile devices, and iOS devices in particular, are nearly impossible to forensically analyze without impacting the device. Unlike desktops, notebooks, and servers, the storage on an iOS device cannot be easily removed. And if the device is powered on, a shutdown of the device or pulling the battery again modifies the data.

When mobile phones were first showing up in investigations, there was very little stored data that could be extracted from the device. Many investigations used traditional approaches such as a search warrant on the wireless carrier to obtain call detail records. It was also possible to remove the SIM card on GSM (global system for mobile communication) devices and extract some data. As phones began to store more data, there developed a deep divide between examiners who advocated the older methods that had little impact on the device and subsequently retrieved only nominal data and those who advocated a fuller exploitation of the device. The techniques used to exploit the devices did modify the device and therefore the ensuing debate.

As of 2011, much of the debate has subsided as the amount of data mobile devices now hold necessitates the more intrusive techniques. The Association of Chief Police Officers in the United Kingdom produced guidelines that address this issue quite clearly. The guide, entitled "Good Practice Guide for Computer-Based Electronic Evidence" establishes four principles of computer-based electronic evidence (ACPO, n.d.):

1. No action taken by law enforcement agencies or their agents should change data held on a computer or storage media which may subsequently be relied upon in court.
2. In circumstances where a person finds it necessary to access original data held on a computer or on storage media, that person must be competent to do so and be able to give evidence explaining the relevance and the implications of their actions.
3. An audit trail or other record of all processes applied to computer-based electronic evidence should be created and preserved. An independent third party should be able to examine those processes and achieve the same result.
4. The person in charge of the investigation (the case officer) has overall responsibility for ensuring that the law and these principles are adhered to.

As mobile devices clearly present a circumstance in which it is necessary to access the original device directly, it is permissible provided the examiner is sufficiently trained, provides valid reasons for the approach, keeps a clear audit trail, and his or her actions are repeatable by a third party. This is certainly good advice and helps provide a solid framework for the forensic investigation of mobile devices.

HANDLING EVIDENCE

Many agencies and first responders have established protocols for securing evidence and the following sections are meant to complement those existing procedures, not replace them. Of course, these represent special procedures, and educating first responders who have many other responsibilities can be quite a challenge.

When an iPhone or other iOS device is seized, or received as evidence, a few precautionary measures should be taken to prevent data from being overwritten. These steps will depend on the current state of the device.

- If the device is powered off, leave it as is. Turning the phone on risks the possibility of data getting overwritten.
- If the device is powered on, be sure to note whether it is passcode-protected (see next section for more details) and what firmware version is running on the device.
- Always be sure to charge the device. However, if the device is powered off, it is important to note that connecting it to a charger will likely power it on. In this case, it is a good idea to wait until you are ready to boot the device into Recovery or Device Failsafe Utility (DFU) mode for an acquisition, and connect the charger at that time (see Chapter 2 for details on booting into various operating modes).

Passcode procedures

Passcode-locked devices are becoming more common as a result of heightened security awareness in consumers and corporations. Circumventing passcodes is not always possible. As such, the first consideration when securing a device is whether an opportunity exists to immediately disable or otherwise circumvent the passcode.

If an iPhone device is encountered and the screen is active, strong consideration should be given to checking and potentially changing its settings. For devices that have passcodes, there is a short period, from 1 minute to "Never," where full access to the device is possible without re-entering the passcode. If a device is in an active state, an examiner may want to consider increasing the screen timeout to prevent or postpone the screen from locking. The location for this setting is in Settings > General > Auto-Lock. From here, be sure to select "Never" so that the device does not auto-lock and require a passcode to log back in.

Of course, these steps make changes to the device and should be thoroughly logged in the case notes with a description of the state of the device, the rationale for the attempted changes, and the outcome of each change. Not only will this assist in future report writing but will likely be an important factor if your decision to change the device is challenged in court.

Network isolation

If a device is found and the screen is still active, it would be ideal to go into the menu and disable the pattern lock and place the device into airplane mode if a Faraday box is not available.

If a device was left running, do not turn it off! Instead attempt to place it into airplane mode, remove the SIM card, turn off Wi-Fi, or get it into a Faraday box as soon as possible to avoid any kind of remote wipe initiation. In addition, depending on the device, evidence can be obtained from the live memory. If the device were shut down, this data would be permanently lost. Memory capturing techniques were covered previously, and while memory recovery on the iPhone is currently not possible, the research community has made major strides and this technique will likely be possible in the future.

Powered-off devices

If a device is powered off and comes to the lab for analysis, the first step in any investigation is noting the model and firmware version of the device. While the model number can be retrieved from the back casing, the examiner will need to boot the device into recovery mode, bypassing the normal boot sequence, to retrieve the running firmware version. This can be equated to performing forensics on a standard computer hard drive. The last thing any investigator would do on a recovered computer is boot it up to determine what operating system is installed. Instead, the hard drive is removed and connected to a write blocker for imaging so as to prevent the destruction of any evidence it might contain. If a phone does not have to be booted into normal mode, why take the chance of overwriting key evidence that could make or break the case? Specific information on how the firmware version can be retrieved is discussed later in this chapter in the "Physical Acquisition" section.

IMAGING AN iPHONE/iPAD

On the iPhone or iPad, there are three methods of acquiring data: backup acquisition, logical acquisition, and physical acquisition.

Backup acquisition

Through a backup acquisition, data that has been backed up from the device onto a computer is retrieved. This method is used when the original device is not available. Because the source of the data is the backup files, only data that are explicitly backed up using Apple's synchronization protocol are recovered.

There are various mobile forensic commercial tools in existence that will perform an acquisition of an iPhone/iPad/iPod Touch backup file. Some of those tools include Paraben Device Seizure, Oxygen Forensic Suite, Mobilyze by BlackBag Tech, Mobile Sync Browser, and iPhone Analyzer. Each of these tools has been tested, and the process is described in depth in Chapter 7. There are also several open-source programs available that allow the contents of a backup file to be extracted, viewed, and analyzed.

As a review from Chapter 2, when a device is backed up through iTunes, the files are stored in a default location depending on the operating system being used (refer to Appendix A for backup locations). The status.plist, info.plist, and manifest.plist are all configuration files containing information about the device, backup files, and status of the backup. The main files that we care about for an acquisition are the *.mddata and *.mdinfo files (or for earlier versions of iTunes, *.mdbackup). These are the binary files that actually contain user data. If the files are opened as they are, they would not be readable. Instead, one of the tools mentioned above is needed in order to convert them to a human-readable form.

Unencrypted

Performing a forensic recovery of the iPhone's backup files can be accomplished using one of the available mobile forensic or open-source tools discussed earlier. In this chapter, we will walk through the process of acquiring this data using two different methods. As Chapter 7 in its entirety is devoted to stepping through each of the different commercial tools, we utilize one of the open-source tools that are currently available. Note that this is just one example of the many free tools available on the Internet that can be used to acquire a backup of a device.

Regardless of the software or method used, the overall process of a backup acquisition remains similar. Each of the binary plists must be converted to XML in order for the content to be legible (for more details on understanding and converting property lists, see Chapter 3). As with any digital forensic examination, all work should be performed on the image of the device rather than the original evidence. In this case, an additional copy can be made of the iTunes backup files prior to analyzing. Once the files are converted, the raw files can then be read as they exist on an iPhone. The iPhone file structure is introduced in this chapter, and then expanded upon in Chapter 6.

Any tool used to analyze an iPhone backup must convert the binary plists into the standard file structure that we see on the iPhone. Many of the commercial tools go one step further and pull some of the data out of these files and incorporate them into a reporting tool. This is helpful for investigators who may not be familiar with the iPhone's data structure. Clicking a button in a user interface that says "SMS" is much easier than navigating through plists and SQLite databases to find the SMS messages (see Appendix B for suggested tools to use for viewing these file types).

We will now walk through the process of acquiring data via an iPhone backup file.

To mimic what a typical user could do, the iPhone Backup Extractor will be used for this acquisition. This is not a mobile forensics tool, but is a free download that allows an individual to simply view the contents of a backup file. It converts the binary plists into files that can be easily viewed on a Macintosh computer. It is important to note that there are alternative open-source tools that will perform a similar extraction, and run on other platforms as well.

Once the iPhone Backup Extractor is started up, the "Read Backups" option will automatically list every iPhone, iPad, or iPod device in which backup files are

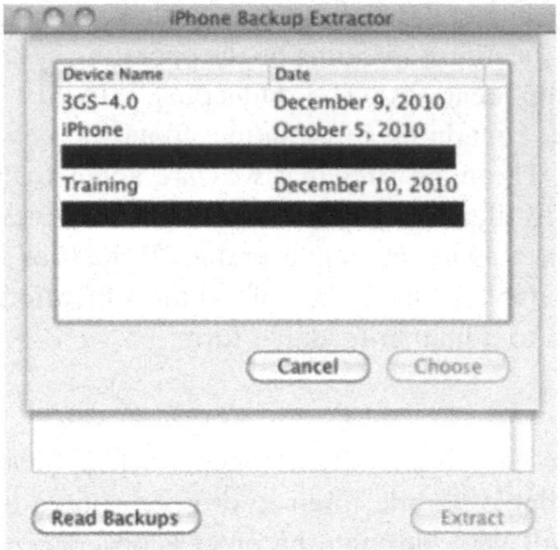

FIGURE 5.1

iPhone Backup Extractor – Read Backups.

currently stored on the host machine. Multiple device backups are shown in Figure 5.1. It must be kept in mind that this software will only list the devices for which the backup files are located in the default location. If the backup was moved or copied to another area, it will not be displayed within the software.

From the list, select the appropriate device (in this example, we are going to select the "3GS-4.0" device). From here, you should see a list of all the applications that are on the device as well as "iOS Files," as shown in Figure 5.2. If you are looking for data specific to an application, you can extract only the files for that particular app.

FIGURE 5.2

iPhone Backup Extractor – List of Files.

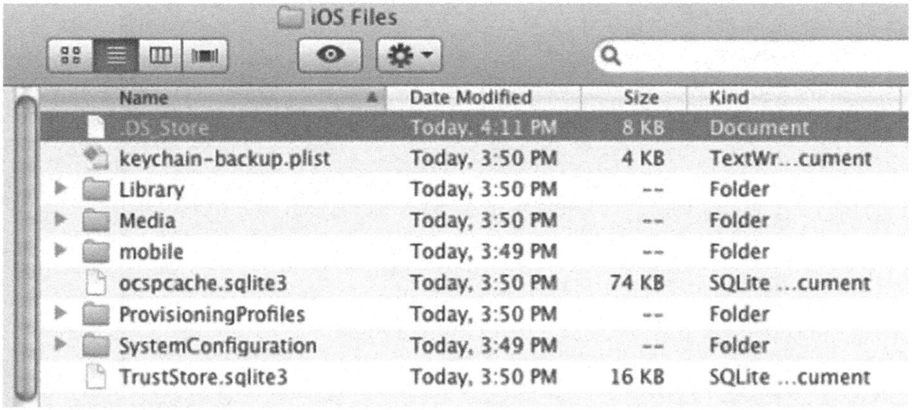

FIGURE 5.3

iPhone Backup Extractor – iOS Files.

However, the iOS Files extraction will provide you with the entire iPhone directory structure (with the exception of any downloaded applications).

In the example shown in Figure 5.2, we are going to select iOS Files and extract those to a selected area on the computer. Those files can now be viewed and are ready to be analyzed as displayed in Figure 5.3.

Encrypted

A user can also initiate an encrypted backup by entering a password prior to syncing the backup files. When a backup is encrypted, a standard forensic or open-source tool is not capable of acquiring data from the *.mddata and *.mdinfo files in most cases, unless a password cracking tool is used.

With the release of iOS version 4, encryption is done differently on the device. If a backup is not passcode-protected, the keychain file (containing user name and password data) is encrypted using hardware keys stored on the iPhone. If the keychain database file is opened, certain information can be viewed, but passwords are encrypted.

If a backup is password-protected, the keychain file is now encrypted using software keys generated from the backup password. What this means is that, as long as the backup passcode is known, it is possible to get the keychain file's encrypted data on a device running firmware version 4.x only.

iPhone Password Breaker exercise

To demonstrate this method, we will use Elcomsoft's iPhone Password Breaker. This software enables forensic access to password-protected backups for iPhone and iPad devices. It recovers the plain-text password that protects encrypted backup files. It can also read and decrypt keychains for devices running iOS version 4.

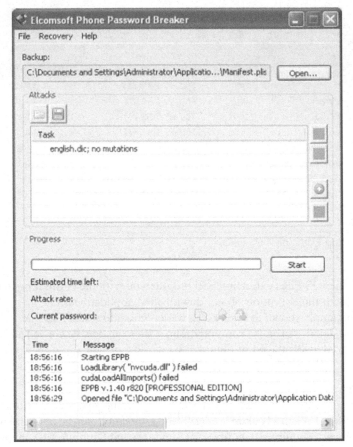

FIGURE 5.4

Elcomsoft Main Screen.

A device is not needed to use this software; only the encrypted backup files (specifically "Manifest.plist") are used. When the software is run, the main screen is displayed as in Figure 5.4. When the user clicks "open," a list of backed up devices is displayed. As we are looking for the encrypted backup file, we would select the device with a lock shown next to it (in Figure 5.5, this is the "3GS-4.0" device).

Next, we did a brute-force attack and selected only five characters and all numerics (see next section for specific testing done on the various brute-force attacks). The four-digit passcode was revealed in less than 1 second and displayed within the main screen of the software (see Figure 5.6).

Another feature of this software is its ability to display passwords or other data that is typically encrypted within the iPhone's keychain database. To view this information, select File > Keychain Explorer from the main menu; then select the

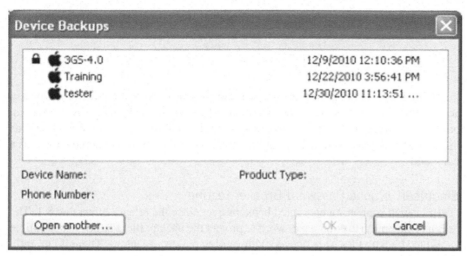

FIGURE 5.5

Elcomsoft – Choose Backup File.

Time	Message
18:56:16	Starting EPPB
18:56:16	LoadLibrary("nvcuda.dll") failed
18:56:16	cudaLoadAllImports() failed
18:56:16	EPPB v.1.40 r820 [PROFESSIONAL EDITION]
18:56:29	Opened file "C:\Documents and Settings\Administrator\Application Data
18:59:12	Password found: "1232". Time elapsed: 0.23 sec.

FIGURE 5.6

Elcomsoft – Passcode Revealed.

encrypted backup once again. The contents of the keychain file are immediately displayed on the screen (Figure 5.7) and can even be exported into a text file:

```
==== GENERIC PASSWORDS ====
PortableStorage (SharingPassword)
    Service:        PortableStorage
    Account:        SharingPassword
    Data:           d7csjAPtRmub
    Access Group:   apple
```

```
AirPort (3Jane)
    Service:       AirPort
    Account:       iPhoneForensicsBook
    Data:          apple765iphone
    Access Group:  apple
```

Using Keychain Explorer, user names and passwords were recovered for wireless access points as well as the voice-mail passcode used on the device. Also recovered, but not displayed in the screenshot, were e-mail accounts and passwords as well as user names and passwords for any applications using Apple's keychain database as a back end.

Elcomsoft iPhone Password Breaker testing

iTunes began supporting encrypted backups ever since the release of version 8.1. The user has the option to enter a password to protect the backup file. For this test, multiple encrypted backup files were created with varying password lengths. There is currently no software available that will read an encrypted backup, so other methods were utilized in order to crack the encryption passcode. ElcomSoft's iPhone Password Breaker can recover the plain-text password by decrypting the Manifest.plist file

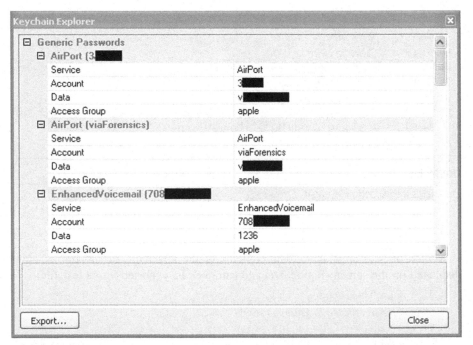

FIGURE 5.7

Elcomsoft Keychain Explorer.

discussed earlier. With the development of iOS 4, Apple has set hardware level encryption. Once a user creates a passcode on the device, he or she has the option to check the "Data protection is enabled" option as mentioned earlier in Chapter 2.

The iPhone Password Breaker supports all models and iOS versions, so the enhanced encryption feature is not an issue in cracking the backup passcode. Table 5.1 outlines the various tests run on the backup file using this software, given the following hardware specifications of the system:

- Windows 7 (64-bit)
- Catalyst 10.3 Drive
- Sapphire graphics card

Each password in the "Numbers only" row started with a "1." This is important because the brute-force attack used within this software systematically checks all possible characters until the correct one is found, starting with the earliest. For example, with a four-digit, all numeric PIN, the attack will start with the number 1, then gradually go up to 9 until the correct number is found. The "expected time remaining" that is shown in the software is assumed to be the longest amount of time expected. For example, using the combination of "all numbers" and a character length of eight, the software reported an expected remaining time of 20 minutes. However, the time was significantly decreased to 5½ minutes, most likely because the password started with a 1.

In the "Alphanumeric" row, with the number of characters being four and five, the software was able to successfully crack the password in a small amount of time. The remaining columns will show an estimated time, as we did not allow the software to run for that long.

In testing, it was noticed that the possibility of an individual instinctively using the iPhone's four-digit PIN code as their backup encryption password is likely. Some individuals might think they need to enter their iPhone PIN instead of creating a brand new password. As you can see in the chart, a numeric, four-digit passcode can be cracked in a very small amount of time.

Logical acquisition

Logical imaging refers to copying the active file system from the device into another file. Through this method, allocated data from the actual device is recovered and can later be analyzed. Logical techniques are often the first type of examination forensic analysts will run because they are easier to execute and often provide sufficient data

Table 5.1 Elcomsoft Backup Encryption Testing

	4 Characters	5 Characters	6 Characters	7 Characters	8 Characters
Numbers only	<1 second	<1 second	5 seconds	20 seconds	5.5 minutes
Alphanumeric	25 seconds	26 minutes	Est. 5.8 days	Est. 341 days	Est. 52 years

for the case. iPhone forensics physical techniques can provide far more data; however, they are more difficult to execute successfully and also take considerably more effort to analyze.

Many of the mobile forensics tools that support iPhone logical acquisitions will also provide a reporting mechanism. Essentially, the tool will execute a logical acquisition of the device, and with this information, it will export commonly viewed files into a graphical user interface (GUI) or report. The problem with some of these tools is that the examiner can see the reported data, but cannot view the source of that data. For example, a report might show a website being visited, but not display the date and time. In such a case, the examiner would need to see the original source of the data in order to see other metadata associated with the file. For reasons such as this, it is helpful if an acquisition tool not only reports the data that was found but also allows the investigator to view the raw files from which it was derived.

The overall steps involved in a logical image of an iPhone, regardless of the software or tool being used, include the following:

1. Run the forensic software of your choice.
2. Connect the device.
3. Begin acquiring an image: this will pull all data from the device that was explicitly backed up using Apple's synchronization protocol. Similar files will be retrieved as from an acquisition of a backup, except that with this method, they are being pulled directly from the device.
4. Depending on the software being used, some or all of this information will be displayed within the software and can later be exported into a report.

In Chapter 7, the reader is guided through a logical acquisition for each of the commercial tools listed. The process begins with installation; then it steps the examiner through the acquisition, reporting, and analysis. As with any forensic tool or technique, it is important for examiners to not only go by the testing and tool validation performed by others but also verify the accuracy of the tool themselves.

Physical acquisition

Physical imaging has been widely used in forensics for many years but is relatively new to the mobile device world. Unfortunately for forensic analysts, iPhone security mechanisms prevent us from being able to extract a physical image from a stock device without first gaining privileged access. However, there are some methods that can be utilized to gain access to the device memory to grab a complete image of the NAND.

A physical acquisition creates a physical bit-by-bit copy of the file system, similar to the way a hard drive would be forensically imaged. For this reason, it has the greatest potential to recover large amounts of data, including deleted files.

The release of iOS 4 brought up many issues from a mobile forensics standpoint. As briefly highlighted in Chapter 2, hardware encryption is offered with iOS 4 on the iPhone 4, 3GS, iPod Touch (3G or later), and all iPad models. What this means is that, even if a full physical disk image is possible, all the data is still encrypted. At the time of writing this book, no solution exists for acquiring an image of a device running iOS 4, or at least a full disk image containing unallocated data.

There are currently three methods available to perform a physical acquisition on an iPhone or iPad: the Zdziarski method, FTS's iXAM software, or through a jailbroken device. With these techniques, a physical acquisition of an iPhone is possible and has been proven to work so long as the firmware version is below 4.x. The first two methods have also been tested by the National Institute of Standards and Technology, and a link to their tool testing site is http://www.cftt.nist.gov/mobile_devices.htm (NIST, 2010).

Preparation

Before jumping into the actual acquisition, there are a few topics that need to be covered to prepare the examiner for the acquisition process, regardless of the tool used.

Locate model and firmware version

One of the first steps for any iPhone acquisition is to locate both the model of the device as well as the running iOS version. This is an important step because many of the commercially available tools only support certain firmware versions. In addition, when using Zdziarski's method, a different set of automated tools is used for each unique model and firmware version combination. For these reasons, it is important to understand what is running on the device.

The model number is easy, as it is displayed on the back of the device. The firmware version can be complex, especially if the device is passcode-protected. If the examiner can access the device (in other words, it is powered on and unlocked), the firmware version can be found under Settings > General > About > Version. In the event that the phone is turned off or it cannot be accessed because it is locked with a passcode, an alternative method must be performed.

iRecovery, which was mentioned earlier in Chapter 2, can be run on the device in order to locate the firmware version. To do this, the device should be placed in Recovery mode (see Chapter 2) and connected to a forensic workstation. Using a terminal window, the examiner will need to change into the directory in which iRecovery was installed. In the example that will follow, iRecovery was located in the Applications directory on a Mac. Next, the iRecovery command was used to identify the iBoot version running on the device. The "-s" flag following the command spawns a shell, displaying general information.

```
Katie-Strzempkas-Macbook:~ kstrzemp$ cd Applications/
Katie-Strzempkas-Macbook:iRecovery kstrzemp$ ./irecovery -s
iRecovery - Recovery Utility
by westbaer
Thanks to pod2g, tom3q, planetbeing and geohot.
========================================
:: iBoot for n82ap, Copyright 2009, Apple Inc.
:: BUILD_TAG: iBoot-636.66.33
```

```
:: BUILD_STYLE: RELEASE
:: USB_SERIAL_NUMBER: CPID:8900 CPRV:30 CPFM:03 SCEP:05 BDID:04
ECID:000003031C18438D IBFL:01 SRNM:[88832BDP1R4]
===========================================
[FTL:MSG] Apple NAND Driver (AND) RO
[NAND] Device ID 0xb655d7ec
[NAND] BANKS_TOTAL 4
[NAND] BLOCKS_PER_BANK 8192
[NAND] PAGES_PER_BANK 104876
[NAND] SECTORS_PER_PAGE 8
[NAND] BYTES_PER_SPARE 128
[FTL:MSG] FIL_Init [OK]
[FTL:MSG] BUF_Init [OK]
[FTL:MSG] FPart Init [OK] read old style signature 0x43303035
(line:371)
[FTL:MSG] VFL Register [OK]
[FTL:MSG] VFL Init [OK]
[FTL:MSG] VFL_Open [OK]
[FTL:MSG] FTL Register [OK]
[FTL:WRN] Failure running _LoadFTLCxt!
[FTL:WRN] Recovering NAND Data Structures - this will take some time!
[FTL:WRN] _FTLRestore OK!
[FL:MSG] FTL_Open [OK]
Boot Failure Count: 1 Panic Fail Count: 0
Entering recovery mode, starting command prompt
```

From the output of iRecovery, the "BUILD_TAG" version can be accessed. In this example, it was iBoot-636.66.33. This is Apple's stage 2 bootloader and, if you recall from Chapter 2, it is this that runs Recovery mode on Apple devices. The iBoot version can be translated to its appropriate firmware version by searching various websites. The iPhone Wiki typically does a decent job of providing the iBoot revisions and their corresponding firmware version. As the links continually change, a direct link is not provided here; however, going to http://theiphonewiki.com and searching for "bootloader" or "iBoot versions" will typically provide the necessary results. In this example, iBoot-636.66.33 is known to run iOS version 3.1.3.

If a device is not found, the iRecovery output will display that information accordingly and report "No iPhone/iPod found."

Install appropriate iTunes version

Most, if not all, forensic acquisition tools rely on iTunes. Therefore, once the firmware version of the device is known, a version of iTunes that supports that iOS version must be installed. If iTunes version 8.2 is installed, and the particular iOS version required is 9.1 or higher, the computer will not recognize that an Apple device is connected and the acquisition will fail.

The question you might be asking yourself is, "Okay, so which iTunes version do I need for each iPhone or iPad firmware version available?" As with many aspects of

Table 5.2 iTunes Version Recommendations

iPhone or iPad Model/iOS Version	Suggested iTunes Version
Model: A1203 iOS: 2.2.1	iTunes version 8.1.1 or lower
Model: A1203 iOS: 3.0	iTunes version 8.1.1 or lower
Model: A1203 iOS: 3.1	iTunes version 8.1.1 or lower
Model: A1203 iOS: 3.1.2	iTunes version 8.1.1 or lower
Model: A1219 iOS: 3.2	iTunes version 8.1.1 and 9.1 or higher
Model: A1241 iOS: 2.2.1	iTunes version 8.1.1
Model: A1241 iOS: 3.0	iTunes version 8.1.1 or lower
Model: A1241 iOS: 3.0.1	iTunes version 8.1.1 or lower
Model: A1241 iOS: 3.1	iTunes version 8.1.1 or lower
Model: A1241 iOS: 3.1.2	iTunes version 8.1.1 or lower
Model: A1241 iOS: 3.1.3	iTunes version 8.1.1 or lower
Model: A1303 iOS: 3.0	iTunes version 8.1.1 or lower
Model: A1303 iOS: 3.0.1	iTunes version 8.1.1 or lower
Model: A1303 iOS: 3.1	iTunes version 8.1.1 or lower
Model: A1303 iOS: 3.1.2	iTunes version 8.1.1 or lower
Model: A1303 iOS: 3.1.3	iTunes version 8.1.1 and 9.1 or higher
Any model running iOS 4.0 or higher	iTunes version 10

mobile forensics, the answer is not always a direct one. However, Table 5.2 provides guidelines that suggest the iTunes version that may be required for the particular device that an examiner might wish to acquire. These suggestions are based on the iTunes versions required by each of Zdziarski's Automated Tools. For a few of Zdziarski's Automated tools, multiple iTunes versions are required; however, if using another commercial tool, it is suggested that the version listed first be installed. If the acquisition process is unsuccessful even after the suggested iTunes version has been installed, it might be worthwhile to either upgrade or downgrade to another version as the computer is evidently not recognizing the connected Apple device. Most of the commercial tools will display an iTunes error, and technical support can help an examiner determine which iTunes version is required.

Once the iTunes version is determined, it needs to be installed. If you need to upgrade to a higher version, a standard install will be sufficient. This will automatically replace the older version with the newer install. If a lower version of iTunes is required than the version currently installed, iTunes will first need to be uninstalled, including the removal of the iTunes helper files. To ensure that all iTunes artifacts are uninstalled from the machine, the following commands can be run in a terminal window:

```
$ sudo rm -rf /Applications/iTunes.app
$ /System/Library/PrivateFrameworks/DeviceLink.framework
```

```
$ /System/Library/Extensions/AppleMobileDevice.kext
$ /System/Library/PrivateFrameworks/iTunesAccess.framework
$ /System/Library/PrivateFrameworks/CoreFP.framework
$ /System/Library/PrivateFrameworks/MobileDevice.framework
```

Once the above commands are run, try to open iTunes in order to make sure that the software was successfully removed (a "?" should appear over the iTunes icon on a Macintosh computer, as there is no longer a linked reference to the software). Next, install the iTunes version that you wish to have running by following the installation wizard. When the installation is complete, the forensic workstation will have to be restarted in order to complete the downgrade. If the machine is not restarted, the acquisition will likely not work.

Acquisition – Zdziarski technique

This method was developed by Jonathan Zdziarski, a former Research Scientist for McAfee, Inc., who has contributed significantly to research into the iPhone and iPod Touch. Using his method, an examiner can acquire a bit-by-bit copy of the user data partition. This process requires modifying a read-only system partition, which is completely separate from where the user data is contained.

The Zdziarski method is run by downloading "Automated Tools" from his website and is strictly command-line driven. The process involves installing a recovery agent within the system partition of the device. Once the live recovery agent becomes active upon reboot, the user initiates a recovery script which creates a copy of the raw disk image on the device and pulls it onto the forensic workstation over a USB connection. The most recently released Automated Tools support all firmware versions for the 2G, 3G, 3G(s), and iPhone 4 up to and including 4.1 as well as all iPad versions. For any device running iOS 4.0 or higher, Zdziarski's method will recover only the logical file system, not a full physical image. Even a logical acquisition of iOS 4.x is a daunting task, as the tools are still being enhanced to work with the encrypted OS.

Once the forensic workstation has been set up with the proper iTunes version and the device model and firmware version is known, the imaging process can begin. In this example, we will refer to an iPhone 3G, running iOS version 3.1.3. It is important to note that around October of 2010, Zdziarski released an update of his tools in which some of the steps are slightly modified. As we step through the acquisition, the differences can be noted by the references to the "Old" Automated Tools in comparison to the "New" Automated Tools.

The general overall process consists of the following steps.

Connect the device

The first step is to connect the iPhone to the computer via a USB cable. If iTunes is automatically launched when the device is connected, be sure to exit the software before proceeding to the next step. Prior to running the script, the iPhone will need to be put in either Recovery or DFU mode, depending on the firmware version. Most versions will require the device to be in DFU mode, but specific instructions provided with the tool will specify this information, as does the output after running each script.

Some of the more recently developed Automated Tools require the use of Linux. The tools for these specific devices are developed to be used only on a Linux workstation (or virtual machine, VM) and do not require the use of iTunes.

Set up the Automated Tools

Prior to running the first scripts, a setup process that downloads the files needed must be completed in order to complete the acquisition process successfully. To ensure you are using the most up-to-date files, it is a good idea to run the setup process prior to each acquisition.

NOTE

The setup step does not need to be performed on the newer automated tools, and the instructions for each module will specify whether this step is needed. If required, a user name and password must be provided to initiate the setup process.

When the setup is complete, a message will indicate that the first script can now be run. The examiner will also be informed about the next step as well as the operating mode the device needs to be in.

Imaging process

The first of three scripts that are required for the imaging process installs a recovery agent onto the device. On most occasions, the phone will need to be in DFU mode for this step; however, there are exceptions for certain models (i.e., the iPhone 3GS running firmware version 3.1.3 as well as the iPad running 3.2.2). These two devices need to be in Recovery mode for the first step. Refer to Chapter 2 for details on how to boot a device into DFU or Recovery mode.

Shortly after running the script, the user will be prompted on-screen to disconnect and reconnect the device from the USB. The examiner will then see additional packets being sent over the USB connection, and when complete, the next step can be completed.

After the device is rebooted, the second script in this process can be run. When executed, the live recovery agent that was installed with the previous command will now become active. Once again, the examiner will need to place the device in the specified operating mode, disconnect and reconnect the device from USB, and follow the on-screen instructions. Once the script has been executed, it should inform the examiner whether the operation was successfully completed, and then the iRecovery tool is initiated to restart the device. Upon restart, the agent should be active.

Now that the recovery agent has been installed and activated, and the iPhone or iPad has been rebooted into normal mode, it is time to initiate the actual recovery.

Prior to October 2010, Zdziarski's Automated Tools contained the setup script within each individual folder (as mentioned in the first step). With the updates released in the third quarter of 2010, some restructuring was done, preventing the module from requiring a setup process. As part of these updates, "usbmux-proxy," which is proprietary for iTunes, is replaced with the open-source version, "usbmuxd." Usbmuxd stands for "USB multiplexing daemon" and it is what allows for communication to the device over USB (Martin, 2011). By replacing usbmux-proxy with the open-source version, Zdziarski is preventing the need for iTunes to be installed in order to successfully run an acquisition. The intention of providing this replacement was so that iTunes versioning would no longer be an issue in imaging an iPhone or iPad device. Because these updated tools are still in their infancy, at times iTunes is still needed for some modules; however, certain devices (such as the iPad running iOS 3.2.2) have been acquired successfully on a Linux machine with no installation of iTunes.

To begin the final acquisition process, the provided recovery script must be used to initiate a physical acquisition of the raw disk image on the device. An image file is created on the forensic workstation, which will continue to slowly grow in size if the process is successful. If the file remains as 0 bytes, it is possible that either the live recovery agent was not installed correctly or not activated properly. Troubleshooting steps would include checking the iTunes version to ensure the workstation was even recognizing that a device was connected. Next, the three scripts are walked through again (after rebooting the device), keeping an eye on the output from the script to ensure that there are no errors during the installation or activation process.

Assuming the device is imaging as expected, do not interrupt the process until it is complete. You will know that the acquisition is finished when the "Cannot connect to usbmux" message appears within the terminal window.

Post-acquisition steps

Once the acquisition is complete, several commands will need to be executed from a separate terminal window in order to properly stop the running processes, as specified in Zdziarski's instructions within the Automated Tools.

Next, the image should be renamed to a case name, number, or other unique identifier. If the image is mounted on a Mac, the extension will also need to be changed to ".dmg". If prompted when the extension is changed, just click "Use dmg," as shown in Figure 5.8.

After modifying the file name, no other changes need to be made to the image file; therefore, it can be marked as read-only. On a Mac, right-click on the file and select "Get Info" (or on the keyboard, hold down "command+i"). This will bring up the properties of the file, and from here the "Locked" check box should be selected, as displayed in Figure 5.9.

Once the image file is locked, it is suggested that the examiner calculate a hash value for the image and document this information in a report. This process can be done through a Terminal window using the following command:

```
# If on a Mac:
$ md5 iPhone.dmg
$ shasum iPhone.dmg

# If using Linux, a hash tool can be installed such as md5sum, sha256sum,
etc.
$ sha256sum iPhone.dmg
$ md5sum iPhone.dmg
```

For either of these commands, the output will be displayed within the Terminal window. If an examiner wishes to copy the hash value directly to a text file, the following can be run to redirect the output:

```
$ md5sum iPhone.dmg > ~/Desktop/md5-hash-value.txt
```

The image is now ready to be mounted and analyzed.

FIGURE 5.8

Modify Extension.

FIGURE 5.9

Modify Image Properties.

Acquisition – iXAM

iXAM was created by Forensic Telecommunications Services Ltd. (FTS). Primarily a forensic technology lab, FTS developed iXAM through independent research and development. iXAM is entirely software-based, requiring the use of only a USB dongle. It runs on Windows only, but will also work in a VM environment that can be run on Linux or Mac. iXAM is installed by running a setup file, provided by FTS on an external USB drive (further installation instructions can be found in Chapter 7). Software updates are retrieved through a secure FTP connection.

The way iXAM works is it executes a custom bootloader on the device. Unsigned code is sent over a USB connection to a device running in DFU mode. Once on the device, the code is executed within RAM and does not touch the user data partition. During the imaging process, iXAM prevents the device from connecting to any external networks. Imaging is done one block at a time, and each block is checked for errors and a hash value is created. Once the imaging process is complete, the bootloader powers off the device. Upon reboot, the program is removed from RAM, which is why iXAM is said to have "Zero-Footprint."

As of version 2, iXAM is known to support all iPhone models including 2G, 3G, 3G(s), and iPhone 4, and all firmware versions up to and including 4.1; however, as with Zdziarski's method, a full physical image is still not supported for iOS 4 devices because of the hardware encryption. The updated version is also anticipated to add greater functionality and drastically improve acquisition times.

The iXAM software arrives on a USB drive, and is installed through an executable file, which then steps the user through the process of downloading prerequisites, purging existing Apple Device drivers, and finally the provisioning and installation process.

The following sections outline the general steps taken to perform a physical acquisition of an iPhone using iXAM software. More details on the installation, acquisition, and reporting process can be found in Chapter 7.

Connect the device

First, the iPhone should be connected to the forensic workstation using a USB cable. In the testing done in Chapter 7, a VM was used that required extra steps to ensure that the iPhone was being seen by the VM rather than the host machine. Once the device is connected and the acquisition process initiated, the examiner is prompted to place the device in DFU mode with the help of a timer in the upper right-hand corner of the software. Next, the wizard walks the examiner through the installation of device drivers.

Imaging process

Moving forward in the process, the next step instructs the user that the Stage 1 bootloader is being sent to the device. The new hardware must first be verified, and then the process repeated for Stage 2 and Stage 3 bootloaders. These preparation steps lead to the start of the actual physical acquisition of the device.

The user is prompted to select the iPhone model that he or she wishes to acquire; then, after selecting the "Forensic Image" option (as opposed to a logical download), the imaging process begins.

Post-acquisition steps
Once the imaging is complete, the examiner is left with a dmg file, which can be mounted and analyzed. Similar to the steps taken for Zdziarski's method, this file should first be marked as read-only and a hash value calculated prior to any type of examination.

Acquisition – Jailbroken device
The reason why Zdziarski and iXAM are able to get a full physical image on an iPhone is that they have developed the means to gain root access on the device, which is difficult to accomplish without modifying the user data partition. Once this is achieved, a simple "dd" function can be performed in order to image the device just as a computer hard drive or other device would be forensically imaged. While the previous two methods do not jailbreak an iOS device in order to perform an acquisition, a physical image can also be taken of a device which has already been jailbroken by the user.

WARNING

Imaging a jailbroken device could potentially overwrite user data, thus modifying evidence on the device. It is suggested that this technique be used only for research.

First of all, it is important to note that acquiring a jailbroken device does modify the user partition, and this method should be used only as a last resort and with the understanding that potential evidence could be overwritten. To physically acquire a jailbroken device, several steps must be taken. The high-level steps are outlined here, and expanded upon in the following sections:

- Create a wireless network
- Remotely connect to iPhone
- Image device

Create a wireless network
Prior to accessing the device in any way, a wireless network must be created (or an existing network used) in order to allow the forensic workstation to remotely connect to the device. For this procedure, a Mac OS X system will be used. While an existing network can also be used, let us go through the steps of creating a separate network for this scenario.

On a Mac, a new wireless network can be created through the system's Network Preferences. For this example, the network was named "iPhone-Book" as shown in Figure 5.10.

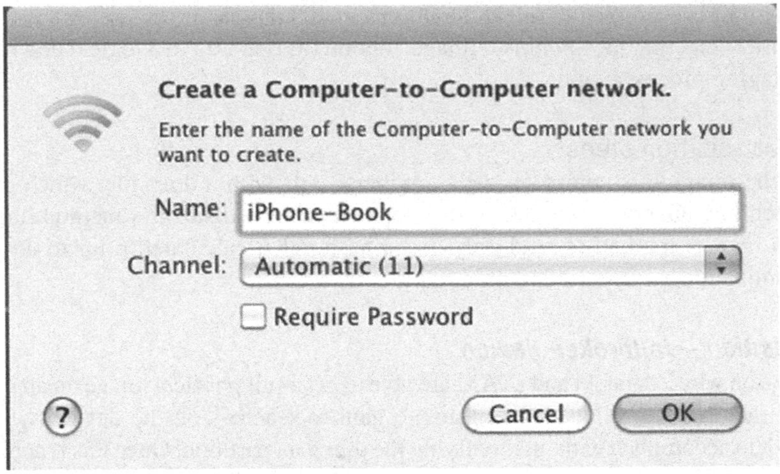

Create a Computer-to-Computer network.

Enter the name of the Computer-to-Computer network you want to create.

Name: iPhone-Book

Channel: Automatic (11)

☐ Require Password

Cancel   OK

FIGURE 5.10

Create Wireless Network.

Next, a static IP address must be set for both the Mac and the iPhone. To set on a Mac, run the following command in a terminal window:

```
$ sudo ifconfig en1 inet 192.168.0.1 netmask 255.255.255.0
```

When running a command beginning with "sudo," the examiner will be prompted to enter the administrator password.

To set the static IP address on the iPhone, navigate to Settings > Wi-Fi, then connect to the newly created network (iPhone-book). Once connected, the user will need to select the right arrow for that network, then "Static" and enter 192.168.0.2 with a netmask of 255.255.255.0 (see Figure 5.11). Once complete, the user selects "Wi-Fi Networks" in the upper left-hand corner to save these settings.

Now that both the Mac and the iPhone are on the same subnet, the two devices should be able to communicate with each other and are ready for the next step.

Remotely connect to iPhone

The examiner can now connect remotely to the device over SSH. On most jailbroken phones, the user name is "root" and the password is "alpine" by default; however, some research will need to be done on the examiner's part to ensure that this is true for the jailbroken device he or she is working with.

Run the following command on the Mac in order to connect to the iPhone:

```
$ ssh root@1923168.0.2
root@192.168.0.2's password:
3GS-40:~ root#
```

If this is not successful, it is most likely because SSH is not installed on the device. As part of the jailbreaking process, most users will take the time to install the source

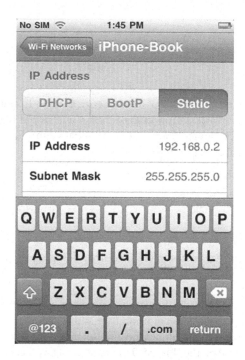

FIGURE 5.11

Set Static IP on iPhone.

packages suggested by the jailbreaking site that instructed them on how to gain root access on the device. However, some users may not complete this step. If SSH is not installed, the examiner will need to do some research on how to manage the Cydia sources on the device (or whatever was used to jailbreak the device, if not Cydia) and install "OpenSSH."

Once connected to the device, let us make sure that we have the necessary files before beginning the imaging process. To do this, we need to make sure both "dd" and "netcat" are installed on the device by running the following commands from the iPhone:

```
3GS-40:~ root# which dd
3GS-40:~ root# which nc
3GS-40:~ root#
```

Typically, if the "which" command is run and the software is installed, the output will display the path to the source file. Since there was no path shown, we can assume that dd and netcat are not yet on the device. We can copy these tools to the iPhone from the Mac. First, we will need to find where these tools are stored on the Mac, and then run the "scp" command to copy the files.

```
Katie-Strzempkas-Macbook:~ kstrzemp$ which nc
/usr/bin/nc
Katie-Strzempkas-Macbook:~ kstrzemp$ which dd
```

```
/bin/dd
Katie-Strzempkas-Macbook:~  kstrzemp$  /usr/bin/scp  /usr/bin/nc
root@192.168.0.2:/bin/nc
Katie-Strzempkas-Macbook:~  kstrzemp$  /usr/bin/scp  /bin/dd
root@192.168.0.2:/bin/dd
```

Those last two commands used "scp" (or "Secure Copy") to transfer the nc and dd tools from the forensic workstation to the iPhone, and stored these tools in the /bin folder on the root of the device. Now, let us SSH back into the iPhone to make sure these files are where they should be:

```
3GS-40:~ root# which dd
/bin/dd
3GS-40:~ root# which nc
/bin/nc
3GS-40:~ root#
```

Now that all of the necessary tools are installed, the imaging process can begin.

Image device

Using this technique, imaging is done over a program called netcat. Netcat creates a tunnel that allows two devices to communicate and transfer files back and forth over a specified port. One end of the tunnel must be set up on the forensic workstation and the other end configured on the iPhone. This process, as well as imaging the raw disk, is all done within two commands (one on the Mac and one on the iPhone).

The first step is to run netcat on the Mac using the following command:

```
Katie-Strzempkas-Macbook:~ kstrzemp$ nc -l 7000 | dd of=~/Desktop/
rdisk0s2.dmg bs=1048576
```

This command tells netcat to "listen" on port 7000 and to create the output file "rdisk0s2.dmg" on the desktop, based on the input from the other end of the tunnel (which is yet to be initiated). Upon hitting enter, it will appear as though nothing is happening; however, the Mac is waiting for the other end of the connection.

Next, let us take a look at the raw disk files on the iPhone to determine which one to create an image of:

```
3GS-40:~ root# cd /dev
3GS-40:/dev root# ls -l rdisk*
crw-r—— 1 root operator 14, 0 Feb 9 10:53 rdisk0
crw-r—— 1 root operator 14, 1 Feb 9 10:54 rdisk0s1
crw-r—— 1 root operator 14, 2 Feb 9 10:53 rdisk0s2
crw-r—— 1 root operator 14, 3 Feb 9 10:54 rdisk0s2s1
```

These files were discussed in the "iPhone Disk Partitions" section of Chapter 3. As a recap, rdisk0 is the entire raw disk (including all partitions). Rdisk0s1 is the firmware partition, and rdisk0s2 is the user data partition (rdisk0s2s1 is unique to the 3GS device). So, when the dd command is initiated, we will want to acquire rdisk0s2 to get a full image of the user data partition.

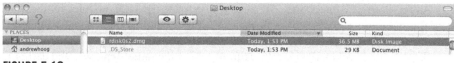

FIGURE 5.12

rdisk0s2.dmg File on Mac.

To begin the acquisition, the following command should be run from the iPhone, which has been connected to over SSH:

```
3GS-40:~ root# /bin/dd if=/dev/rdisk0s2 bs=1M | /bin/nc 192.168.0.1 7000
```

Let us break down this command to gain a better understanding:

- */bin/dd*: This runs the dd command, which is stored in the /bin directory.
- *if=/dev/rdisk0s2*: This specifies the "input file" as rdisk0s2, the raw disk for the user data partition (slice 2).
- *bs=1M*: Sets a "byte size" of 1 MB.
- */bin/nc 192.168.0.1 7000*: This runs the netcat command, instructing the device to connect to 192.168.0.1 (the Mac) over port 7000 (the port the Mac is listening on).

To summarize, we initiated the dd command to image the "rdisk0s2" file, took that output, and sent it through a netcat tunnel, which is connected to our forensic workstation. As soon as this command is run, we should see the "rdisk0s2.dmg" file created on the desktop of the Mac and it should be increasing in size (see Figure 5.12).

Post-acquisition steps

Once the imaging process is complete (it will likely take several hours to acquire depending on the size of the device), the image file can be marked as read-only, mounted, hash value calculated, and analyzed.

IMAGING OTHER APPLE DEVICES

It is also possible to image other Apple iOS devices such as the iPod Touch and Apple TV. Other devices, specifically the iPod, run either HFS+ or FAT32 depending on the operating system on which the device was initialized.

iPad

While the examples provided in this chapter did not specifically show a backup, logical, or physical acquisition of an iPad, the very same techniques used on the iPhone can be applied to this device.

When an iPad is connected to iTunes, a user can initiate a backup which is stored in the same location as that of an iPhone backup file. Again, this backup can be analyzed using the commercial tools highlighted in Chapter 7, or even the open source tools available on the Internet. The same applies for a logical acquisition.

As for a physical extraction, Zdziarski also provides specific modules for the iPad, and the same process and scripts are run. iXAM does not list the iPad as a supported device; however, according to the website, this device will be added in the near future.

Finally, a jailbroken iPad can be acquired using the same steps outlined earlier in this chapter for the iPhone.

iPod Touch

The iPod Touch is a portable media player and personal digital assistant, which allows the capability to connect to Wi-Fi, store and take photos and videos, and download apps for the App Store (among other features). While it does not have network access to allow for phone calls and text messages, acquiring data from this device could be extremely beneficial in the course of an investigation.

The iPod Touch runs iOS and can therefore be acquired by many of the tools that support the iPhone. While this particular device was not tested on the tools within Chapter 7, most list the iPod Touch as a supported device.

Apple TV

The first-generation Apple TV ran a modified version of OS X. The second generation, however, runs a version of iOS that is almost identical to the fourth-generation iPod Touch. Technically, Apple TV (2G) does not run a standard iOS; however, the operating system is very similar to that of the iPod Touch, iPhone, and iPad ("What Operating System. . .", 2010).

The original Apple TV is essentially a hard drive running Mac OS X, and thus the drive can be removed and imaged the way a typical hard drive would. Many details on this version of the Apple TV, including how it works and where forensic data can be discovered, can be found by searching the Internet for "hacking the Apple TV and where your forensic data lives." This set of information was presented at Defcon in July 2009 (Estis & Robbins, 2009). The second-generation Apple TV is a bit different. It lacks the hard drive storage; however, 8 GB of NAND Flash storage is available for caching.

SUMMARY

The first step in any mobile forensic examination is to image or acquire data from the device. With so many different models and operating system versions, the process for one device may not be the same as that for another. In addition, some of the commercial tools do not yet support the latest firmware versions, leading the investigator to turn to other methods of data acquisition, such as from an iTunes backup file.

This chapter covered the various types of forensic acquisitions that can be performed on the iPhone, iPad, and other iOS devices. The importance of forensic imaging was discussed, followed by the different ways in which a device can be imaged. Two different methods of data retrieval through the iPhone's backup files were stepped through in detail, followed by a logical acquisition and, finally, a physical extraction of the device. The methods of imaging other iOS devices, including the iPod Touch and Apple TV, were also outlined.

References

ACPO Good Practice Guide for Computer-Based Electronic Evidence – 7Safe Information Security. (n.d.). 7Safe Information Security. Retrieved February 19, 2011, from http://7safe.com/electronic_evidence/index.html#

Estis, K., & Robbins, R. (2009, July 30). Hacking the Apple TV and where your forensic data lives. Def Con Hacking Conference. Retrieved February 23, 2011, from www.defcon.org/images/defcon-17/dc-17-presentations/defcon-17-kevin_estis-apple_tv.pdf

Government Employment & Payroll. (n.d.). Census Bureau home page. Retrieved February 19, 2011, from http://www.census.gov/govs/apes/

Martin, H. (n.d.). Abort, retry, hack? » usbmuxd. Abort, retry, hack? Retrieved January 10, 2011, from http://marcansoft.com/blog/iphonelinux

National Institute of Standards and Technology. (2010, November). Mobile devices. NIST Computer Forensic Tool Testing Program. Retrieved January 10, 2011, from http://www.cftt.nist.gov/mobile_devices.htm

What operating system do the Apple TV models use? Can Apple TV run Mac OS X software? Can it run iOS applications? Can Apple TV run Windows? Can it play iPod games? @ EveryMac.com. (2010, October 8). Mac specs, prices, answers, & comparison @ EveryMac.com – Est. 1996. Retrieved January 10, 2011, from http://www.everymac.com/systems/apple/apple-tv/apple-tv-faq/apple-tv-operating-system-mac-os-x-applications-running-windows-ipod-games.html

Data and application analysis

INTRODUCTION

A lot of material has been covered up to this point in the book including an overview of an iOS device, the file system used, the types of data storage, device and application security, and an in-depth review of the various forensic acquisition methods. All this information has been important in leading up to this chapter, which covers the analysis of the data recovered from the device.

ANALYSIS TECHNIQUES

This section provides an overview of the analysis techniques that can be used on an image in order to recover the greatest amount of data possible.

Mount disk image

As discussed throughout this book, the directories and files in the device's file system are the primary focus of a forensic investigation. The final section of this chapter, iPhone Application Analysis and Reference, provides a detailed analysis of both default and downloaded iPhone apps. Combining this information with the techniques demonstrated in Chapter 3, File System and Data Storage, will provide the most significant results for an investigation.

After performing a physical acquisition on an iOS device using one of the available methods, the resulting file will be in a disk image (.dmg) format. On a Mac, this file can be marked as read-only (see Chapter 5, section on "Postacquisition Steps") and mounted by double-clicking the file. By default, this should launch the DiskImageMounter on a Mac.

Oftentimes, an iPhone image may be corrupt or, for one reason or another, will not mount successfully on a Mac. In this case, Linux can also be used to mount a dmg file. The following command will mount an HFS Plus disk image on a Linux workstation or virtual machine (VM):

```
kstrzempka@linux-wks:~$ sudo mount -t hfsplus -o ro,loop ~/Desktop/
iPhone.dmg ~/Desktop/mount-
```

To mount the dmg, a folder needs to be created first in the location where the image should be mounted. Above, the "mount" folder was created on the user's desktop. Now, let us walk through the previous command to make sure we understand all of the options listed:

- sudo: Provides extended security privileges to the user.
- -t hfsplus: Specifies the file system type of HFS Plus.
- -o ro,loop: Specifies the option to open the device as read-only (ro) and as a loopback device, which makes the file accessible as a block device.
- ~/Desktop/iPhone.dmg: Source path where the dmg file is stored.
- ~/Desktop/mount: Destination path to the folder where the image is to be mounted.

Once the image is mounted on either a Mac or a Linux workstation, the examiner will see the entire file system of the device (see Appendix C to view the full iPhone file system). The analysis of folders and files within these directories is discussed in the "iPhone Data Storage Locations" section later in this chapter.

File carving

File carving is a process in which specified file types are searched and extracted across binary data, often a forensic image of an entire disk or partition. File carving works by examining the binary data and identifying files based on their known file headers. If the file format has a known footer, it will scan from the header until it finds the footer (or hits a maximum file length set by the configuration file), and then it saves the carved file to disk for further examination.

Traditional file carving techniques require that the data is sequential in the image and therefore they cannot produce the full file if it is fragmented. There are many reasons why files are fragmented, as the process for saving the file to nonvolatile storage varies by file system type as well as by the strong influence of the memory type such as NAND Flash. This also means that files that are very large (such as videos) will be more difficult to recover.

Newer file carving techniques are being researched and developed to address the limitations experienced with file fragmentation. One such technique has been developed by Digital Assembly, a digital forensics solutions company based in New York. Their technique, called SmartCarving, profiles the fragmentation characteristics of several popular file systems and uses this information to carve even fragmented photos. Their product, Adroit Photo Forensics, can also carve images from unknown file systems (Digital Assembly, n.d.).

The process of data carving typically involves a data carving tool, a configuration file for that tool, and a disk image containing the desired data. The configuration file contains details related to the file types that are to be carved out of the image. The tool will then search the raw data for file signatures of the file types referenced in the configuration file.

Once the data carving process is complete, the output is typically grouped by file type. The following is an example of the resulting file types after file carving was performed on an iPhone disk image file. If there are more than 1000 files, a new folder is created. For example, thousands of jpg images were contained on the device, and therefore a large number of jpg folders were created (jpg-2-0 through jpg-3-2). The "amr" file type stands for Adaptive Multi-Rate and this is where media files are commonly stored.

```
kstrzcmpka@linux-001:~# tree -L 1 scalpel-output/
scalpel-output/
├── amr-16-0
├── audit.txt
├── bplist-8-0
├── bplist-8-1
├── bplist-8-2
├── bplist-8-3
├── bplist-8-4
├── bplist-8-5
├── bplist-8-6
├── bplist-8-7
├── bplist-8-8
├── bplist-8-9
├── dat-6-0
├── email-10-0
├── email-10-1
├── gif-0-0
├── gif-1-0
├── htm-13-0
├── jpg-2-0
├── jpg-2-1
├── jpg-2-2
├── jpg-2-3
├── jpg-2-4
├── jpg-2-5
├── jpg-2-6
├── jpg-2-7
├── jpg-2-8
├── jpg-2-9
├── jpg-3-0
├── jpg-3-1
```

```
├── jpg-3-2
├── mov-11-0
├── pdf-15-0
├── plist-7-0
├── plist-7-1
├── plist-7-2
├── plist-7-3
├── plist-7-4
├── png-5-0
├── png-5-1
├── png-5-2
├── process
├── sqlitedb-9-0
└── sqlitedb-9-1
```

One popular tool used for carving data files is known as scalpel. Scalpel is an open source high-performance file carving utility written by Golden G. Richard III. It reads a database of header and footer definitions in order to extract files from a raw image. This utility is filesystem-independent and will work on FATx, NTFS, ext2/3, HFS, or raw partitions. Scalpel was rewritten based on foremost 0.69, which is another popular open source file carving utility. It is written in C and runs on Linux, Windows, Mac OS X, and other operating systems that can compile the C code (Richard, 2006).

Installing scalpel

The source code for scalpel can be downloaded from http://www.digitalforensicssolutions.com/Scalpel/ or installed via command line. The latter will automatically install the latest version. The following command must be run on the Linux workstation to install scalpel.

```
sudo apt-get install scalpel
```

Alternatively, one can compile from source, which will allow the installation of the latest version on Linux or other platforms without waiting for the specific platform maintainer to update the prepackaged version. In this method, the package must be compiled and built from the source code using the specific commands. First, the archive must be extracted using the tar command (-x will extract the files, -z unzips the files, -v signifies verbose output, and -f specifies the archived file). The following commands should be run to extract the files and compile the program. In this example, Scalpel version 1.60 was used. The most up-to-date software available at the time should be used.

```
$ cd ~
$ wget http://www.digitalforensicssolutions.com/Scalpel/scalpel-
1.60.tar.gz
$ tar xzvf scalpel-1.60.tar.gz
$ cd scalpel-1.60/
$ make
```

The scalpel executable is now in ~/scalpel-1.60 and is simply called scalpel. In addition, there is a sample scalpel.conf in the same directory, which is needed for scalpel to run and to extend the supported file definitions. Here is a starter scalpel.conf for an iPhone device:

```
#ext    case size       header                          footer
gif     y    5000000     \x47\x49\x46\x38\x37\x61        \x00\x3b
gif     y    5000000     \x47\x49\x46\x38\x39\x61        \x00\x3b
jpg     y    200000000   \xff\xd8\xff\xe0\x00\x10        \xff\xd9
jpg     y    5000000     \xff\xd8\xff\xe1                \x7f\xff\xd9

png     y    102400      \x50\x4e\x47?                   \xff\xfc\xfd\xfe
png     y    102400      \x89PNG

tif     y    20000000    \x49\x49\x2a\x00

db      y    409600      SQLite\x20format

dat     y    8192        DynamicDictionary-
plist   y    4096        <plist                          </plist
bplist  y    4096        \x62\x70\x6c\x69\x73\x74\x30\x30
sqlitedb y   819200      SQLite\x20format
email   y    10240       From:
mov     y    8192000     \x00\x00\x00\x14\x66\x74\x79\x70\x71\x74\x20
\x20\x00\x00\x00\x00

doc     y    10000000    \xd0\xcf\x11\xe0\xa1\xb1\x1a\xe1\x00\x00 \xd0
\xcf\x11\xe0\xa1\xb1\x1a\xe1\x00\x00 NEXT
doc     y    10000000    \xd0\xcf\x11\xe0\xa1\xb1

htm     n    50000       <html                           </html>

pdf     y    5000000     %PDF %EOF\x0d   REVERSE
pdf     y    5000000     %PDF %EOF\x0a   REVERSE

wav     y    200000      RIFF????WAVE
amr     y    200000      #!AMR

zip     y    10000000    PK\x03\x04                      \x3c\xac

java    y    1000000     \xca\xfe\xba\xbe
```

As one can tell, the headers for this configuration file define the extension or file type, whether it is case sensitive, the maximum size to carve, the header definition (in ASCII, hex, and other supported notations), and the footer (if it exists). A targeted file type for carving does not need to define each setting. For additional information, see the sample configuration file in the downloaded source files, as there are many additional options that are quite powerful. Your workstation now has the software needed for file carving.

It is worth pointing out that a large number of file signatures have already been assembled. Gary Kessler, an independent consultant and practitioner of digital forensics, actively maintains a table of file signatures on his website. He references the "magic file," which is found on most Unix systems and is located at /usr/share/file/magic on the Ubuntu workstation. On the workstation, one can run the "file" command, which takes a file as an argument and attempts to determine the file type based on the signatures in the magic file (Kessler, 2011).

A simple example would include looking at an unknown file that cannot be easily identified by the file name (of course, some people might try to hide file types by changing the extension, but this is easily discovered by examining the file signature):

```
root@linux-wks:~/Desktop/iPhone-mount/run# file syslog.pid
syslog.pid: ASCII text
```

Looking at the "syslog.pid" file found in the "run" directory at the root of the device, the file command shows that this file contains ASCII characters.

Usage

To use scalpel, you will first need to have the program installed and compiled and also have access to a dmg (or other image file) and the scalpel configuration file. By default, scalpel will create a "scalpel-output" directory in the current folder, so make sure you are cd'd into the directory where you would like the output to go. Run the following command:

```
kstrzempka@linux-wks:~/Desktop$ time scalpel -c /home/kstrzempka/
Documents/scalpel-iphone.conf iPhone.dmg
Scalpel version 1.60
Written by Golden G. Richard III, based on Foremost 0.69.

Opening target "iPhone.dmg"

Image file pass 1/2.
iPhone.dmg: 100.0%
|****************************************************************
****| 14.6 GB   00:00 ETAAllocating work queues...
Work queues allocation complete. Building carve lists...
Carve lists built. Workload:
gif with header "\x47\x49\x46\x38\x37\x61" and footer "\x00\x3b" -->
0 files
gif with header "\x47\x49\x46\x38\x39\x61" and footer "\x00\x3b" -->
31 files
jpg with header "\xff\xd8\xff\xe0\x00\x10" and footer "\xff\xd9" -->
45 files
jpg with header "\xff\xd8\xff\xe1" and footer "\x7f\xff\xd9" -->
13 files
```

```
png with header "\x50\x4e\x47\x3f" and footer "\xff\xfc\xfd\xfe" -->
0 files
png with header "\x89\x50\x4e\x47" and footer "" --> 955 files
dat with header "\x44\x79\x6e\x61\x6d\x69\x63\x44\x69\x63\x74\x69
\x6f\x6e\x61\x72\x79\x2d" and footer "" --> 1 files
plist with header "\x3c\x70\x6c\x69\x73\x74" and footer "\x3c\x2f
\x70\x6c\x69\x73\x74" --> 802 files
bplist with header "\x62\x70\x6c\x69\x73\x74\x30\x30" and footer ""
--> 1273 files
sqlitedb with header "\x53\x51\x4c\x69\x74\x65\x20\x66\x6f\x72\x6d
\x61\x74" and footer "" --> 56 files
email with header "\x46\x72\x6f\x6d\x3a" and footer "" --> 13 files
mov with header "\x00\x00\x00\x14\x66\x74\x79\x70\x71\x74\x20\x20
\x00\x00\x00\x00" and footer "" --> 0 files
doc with header "\xd0\xcf\x11\xe0\xa1\xb1" and footer "" --> 0 files
htm with header "\x3c\x68\x74\x6d\x6c" and footer "\x3c\x2f\x68\x74
\x6d\x6c\x3e" --> 8 files
pdf with header "\x25\x50\x44\x46" and footer "\x25\x45\x4f\x46\x0d"
--> 0 files
pdf with header "\x25\x50\x44\x46" and footer "\x25\x45\x4f\x46\x0a"
--> 0 files
amr with header "\x23\x21\x41\x4d\x52" and footer "" --> 0 files
Carving files from image.
Image file pass 2/2.
iPhone.dmg: 100.0%
|*****************************************************************
****|  14.6 GB    00:00 ETAProcessing of image file complete. Cleaning
up...
Done.
Scalpel is done, files carved = 3197, elapsed = 409 seconds.

real 6m48.487s
user 4m28.320s
sys 0m25.050s
```

The command is broken down as follows:

- time: This is optional and will simply document how long the process took (see the previous output for the real, user, and sys times).
- scalpel: Runs the scalpel program.
- -c /home/kstrzempka/Documents/scalpel-iPhone.conf: Points the scalpel program to the appropriate configuration file: in this case, "scalpel-iPhone.conf."
- iPhone.dmg: Tells scalpel to run against the specified dmg file. If the dmg is not in the current directory, a path can also be specified, such as "/home/kstrzempka/ Desktop/iPhone.dmg."

When scalpel has finished, a "scalpel-output" folder is created in the current directory, which contains all the recovered files, sorted by file type. Table 6.1 contains a

Table 6.1 Files Recovered through Scalpel

File Type	Description
amr	Voicemails will typically be stored here. AMR stands for "Adaptive Multi-Rate Codec" File which is a compressed audio format.
bplist/plist	Binary plist and XML plist files recovered from the device.
dat	This is a "Data" file; the dynamic dictionary file is a common file found in this category (containing a list of key words unique to the user).
email	Recovered email files are stored here. Because there is a set file size that is extracted from the dmg, there are usually multiple emails within each ".email" file.
gif/jpg/png	Various images, photos, and icons recovered from the device are stored in these folders.
htm	Cached web history files.
mov	Videos taken from the device or synced to the device can be found in the "mov" directory.
doc/pdf	Documents or PDF files.
sqlitedb	SQLite database files are stored here and can be queried to recover data.

breakdown of the standard file types recovered from an iPhone using scalpel and the type of information that may be found within these files.

Strings

The strings command on a Linux workstation will extract, by default, ASCII printable strings at least four characters long from any file, text, or binary. While this technique is not terribly elegant or sophisticated, it is quite effective at quickly examining binary data to determine whether information of interest might be contained in the file.

There are several options that have a great impact on what the strings command will output. First, let us take a look at the synopsis section of the command's man page (manual):

```
STRINGS(1)          GNU Development Tools          STRINGS(1)

NAME
    strings - print the strings of printable characters in files.

SYNOPSIS
    strings [-afovV] [-min-len]
        [-n min-len] [--bytes=min-len]
        [-t radix] [--radix=radix]
        [-e encoding] [--encoding=encoding]
        [-] [--all] [--print-file-name]
```

```
[-T bfdname] [--target=bfdname]
[--help] [-version] file...
```

There are a few options you should always consider using when executing strings. First, the "--all" option tells strings to examine the entire file (on certain files, it only examines certain portions of the file. Second, the "--radix=" option tells strings to print the offset within the file where the string was found. This is extremely helpful when you combine strings and a hex editor to examine possible evidence found in the file. The radix option can print the offset in octal (--radix=o), hex (--radix=x), or decimal (--radix=d). For most hex editors, you should consider hex, or perhaps decimal, offsets.

Another extremely important option controls the character encoding of the strings that provide support for Unicode characters in both big endian and little endian formats:

```
--encoding=encoding
    Select the character encoding of the strings that are to be found.
    Possible values for encoding are: s = single-7-bit-byte characters
    (ASCII, ISO 8859, etc., default), S = single-8-bit-byte
    characters,
    b = 16-bit bigendian, l = 16-bit littleendian, B = 32-bit
    bigendian, L = 32-bit littleendian. Useful for finding wide
    character strings. (l and b apply to, for example, Unicode
    UTF-16/UCS-2 encodings).
```

An example of utilization of the strings command on an iPhone.dmg file is given as follows:

```
kstrzempka@linux-wks:~$ strings --all --radix=x iPhone-book.dmg |
less
    8bd586a  Message-ID:    <0FBEB6FB-E72A-42A5-BDD5-CE36DE853A8B@
    viaforensics.com>
    8bd58a7 From: <testaccount@viaforensics.com>
    8bd58cd thread-topic: Test
    8bd58e0 thread-index: AcsOOTXUVxQEEp2BTLq8uC1Or43JSA==
    8bd590f To: <viaforensics-test-account@gmail.com>
    8bd5931 Content-Type: text/plain; format=flowed; charset="us-
    ascii"
    8bd596d Content-Transfer-Encoding: 7bit
    8bd598d MIME-Version: 1.0 (iPhone Mail 7D11)
    8bd59b2 Subject: Test
    8bd59c0 Date: Thu, 5 Aug 2010 14:05:42 -0500
    8bd59e5 Return-Path: testaccount@viaforensics.com
    8bd5a05 X-OriginalArrivalTime: 05 Aug 2010 19:05:46.0948 (UTC)
    8bd5a3c FILETIME=[3607C840:01CB34D1]
    8bd5a5b This is a test message that will be deleted from the gmail
    account
    8bd5a9f Sent from my iPhone
```

In this example, the first lines of the results were omitted; however, a known deleted e-mail was located on the dmg. The message content says "This is a test message that will be deleted from the Gmail account" and it is at offset 0x8bd5a5b. By jumping to this section in a hex editor, further information can be revealed (as discussed in the "Advanced Forensic Analysis" section).

Now, let us change the encoding parameter and look for the following:

```
kstrzempka@linux-wks:~$ strings --all --radix=x -encoding=b
iPhone-book.dmg | less
    5e8a1e 0-www.groupon.com-api-v1-users-katie-strzempka-
groupons-5620002-0-1-29169321.png
    5e8ad0 bakin-eggs-chicago.plist
    5e8b10 0www.groupon.com-images-site_images-avatars-deals-
bakin-eggs-chicago_sidebar.jpg
    5e8bc0 0-www.groupon.com-api-v1-users-katie-strzempka-
groupons-6290319-0-1-78638381.png
    5e8c70 &southport-lanes-seven-ten-lounge.plist
    5e8cce ]www.groupon.com-images-site_images-avatars-deals-
southport-lanes-seven-ten-lounge_sidebar.jpg
    5e8d9c gap-inc-chicago.plist
```

In this example, we are looking for 16-bit big endian characters. In this case, an example was pulled from the results related to the Groupon mobile application (which allows users to purchase coupons for local businesses from their mobile device). The string results revealed three groupons that were potentially purchased. In a hex editor, an examiner could jump to 0x5e8a1e and view further details, perhaps the date and time of the purchase.

Strings is a very powerful command that, when combined with searching and filters, can quickly determine whether phone numbers, names, locations, GPS coordinates, dates, and many more pieces of information are easily extractable in a data file. It is strongly encouraged to explore other encoding options in order to locate the greatest amount of data.

Timeline development and analysis

Many files and directories have times associated with them. For this reason, timeline analysis should be a key component of any investigation, as the timing of events is nearly always relevant. There are many ways to build a forensic timeline; however, most are manual and quite tedious. The creation of a timeline provides a high-level look at system activity, such as when files were compiled and when archives were opened.

For supported file systems, a number of tools are available that can create the timeline. The primary source of timeline information is the file system metadata including the date modified (file metadata), accessed, changed (file contents), and created. This metadata is often referred to as MAC times or sometime MACB, where the "B" represents when a file was created (birthed). File systems track different timestamps and have nuances that must be taken into account when performing forensic analysis.

One tool used in this book for timeline analysis is The Sleuth Kit (TSK), which supports several file systems, including hfs/hfs+. TSK contains various forensic tools, including the ability to create a timeline. This process involves two steps, which require the use of the tools within TSK (Carrier, 2009):

- First, the "fls" tool is used to list file and directory names in a disk image. The fls command gathers data from sources such as file systems, registries, logs, etc. and saves them into a "body file" format.
- The "mactime" script is then used to sort and merge this data into a timeline.

Details on how to install, create, and analyze a timeline are covered in the following sections.

Download, compile, and install TSK

In this example, TSK is going to be installed on a Linux machine. To install and compile on a Mac, Apple's Developer Tools are first required (specifically, XCode 3 must be installed from developer.apple.com). Details on compiling TSK on a Mac can be found on www.appleexaminer.com, a site developed by Ryan Kubasiak, which contains a wide range of free tools and information dedicated to Apple device forensics.

The source code for TSK can be downloaded from http://www.sleuthkit.org/sluethkit/download.php. Once downloaded, the examiner can extract, compile, and install the software. The following command will extract the contents of the tar file (-x) in verbose mode (-v) to a file (-f), with much of the output removed for simplicity. In this example, TSK version 3.2.0 was downloaded, as this was the most recent version available.

```
Katie-Strzempkas-MacBook:Downloads kstrzemp$ tar xvf sleuthkit-
3.2.0.tar
x sleuthkit-3.2.0/
x sleuthkit-3.2.0/aclocal.m4
x sleuthkit-3.2.0/ChangeLog.txt
x sleuthkit-3.2.0/config/
x sleuthkit-3.2.0/configure/
x sleuthkit-3.2.0/configure.ac
x sleuthkit-3.2.0/docs/
x sleuthkit-3.2.0/INSTALL.txt
x sleuthkit-3.2.0/licenses/
...
```

Next, the software must be compiled. The following commands will complete this process; however, it must be kept in mind that one will first need to "cd" into the sleuthkit directory that was created in the previous step. Once again, most of the output for this command was removed.

```
Katie-Strzempkas-MacBook:Downloads kstrzemp$ cd sleuthkit-3.2.0/
Katie-Strzempkas-MacBook:sleuthkit-3.2.0 kstrzemp$ ./configure
checking for a BSD-compatible install... /usr/bin/install -c
checking whether build environment is sane... yes
```

```
checking for a thread-safe mkdir -p... config/install-sh -c -d
checking for gawk... no
checking for mawk... no
checking for nawk... no
checking for awk... awk
checking whether make sets $(MAKE)... yes
...

Katie-Strzempkas-MacBook:sleuthkit-3.2.0 kstrzemp$ make
Making all in tsk3
make all-recursive
Making all in base
/bin/sh ../../libtool --tag=CC --mode=compile gcc -DHAVE_CONFIG_H
-I. -I../../tsk3
-I../.. -Wall -g -O2 -I/usr/local/include -MT md5c.lo -MD -MP -MF
.deps/md5c.Tpo -c -o md5c.lo md5c.c
libtool: compile: gcc -DHAVE_CONFIG_H -I. -I../../tsk3 -I../.. -Wall
-g -O2 -I/usr/local/include
-MT md5c.lo -MD -MP -MF .deps/md5c.Tpo -c md5c.c -fno-common -DPIC -o
.libs/md5c.o
libtool: compile: gcc -DHAVE_CONFIG_H -I. -I../../tsk3 -I../.. -Wall
-g -O2 -I/usr/local/include -MT
md5c.lo -MD -MP -MF .deps/md5c.Tpo -c md5c.c -o md5c.o >/dev/null 2>&1
...
```

Finally, the program can be installed:

```
Katie-Strzempkas-MacBook:sleuthkit-3.2.0    kstrzemp$    sudo    make
install
Password:
Making install in tsk3
Making install in base
make[3]: Nothing to be done for 'install-exec-am'.
make[3]: Nothing to be done for 'install-data-am'.
...
```

The two specific tools used to create a timeline, fls and mactime, should be installed in /usr/local/bin/ (if installed on a Mac). If installed on Linux, scalpel will be installed in /usr/bin/scalpel. This means that the commands can be run from any directory, rather than having to "cd" into the folder in which the tools were downloaded or installed.

Usage
Once the install is successfully completed, the first step in timeline creation is to run the "fls" tool. "fls" goes through the entire directory structure on an image and lists each file contained on the file system, both allocated and unallocated. This command accepts several different arguments, and the general command contains the following parameters:

```
fls -z EST5EDT -s 0 -m '/' -f hfs -r ~/Desktop/iPhone_3GS.dmg > ~/
Desktop/iPhone3GS.body
```

Table 6.2 fls Options

Argument	Description
-z EST5EDT	Specifies the time zone of the data on the device; in this example, the phone was in the Eastern time zone (or Greenwich mean time minus 5 hours (GMT − 5)).
-s 0	This option sets the time skew, or the minutes that are to be added or subtracted to/from the times. The skew is used in the event that the time on the clock was incorrect.
-m '/'	Sets the character(s) that all file paths should begin with: for example, if the timeline was performed on a Windows local drive, "C:/" could be specified.
-f hfs	Specifies the file system running on the image: whether the file system is HFS or HFS+, "-f hfs" should be utilized.
-r	This option allows fls to recursively follow directories.
~/Desktop/ iPhone_3GS.dmg	Path to the source of the image file.
> ~/Desktop/ iPhone3GS.body	Directs the data output to a file named "iPhone3GS.body" on the desktop of the current user (destination path).

A description of the options can be found in Table 6.2 (Kubasiak, n.d.).

The body file is simply a listing of all the files, file paths, and metadata that were gathered using the fls command. This file is not organized in a manner that allows an examiner to easily read its contents. A small section of the body file is shown below. While the directory path and file can easily be read, the remaining data are difficult to determine. Many of the numbers shown are various timestamps, but let us hold off on analyzing this data until it is organized a little better.

```
0|/mobile/Library/Caches/com.apple.itunesstored/url-resolution
.plist|1394|r/rrw-r--r--
|501|501|1531|1282758918|1282758918|1282758918|1282758918
0|/mobile/Library/Caches/com.apple.mobile.installation.
plist|6337|r/rrw-r-r-
|501|501|10260|1282782974|1282782974|1282782974|1282782974
0|/mobile/Library/Caches/com.apple.notes.sharedstore.lock|721|r/
rrwx------
|501|501|0|1282757434|1282757434|1282757434|1282757434
0|/mobile/Library/Caches/com.apple.pep.configuration.plist|751|r/
rrw-r--r--
|501|501|924|1282757563|1282757563|1282757563|1282757563
0|/mobile/Library/Caches/com.apple.persistentconnection.cache.
plist|11378|r/rrw-r--r--
|501|501|294|1282927983|1282927983|1282927983|1282927983
0|/mobile/Library/Caches/com.apple.springboard.displaystate.
plist|11058|r/rrw-r--r--
|501|501|781|1282927293|1282927293|1282927293|1282927293
```

```
0|/mobile/Library/Calendar|143|d/drwx------
|501|501|0|1282755309|1282927980|1282927980|1282755309
0|/mobile/Library/Calendar/Calendar.sqlitedb|185|r/rrw-r--r--
|501|501|110592|1282755315|1282927980|1282927980|1282755315
0|/mobile/Library/CallHistory|170|d/drwx------
|501|501|0|1282755314|1282926559|1282926559|1282755314
0|/mobile/Library/CallHistory/call_history.db|171|r/rrw-r--r--
|501|501|28672|1282755314|1282926559|1282927981|1282755314
```

Next, the mactime command must be run in order to sort, merge, and otherwise organize the data into a readable format so that an examiner can more easily analyze the data. Similar to the fls command, mactime accepts a few different arguments with the following general format:

```
mactime -b ~/Desktop/iPhone3GS.body -z EST5EDT -d > ~/Desktop/
iPhone3GS-Timeline.csv
```

A description of these parameters is shown in Table 6.3 (Kubasiak, n.d.).

Timeline analysis

Once the timeline.csv file is opened, the examiner can see all actions taken on the device including the file, file path, whether it was created, modified, or deleted, as well as the date and time on which this action occurred. A timeline is especially helpful in an investigation when an examiner can jump to a specific date and time to determine what actions took place. As you can see in Figure 6.1, there are many different fields within an fls timeline including Date, Size, Type, Mode, UID, GID, Meta, and File Name. While some of those columns are fairly straightforward, let us discuss the contents within each column and what they represent.

The Date column is pretty clear. It contains the date and time (time zone specified when running the command) that the event occurred. The next field contains the size of the file in bytes. Following that is the "Type" column which plays an important role in the timeline analysis. These are the MACB times which tell whether the specified file was modified, accessed, created, or birthed. Let us describe these a

Table 6.3 Mactime Options

Argument	Description
-b ~/Desktop/ iPhone3GS.body	Specifies the path to the previously created body file.
-z EST5EDT	Specifies the time zone (GMT − 5).
-d	Creates a delimited file, which can be opened in Microsoft Excel (or a similar product).
> ~/Desktop/ iPhone3GS-Timeline.csv	Directs the output of the modified body file to a.csv file named "iPhone3GS-Timeline.csv" on the desktop of the current user (destination path).

Date	Size	Type	Mode	UID	GID	Meta	File Name
Sun Dec 31 2000 18:00:00	15872	ma.b	r/rrw-r--r--	501	501	230	/mobile/Library/Caches/SpringBoardIconCache/com.apple.WebSheet
Sun Dec 31 2000 18:00:00	3712	ma.b	r/rrw-r--r--	501	501	231	/mobile/Library/Caches/SpringBoardIconCache-small/com.apple.Web
Sun Dec 31 2000 18:00:00	15872	ma.b	r/rrw-r--r--	501	501	244	/mobile/Library/Caches/SpringBoardIconCache/com.apple.DemoApp
Sun Dec 31 2000 18:00:00	3712	ma.b	r/rrw-r--r--	501	501	245	/mobile/Library/Caches/SpringBoardIconCache-small/com.apple.Dem
Sun Dec 31 2000 18:00:00	15872	ma.b	r/rrw-r--r--	501	501	248	/mobile/Library/Caches/SpringBoardIconCache/com.apple.fieldtest
Sun Dec 31 2000 18:00:00	3712	ma.b	r/rrw-r--r--	501	501	249	/mobile/Library/Caches/SpringBoardIconCache-small/com.apple.field
Sun Dec 31 2000 18:00:00	15872	ma.b	r/rrw-r--r--	501	501	266	/mobile/Library/Caches/SpringBoardIconCache/com.apple.springboar
Sun Dec 31 2000 18:00:00	3712	ma.b	r/rrw-r--r--	501	501	267	/mobile/Library/Caches/SpringBoardIconCache-small/com.apple.sprir
Fri Dec 18 2009 05:15:07	3712	ma.b	r/rrw-r--r--	501	501	259	/mobile/Library/Caches/SpringBoardIconCache-small/com.apple.stocl
Fri Dec 18 2009 05:15:11	15872	ma.b	r/rrw-r--r--	501	501	258	/mobile/Library/Caches/SpringBoardIconCache/com.apple.stocks
Fri Dec 18 2009 05:16:05	3712	ma.b	r/rrw-r--r--	501	501	263	/mobile/Library/Caches/SpringBoardIconCache-small/com.apple.weal
Fri Dec 18 2009 05:16:09	15872	ma.b	r/rrw-r--r--	501	501	262	/mobile/Library/Caches/SpringBoardIconCache/com.apple.weather
Fri Dec 18 2009 05:16:10	3712	ma.b	r/rrw-r--r--	501	501	227	/mobile/Library/Caches/SpringBoardIconCache-small/com.apple.calcu
Fri Dec 18 2009 05:16:21	15872	ma.b	r/rrw-r--r--	501	501	226	/mobile/Library/Caches/SpringBoardIconCache/com.apple.calculator

FIGURE 6.1

fls Timeline.

bit further as they are very important in analyzing the data in this timeline. The MACB time can be defined as follows (Kubasiak, 2009):

- m: modified (metadata modified about the file)
- a: accessed (file itself has been accessed)
- c: changed (content of the file has been changed)
- b: birth (file created)

The fourth column, Mode, contains file permissions in Unix format. Every file on the file system has a set of permissions that determine read, write, and execute permissions for a user, group, or other. The "user" is the owner of the file, a "group" may contain multiple users that have elevated privileges on the file, and "other" refers to everyone else with an account on that system. In Table 6.4, file permission values are explained (Dartmouth, n.d.). So, looking back at the fourth column in Figure 6.1, the file permissions show "r/rrw-r--r--." The user has "rw" or read and write access, while the group and others have "r" or read access.

The UID and GID columns are the user and group IDs, and the Meta column, or metadata address, is the inode number of the file, which contains information about the object. Finally, the File Name column represents the path and file name on which the action occurred.

As an example, let us take a look at the timeline of events for August 25, 2010, around noon. A portion of this time frame has been extracted from a timeline.csv file created using the fls and mactime commands. For simplicity and readability, the following columns have been removed: Size, Mode, UID, GID, and Meta.

Table 6.4 File Permissions	
-	flag is not set
r	user, group, or other has read access
w	user, group, or other has write access
x	user, group, or other has execute permissions (only applicable for programs and scripts, not data files)

```
Wed Aug 25 2010 12:02:02 .a.b /mobile/Media/DCIM/.MISC
Wed Aug 25 2010 12:02:02 .a.b /mobile/Media/DCIM/.MISC/Info.plist
Wed Aug 25 2010 12:02:02 .a.b /mobile/Media/DCIM/100APPLE
Wed Aug 25 2010 12:02:02 ma.b /mobile/Media/DCIM/100APPLE/IMG_0001.JPG
Wed Aug 25 2010 12:02:03 .a.b /mobile/Media/DCIM/100APPLE/.MISC
Wed Aug 25 2010 12:02:04 ..c. /mobile/Media/DCIM/100APPLE/IMG_0001.JPG
Wed Aug 25 2010 12:02:04 macb /mobile/Media/DCIM/100APPLE/.MISC/
IMG_0001.THM
Wed Aug 25 2010 12:02:04 macb /mobile/Media/DCIM/100APPLE/.MISC/
IMG_0001.BTH
Wed Aug 25 2010 12:04:27 .a.b /root/Library/Caches/locationd/cells.
plist
Wed Aug 25 2010 12:04:27 .a.b /root/Library/Caches/locationd/cells-
local.plist
Wed Aug 25 2010 12:04:27 .a.b /root/Library/Caches/locationd/cache.
plist
Wed Aug 25 2010 12:04:27 .a.b /root/Library/Caches/locationd/stats.
plist
Wed Aug 25 2010 12:11:01 .a.b /mobile/Library/DataAccess
Wed Aug 25 2010 12:11:01 .a.b /mobile/Library/Caches/Snapshots
Wed Aug 25 2010 12:16:02 macb /mobile/Library/Preferences/com.apple.
dataaccess.launchd
Wed Aug 25 2010 12:16:10 m.c. /mobile/Library/Keyboard
Wed Aug 25 2010 12:16:10 .a.b /mobile/Library/Keyboard/dynamic-text.dat
Wed Aug 25 2010 12:16:57 macb /mobile/Library/Mail/Mailboxes
Wed Aug 25 2010 12:16:57 macb /mobile/Library/Mail/Mailboxes/
.mboxCache.plist
Wed Aug 25 2010 12:23:30 .a.b /mobile/Library/Mail/IMAP-
viaforensicstest@gmail.com@imap.gmail.com
Wed Aug 25 2010 12:23:30 .a.b /mobile/Library/Mail/IMAP-
viaforensicstest@gmail.com@imap.gmail.com/.mboxCache.plist
Wed Aug 25 2010 12:23:31 macb /mobile/Library/Mail/AutoFetchEnabled
Wed Aug 25 2010 12:23:40 .a.b /mobile/Library/Mail/MFData
Wed Aug 25 2010 12:30:20 .a.b /mobile/Library/Notes
Wed Aug 25 2010 12:30:20 .a.b /mobile/Library/Notes/notes.db
Wed Aug 25 2010 12:30:34 macb /mobile/Library/Caches/com.apple.
notes.sharedstore.lock
Wed Aug 25 2010 12:30:34 .a.b /mobile/Library/Notes/notes.idx
Wed Aug 25 2010 12:31:55 m.c. /mobile/Library/Notes
Wed Aug 25 2010 12:31:55 m.c. /mobile/Library/Notes/notes.db
Wed Aug 25 2010 12:31:55 m.c. /mobile/Library/Notes/notes.idx
Wed Aug 25 2010 12:32:04 macb /mobile/Library/Caches/Snapshots/com.
apple.mobilenotes-Default.jpg
```

As you can see, the date and time is shown in the first column, followed by the MACB times, and finally the path/file name in the third. Analyzing the files within a timeline can be very time consuming, as it requires a lot of research to understand what the files signify. For the first example, we will start with an easy one. Starting at the top, we see a list of files within the /mobile/Media/DCIM folder. On the iPhone, this folder contains photos either taken on the device or synced to the device. Let us jump straight to the first jpeg file: IMG_0001.JPG. The timeline shows that this file was created, accessed, and metadata modified at 12:02:04. It is known that photos within the "100APPLE" folder were those taken from the on-board camera, so it would be safe to assume that this particular photo was taken at that time. To see which picture this was, an examiner could navigate to that file on the file system.

Moving down further in the timeline, the Mail app appears to have been used in some way. It shows that the viaforensicstest Gmail account was accessed and birthed (created) around 12:23 p.m. The next line shows "AutoFetchEnabled" which is updated when the e-mail is synced between the device and the mail server. It is likely that the Gmail account was originally synced with the device at this time.

As a final example, let us look at the final three lines. The timeline shows that the notes database was changed and the metadata modified, which implies that a note was viewed, created, or deleted from that particular database. The last line shows that a snapshot was taken of the notes application. Snapshots of applications on the device are taken at random points in time (this is discussed in more detail later in this chapter). This particular snapshot was most likely taken of the Notes application while it was open. Assuming the examiner is able to get a physical image of the device, this snapshot could very possibly be recovered through file carving.

This portion of the timeline contained merely 31 records out of the several thousand that were available in the timeline.csv file. To truly benefit from timeline analysis, it is important to have a specific time frame in mind and jump straight to that section.

Forensic analysis

In many forensic investigations, a logical acquisition or a logical file system analysis from a physical acquisition will provide more than enough data for the case. However, certain cases require a deeper analysis to find deleted data or unknown file structures. This is also necessary when the file system has little or no support in standard forensic tools.

Understandably, many forensic analysts would prefer not to perform a deeper analysis because it requires a significant amount of time, is extremely tedious, and requires a fairly deep understanding and curiosity of data structures. But the results from this type of analysis are often quite amazing, and important information learned from individual cases might generally be applicable to many cases in the future.

For these reasons, every forensic analyst should be comfortable using a hex editor, if the need arises. This allows the analysts to see exactly what data is being stored, to look for patterns and, perhaps, to identify deleted or previously understood data structures.

This can be explained better with an example. First, it is essential to install the following package on a Linux workstation:

```
kstrzempka@linux-wks:~$ sudo apt-get install hexedit
```

This is a very fast, terminal-based hex editor. Of course, one can use any hex editor one is comfortable with. Next, the strings command is used to look at the sms.db file, which is located in the /mobile/Library/SMS directory, to see whether some deleted text messages are found. In this sample case, it is known that text messages to 3128781100 were deleted from the device. First, let us use strings to see whether we find that phone number in the SQLite file:

```
kstrzempka@linux-wks:~$ strings --all --radix=x sms.db | grep -A 1
3128781100|wc -l
28
```

In this command, we use the pipe ("|") operator, which takes the output from one command and sends it to the next command. In this way, we can chain many commands together, which can be a very powerful analysis technique. So the above command does the following:

1. Runs the strings command on the SQLite database.
2. Takes the output of the strings command and runs it through the grep program, which filters the output-based patterns provided. In this case, we provide the phone number in question; however, you can create very powerful search strings for grep including regular expressions.
3. Takes the output from the grep command and sees how many lines are returned, but pipes the output to the word count program ("wc"). It then instructs it to count by line instead of by word.

The result is that 28 entries for that phone number are found, obviously indicating that the phone number was indeed communicated with on the device. Next, we want to take a close look at the messages, so instead of piping the output to the wc program, we look at the results directly and include one line of text after the phone number by adding the option "-A 1" to grep (also, we pipe the output to the "less" command in order to display it one page at a time):

```
kstrzempka@linux-wks:~$ strings --all --radix=x sms.db | grep -A 1
3128781100|less
    2462 +13128781100Lv
    2471 Great. I may need to head out around 830
--
    24e0 +13128781100Lv
    24f0 Sure ill meet you at the Italian place on the corner
--
    2542 +13128781100Lv
    2552 Dinner at 7?
```

```
- -
    257c +13128781100Lv
    258c Working until 6.
```

So, we know we have a SQLite database with the targeted number and messages.
Let us use SQLite 3 to better understand the database. Here we will use a command
line, but you can use a SQLite viewer with a graphical front end if you prefer (such as
SQLite Database Browser).

```
kstrzempka@linux-wks-001:~/Desktop$ sqlite3 mms-example.db
SQLite version 3.6.22
Enter ".help" for instructions
Enter SQL statements terminated with a ";"

sqlite> .tables
_SqliteDatabaseProperties msg_group
group_member              msg_pieces
message

sqlite> .schema message
CREATE TABLE message (ROWID INTEGER PRIMARY KEY AUTOINCREMENT,
address TEXT, date INTEGER, text TEXT, flags INTEGER, replace INTEGER,
svc_center TEXT, group_id INTEGER, association_id INTEGER, height
INTEGER, UIFlags INTEGER, version INTEGER, subject TEXT, country
TEXT, headers BLOB, recipients BLOB, read INTEGER);
CREATE INDEX message_flags_index ON message(flags);
CREATE INDEX message_group_index ON message(group_id, ROWID);
CREATE TRIGGER delete_message AFTER DELETE ON message WHEN NOT read
(old.flags) BEGIN UPDATE msg_group SET unread_count = (SELECT
unread_count FROM msg_group WHERE ROWID=old.group_id) -1 WHERE ROWID
= old.group_id; END;
CREATE TRIGGER delete_newest_message AFTER DELETE ON message WHEN
old.ROWID = (SELECT newest_message FROM msg_group WHERE ROWID = old.
group_id) BEGIN UPDATE msg_group SET newest_message = (SELECT ROWID
FROM message WHERE group_id = old.group_id AND ROWID = (SELECT max
(ROWID) FROM message WHERE group_id = old.group_id)) WHERE ROWID =
old.group_id; END;
CREATE TRIGGER delete_pieces AFTER DELETE ON message BEGIN DELETE from
msg_pieces where old.ROWID == msg_pieces.message_id; END;
CREATE TRIGGER insert_newest_message AFTER INSERT ON message WHEN
new.ROWID >= IFNULL((SELECT MAX(ROWID) FROM message WHERE message.
group_id = new.group_id), 0) BEGIN UPDATE msg_group SET newest_
message = new.ROWID WHERE ROWID = new.group_id; END;
CREATE TRIGGER insert_unread_message AFTER INSERT ON message WHEN NOT
read(new.flags) BEGIN UPDATE msg_group SET unread_count = (SELECT
unread_count FROM msg_group WHERE ROWID = new.group_id) +1 WHERE ROWID
= new.group_id; END;
```

```
CREATE TRIGGER mark_message_read AFTER UPDATE ON message WHEN NOT read
(old.flags) AND read(new.flags) BEGIN UPDATE msg_group SET unread_
count = (SELECT unread_count FROM msg_group WHERE ROWID = new.
group_id) - 1 WHERE ROWID = new.group_id; END;
CREATE TRIGGER mark_message_unread AFTER UPDATE ON message WHEN read
(old.flags) AND NOT read(new.flags) BEGIN UPDATE msg_group SET
unread_count = (SELECT unread_count FROM msg_group WHERE ROWID =
new.group_id) + 1 WHERE ROWID = new.group_id; END;

sqlite> .mode line

sqlite> select * from message limit 1;
  ROWID = 4
        address = (312) 878-1100
           date = 1282844546
           text = Sure is a nice day out
          flags = 3
        replace = 0
     svc_center =
       group_id = 3
 association_id = 1282844546
         height = 0
         UIFlags = 4
        version = 0
        subject =
        country = us
        headers =
     recipients =
           read = 1

sqlite> .quit
```

In the previous sqlite3 sessions, the following was done to better understand the data:

1. sqlite3 sms.db: Opened database for querying.
2. .tables: Listed off the tables in the database.
3. .schema sms: Focused on the sms table and asked database for the structure (schema) of the table. The schema was quite long and truncated.
4. .mode line: Set the display mode to line for easier viewing.
5. select * from sms limit 1: Instructed sqlite3 to display one record to the screen (limit 1) from the sms table showing all columns.
6. .quit: Exited the program.

So, we can now see that there are a number of fields in the sms table, but that after the phone number (address), there is a timestamp, followed by the text content. Using a hex editor, let us see whether we can determine the date/time stamp from the message regarding the meeting at the Italian place on the corner. First, let us open the sms.db in the hex editor we have just installed:

```
kstrzempka@linux-wks:~$ hexedit sms.db
```

which will then show the beginning of the file in hex as well as the printable ASCII strings in the right column:

```
00000000  53 51 4C 69  74 65 20 66  6F 72 6D 61  74 20 33 00  SQLite format 3.
00000010  08 00 01 01  00 40 20 20  00 00 00 FA  00 00 00 00  .....@.........
00000020  00 00 00 00  00 00 00 00  00 00 00 0F  00 00 00 01  ...............
00000030  00 00 00 00  00 00 00 0C  00 00 00 01  00 00 00 00  ...............
00000040  00 00 00 00  00 00 00 00  00 00 00 00  00 00 00 00  ...............
00000050  00 00 00 00  00 00 00 00  00 00 00 00  00 00 00 00  ...............
00000060  00 00 00 00  05 00 00 00  01 07 FB 00  00 00 00 0E  ...............
00000070  07 FB 05 72  04 C6 04 2D  03 0E 02 A9  02 4F 01 3E  ...r...-.....O.>
00000080  00 00 00 00  00 00 00 00  00 00 00 00  00 00 00 00  ...............
00000090  00 00 00 00  00 00 00 00  00 00 00 00  00 00 00 00  ...............
000000A0  00 00 00 00  00 00 00 00  00 00 00 00  00 00 00 00  ...............
000000B0  00 00 00 00  00 00 00 00  00 00 00 00  00 00 00 00  ...............
000000C0  00 00 00 00  00 00 00 00  00 00 00 00  00 00 00 00  ...............
000000D0  00 00 00 00  00 00 00 00  00 00 00 00  00 00 00 00  ...............
000000E0  00 00 00 00  00 00 00 00  00 00 00 00  00 00 00 00  ...............
000000F0  00 00 00 00  00 00 00 00  00 00 00 00  00 00 00 00  ...............
00000100  00 00 00 00  00 00 00 00  00 00 00 00  00 00 00 00  ...............
00000110  00 00 00 00  00 00 00 00  00 00 00 00  00 00 00 00  ...............
00000120  00 00 00 00  00 00 00 00  00 00 00 00  00 00 00 00  ...............
00000130  00 00 00 00  00 00 00 00  00 00 00 00  00 00 82 0E  ...............
00000140  0A 07 1B 37  1B 01 83 53  74 72 69 67  67 65 72 69  ...7...Striggeri
00000150  6E 73 65 72  74 5F 75 6E  72 65 61 64  5F 6D 65 73  nsert_unread_mes
00000160  73 61 67 65  6D 65 73 73  61 67 65 00 43 52 45 41  sagemessage.CREA
```

We can press "Enter" to specify an offset in the file. In this case, the previous strings command included the --radix=x, so we have the offset in hex (0x24F0) to be searched:

```
000000A0   00 00 00 00 00 00 00 00 00 00 00 00 00 00 00 00 00 00 00 00
..................
000000B4   00 00 00 00 00 00 00 00 00 00 00 00 00 00 00 00 00 00 00 00
..................
000000C8   00 00 00 00 00 00 00 00 00 00 00 00 00 00 00 00 00 00 00 00
..................
000000DC   00 00 00 00 00 00 00 00 00 00 00 00 00 00 00 00 00 00 00 00
..................


                    New position ? 0x24F0


0000012C   00 00 00 00 00 00 00 00 00 00 00 00 00 00 00 00 00 00 82 0E
..................
00000140   0A 07 1B 37 1B 01 83 53 74 72 69 67 67 65 72 69 6E 73 65 72
...7...Striggerinser
00000154   74 5F 75 6E 72 65 61 64 5F 6D 65 73 73 61 67 65 6D 65 73 73
t_unread_messagemess
00000168   61 67 65 00 43 52 45 41 54 45 20 54 52 49 47 47 45 52 20 69  age.
CREATE TRIGGER i
```

The hex editor is extremely responsive and jumps to the offset:

```
000024B8  79 20 6F 66 20 74 69 6D 65 20 03 00 04 00 00 00 00 75 73 01  y of time
.......us.
000024CC  60 08 12 00 25 04 75 01 01 00 01 01 01 01 01 00 11 00 00 01  '...%.
u...........
000024E0  2B 31 39 32 30 32 37 37 31 38 36 39 4C 76 AC 01 53 75 72 65  +19202771869Lv..Sure
000024F4  20 69 6C 6C 20 6D 65 65 74 20 79 6F 75 20 61 74 20 74 68 65   ill meet
you at the
00002508  20 49 74 61 6C 69 61 6E 20 70 6C 61 63 65 20 6F 6E 20 74 68   Italian
place on th
0000251C  65 20 63 6F 72 6E 65 72 02 00 04 00 00 00 00 75 73 01 38 07  e
corner.......us.8.
00002530  12 00 25 04 25 01 01 00 01 01 01 01 01 00 11 00 00 01 2B 31  ..%.
%............+1
00002544  39 32 30 32 37 37 31 38 36 39 4C 76 AB DC 44 69 6E 6E 65 72  9202771869Lv..Dinner
00002558  20 61 74 20 37 3F 03 00 04 00 00 00 00 75 73 01 3C 06 12 00   at
7?......us.<...
0000256C  25 04 2D 01 01 00 01 01 01 01 01 00 11 00 00 01 2B 31 39 32  %.-
............+192
00002580  30 32 37 37 31 38 36 39 4C 76 AB BE 57 6F 72 6B 69 6E 67 20  02771869Lv..Working
00002594  75 6E 74 69 6C 20 36 2E 02 00 04 00 00 00 00 75 73 01 49 05  until
6........us.I.
```

Looking at the hex data above, we can see the phone number and it ends at 0x24EB. After that, we should see a timestamp field, which takes up the next 4 bytes. In hex, this is 0x4C76AC01. When translated to decimal, the resulting number is 1282845697. Finally, we can use a couple of techniques to convert this time to a date/time more easily read by examiners. One technique is to use the built-in date command on a Mac:

```
Katie-Strzempkas-MacBook:~ kstrzemp$ date -r @ 1282845697
Thu Aug 26 12:01:37 CDT 2010
```

The date command automatically displays the date in the current system timezone. Another quick way to convert the time is to use a website designed to convert Unix Epoch time at http://www.epochconverter.com/. This site handles both Unix epoch in seconds and milliseconds. To convert, copy the timestamp into the website text box and click "Timestamp to Human date":

A third timestamp conversion technique that can be used is the CFAbsolute-TimeConverter utility. On an Apple device, Core Foundation (CF) measures time in seconds, similar to Unix Epoch time (which is the number of seconds since January 1, 1970). The CFAbsoluteTime data type represents the number of seconds since January 1, 2001. The CFAbsoluteTimeConverter software will convert only the OS X Epoch time into a human-readable time (Apple Inc., 2007). If a Unix

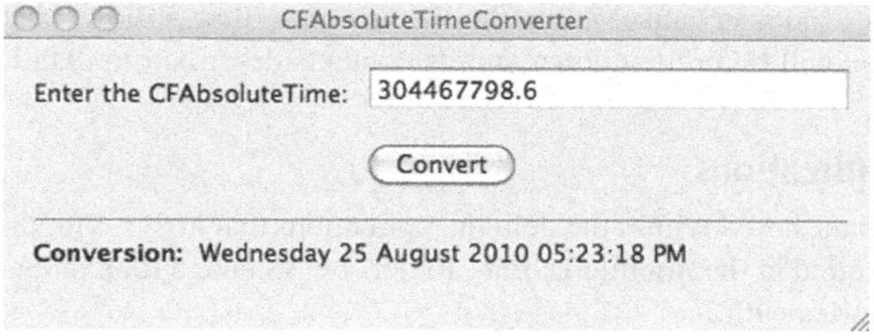

FIGURE 6.2

CFAbsoluteTimeConverter.

Epoch timestamp is converted using this utility, the date and time will be accurate, but the year will be 31 years off. The timestamps recovered from the sms.db are in Unix Epoch time; however, many of the timestamps within files on the iPhone and other iOS devices are in the unique OS X Epoch format. Be sure to pay attention to the differences when attempting to convert those numbers.

For the example shown in Figure 6.2, a different timestamp is used than in the previous examples as it requires an OS X Epoch timestamp for an accurate conversion. The timestamp selected is from the Safari History plist file.

iPHONE DATA STORAGE LOCATIONS

When an iPhone dmg is first mounted, the following directory structure is displayed at the root of the device:

```
├── CommCenter
├── db
├── ea
├── empty
├── folders
├── Keychains
├── log
├── logs
├── Managed Preferences
├── mobile
├── MobileDevice
├── msgs
├── preferences
├── root
├── run
├── tmp
└── vm
```

While evidence is scattered throughout these directories, a great majority of the data is going to be found in the /mobile folder, which consists of three subdirectories:

Applications, Library, and Media. In the sections that follow, each of these subdirectories will be broken down and its contents described in detail.

Default applications

Most of the data stored within the default applications that arrive with the device are going to be found in the /mobile/Library folder. Let us take a look at the breakdown of the directories within:

```
kstrzempka@linux-wks:/home/kstrzempka/Desktop/iPhoneapp-mount/
mobile# tree -L 2 Library/
Library/
├── AddressBook
│   ├── AddressBookImages.sqlitedb
│   └── AddressBook.sqlitedb
├── Caches
│   ├── AccessToMigrationLock
│   ├── AccountMigrationInProgress
│   ├── com.apple.AppStore
│   ├── com.apple.itunesstored
│   ├── com.apple.mobile.installation.plist
│   ├── com.apple.notes.sharedstore.lock
│   ├── com.apple.pep.configuration.plist
│   ├── com.apple.persistentconnection.cache.plist
│   ├── com.apple.springboard.displaystate.plist
│   ├── com.apple.UIKit.pboard
│   ├── com.apple.WebAppCache
│   ├── Maps
│   ├── MapTiles
│   ├── Safari
│   ├── SBShutdownCookie
│   ├── Snapshots
│   ├── SpringBoardIconCache
│   └── SpringBoardIconCache-small
├── Calendar
│   └── Calendar.sqlitedb
├── CallHistory
│   └── call_history.db
├── Carrier Bundle.bundle -> /System/Library/Carrier Bundles/310410
├── com.apple.iTunesStore
│   └── LocalStorage
├── com.apple.itunesstored
│   ├── itunesstored2.sqlitedb
│   └── itunesstored_private.sqlitedb
├── ConfigurationProfiles
│   ├── EASPolicies.plist
│   ├── PasswordHistory.plist
│   └── PayloadManifest.plist
├── Cookies
```

```
|    ├── com.apple.itunesstored.plist
|    └── Cookies.plist
├── DataAccess
|    ├── AccountInformation.plist
|    ├── ASFolders-492BF7DC-7739-47B8-9B5D-01111DF482C9
|    └── ASFolders-D9D2E90A-5A76-4C92-B598-012C2BA348F6
├── Keyboard
|    └── dynamic-text.dat
├── Logs
|    ├── ADDataStore.sqlitedb
|    ├── ADDataStore.sqlitedb-journal
|    ├── AppleSupport
|    ├── CrashReporter
|    └── MobileInstallation
├── Mail
|    ├── AutoFetchEnabled
|    ├── Envelope Index
|    ├── IMAP-viaforensicstest@gmail.com@imap.gmail.com
|    ├── Mailboxes
|    ├── metadata.plist
|    └── MFData
├── Maps
|    ├── Directions.plist
|    └── History.plist
├── MobileInstallation
|    └── ApplicationAttributes.plist
├── Notes
|    ├── notes.db
|    └── notes.idx
├── Operator Bundle.bundle -> /System/Library/Carrier Bundles/310410
├── Preferences
|    ├── com.apple.accountsettings.plist
|    ├── com.apple.aggregated.plist
|    ├── com.apple.AppStore.plist
|    ├── com.apple.AppSupport.plist
|    ├── com.apple.apsd.plist
|    ├── com.apple.BTServer.airplane.plist
|    ├── com.apple.BTServer.plist
|    ├── com.apple.carrier.plist -> /System/Library/Carrier Bundles/
310410/carrier.plist
|    ├── com.apple.commcenter.plist
|    ├── com.apple.dataaccess.launchd
|    ├── com.apple.GMM.plist
|    ├── com.apple.iqagent.plist
|    ├── com.apple.itunesstored.plist
|    ├── com.apple.locationd.plist
|    ├── com.apple.Maps.plist
|    ├── com.apple.mobilecal.alarmengine.plist
|    ├── com.apple.mobilecal.plist
```

```
|   ├── com.apple.MobileInternetSharing.plist
|   ├── com.apple.mobileipod.plist
|   ├── com.apple.mobilemail.plist
|   ├── com.apple.mobilenotes.plist
|   ├── com.apple.mobilephone.plist
|   ├── com.apple.mobilephone.speeddial.plist
|   ├── com.apple.mobilesafari.plist
|   ├── com.apple.mobileslideshow.plist
|   ├── com.apple.MobileSMS.plist
|   ├── com.apple.mobile.SyncMigrator.plist
|   ├── com.apple.mobiletimer.plist
|   ├── com.apple.operator.plist -> /System/Library/Carrier
Bundles/310410/carrier.plist
|   ├── com.apple.PeoplePicker.plist
|   ├── com.apple.persistentconnection.plist
|   ├── com.apple.preferences.datetime.plist
|   ├── com.apple.preferences.network.plist
|   ├── com.apple.Preferences.plist
|   ├── com.apple.springboard.plist
|   ├── com.apple.voicemail.plist
|   ├── com.apple.weather.plist
|   ├── com.apple.youtubeframework.plist
|   ├── com.apple.youtube.plist
|   └── dataaccessd.plist
├── RemoteNotification
|   └── Clients.plist
├── Safari
|   ├── Bookmarks.plist
|   ├── History.plist
|   └── SuspendState.plist
├── SMS
|   ├── Drafts
|   ├── Parts
|   ├── sms.db
|   └── sms-legacy.db
├── Voicemail
|   ├── 1.amr
|   ├── 4.amr
|   ├── _subscribed
|   └── voicemail.db
├── Weather
├── WebClips
├── WebKit
|   ├── Databases
|   └── LocalStorage
└── YouTube
45 directories, 85 files
```

As seen from this listing, many of the file names are fairly straightforward. The AddressBook, Calendar, Call History, Notes, SMS, and Voicemail data are all stored in a database. These files can be opened within SQLite Database Browser (as demonstrated in Chapter 3) to view the data contents within the tables. As an example, let us take a look at the calendar.sqlitedb file. When opened in a SQLite browser, the database structure is shown, including the table names and schema (see Figure 6.3).

Next, click on "Browse Data" to select a specific table. As can be seen from the database structure, this particular database contains a large number of tables. Sometimes it is necessary to go through each table one by one in order to see what kind of data can be recovered from each. The calendar events are going to be found in the "Event" table. Here, a summary of the event is shown as well as a start date, end date, time zone, and other optional information that the user may or may not have entered (such as location and description). In Figure 6.4, the Event table is displayed with a

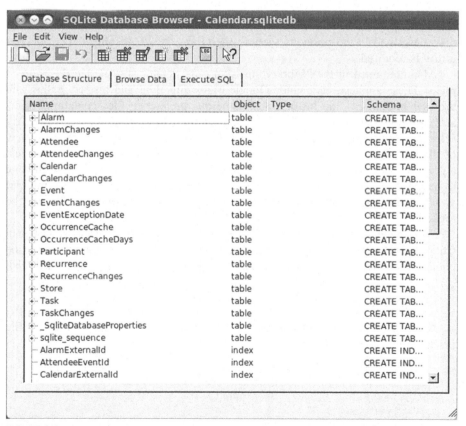

FIGURE 6.3

Calendar.sqlitedb – Database Structure.

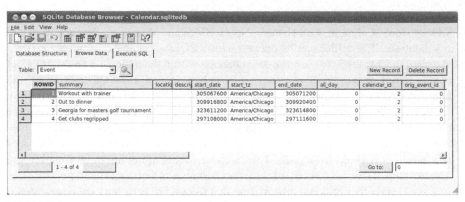

FIGURE 6.4

Calendar.sqlitedb – Event Table.

few items populated. The timestamp used in this particular file is the OS X Epoch time described in the previous section; therefore, the CFAbsoluteTimeConverter utility is required.

Also contained in the "Library" directory are default app files in the form of plists. These applications include Google Maps directions and history, Safari web browser bookmarks and history, and numerous preference files containing items such as speed dial numbers, YouTube data, and a list of installed applications. By selecting a plist and hitting the space bar, the examiner can quickly get a preview of the file. This is the quickest way to view the data contents. However, it is just a preview, so if the examiner wishes to search the text within the plist, it will have to be opened in TextEdit, Text Wrangler, or another text editor. As an example of viewing and interpreting data within a plist, the Safari History.plist file will be looked at.

First, since it is a binary plist, it will need to be converted to XML (as described in Chapter 3). Since the dmg is mounted as read-only, this file will first need to be copied elsewhere, in this case to the desktop, prior to converting to an ASCII plist.

```
Katie-Strzempkas-MacBook:Desktop kstrzemp$ plutil -convert xml1
History.plist
```

Now, it is in XML format and can be easily read. The beginning section of this file is shown in the following text:

```
<?xml version="1.0" encoding="UTF-8"?>
<!DOCTYPE plist PUBLIC "-//Apple//DTD PLIST 1.0//EN"
"http://www. apple.com/DTDs/PropertyList-1.0.dtd">
<plist version="1.0">
<dict>
   <key>WebHistoryDates</key>
   <array>
      <dict>
```

```
<key></key>
<string>http://viaforensics.com</string>
<key>D</key>
<array>
    <integer>1</integer>
</array>
<key>WebViewportArguments</key>
<dict>
    <key>height</key>
    <real>-1</real>
    <key>initial-scale</key>
    <real>-1</real>
    <key>maximum-scale</key>
    <real>-1</real>
    <key>minimum-scale</key>
    <real>-1</real>
    <key>user-scalable</key>
    <real>-1</real>
    <key>width</key>
    <real>-1</real>
</dict>
<key>lastVisitedDate</key>
<string>304467798.6</string>
<key>redirectURLs</key>
<array>
    <string>http://viaforensics.com</string>
</array>
<key>title</key>
<string>viaForensics</string>
<key>visitCount</key>
<integer>1</integer>
</dict>
```

Within History.plist, each visited website is organized within its own section, noted by the <dict> and </dict> tags. Within these tags, the website URL and last visited date are both shown as a string. The date is in OS X Epoch time, so it will need to be converted using CFAbsoluteTimeConverter. From the information shown here, it can be said that the user visited http://viaforensics.com on Thursday, August 26, 2010, at 6:21:50 PM (CST).

The Library directory contains a significant amount of valuable data in plist, SQLite, and other formats. Many of the default applications that are found in this folder have been analyzed and described in great detail. These results are included in the "iPhone Application Analysis and Reference" section later in this chapter.

Moving on to the "Media" folder, this is where any type of photo, video, or music files are stored. Here, the subdirectories are broken down further:

```
kstrzempka@linux-wks:/home/kstrzempka/Desktop/iPhoneapp-mount/
mobile# tree -L 3 Media/
```

```
Media/
├── com.apple.itdbprep.postprocess.lock
├── com.apple.itunes.lock_sync
├── DCIM
│   └── 100APPLE
│       ├── IMG_0001.JPG
│       ├── IMG_0002.JPG
│       ├── IMG_0003.JPG
│       └── IMG_0004.JPG
├── Downloads
│   └── manifest.plist
├── iTunes_Control
│   ├── iTunes
│   │   ├── IC-Info.sidb
│   │   ├── IC-Info.sidv
│   │   ├── iTunesCDB
│   │   ├── iTunesControl
│   │   ├── iTunesDB
│   │   ├── iTunes Library.itlp
│   │   ├── iTunesPrefs
│   │   ├── iTunesPrefs.plist
│   │   ├── PhotosFolderAlbums
│   │   ├── PhotosFolderName
│   │   ├── PhotosFolderPrefs
│   │   ├── Rentals.plist
│   │   ├── Ringtones.plist
│   │   └── VoiceMemos.plist
│   └── Music
│       ├── F00
│       ├── F01
│       ├── F02
│       ├── F03
│       ├── F04
│       ├── F05
│       └── F06
├── Photos
│   ├── Photo Database
│   └── Thumbs
│       ├── F3004_1.ithmb
│       ├── F3008_1.ithmb
│       ├── F3009_1.ithmb
│       └── F3011_1.ithmb
├── Podcasts
├── Purchases
├── Recordings
└── Safari
    └── goog-phish-shavar.dat
```

Pictures taken from the device itself, using the on-board camera, are stored in one central location: Media/DCIM/100Apple. When a photo is taken, the file is stored as a jpeg in that location, with a filename of "IMG_000X.JPG." The number in the file name increments by 1 with each new picture taken. When a file is deleted and a new picture is taken, the number of the deleted file will not be reused, but the next number in sequence will be assigned. For example, looking at the previous output, images IMG_0001 through IMG_0004 are listed. If IMG_003 is deleted, this number will not be reused. Instead, IMG_0005 will be the file name assigned to the next photo. Since the device uses this technique to save files, it is easy to identify whether any photos were deleted by simply noting if there are any numbers missing.

While this is not shown in the "tree" output, there is also a special location for screen shots that have been taken from the device. On the iPhone, if the user holds down the "Home" button and presses "Power," a screen shot of the phone is taken and stored. These images are saved in Media/DCIM/999Apple.

A third storage format for photos involves those pictures that were synced to the device through iTunes. These are stored in a Photo Database on the iPhone (as shown in the "tree" output under Photos > Photo Database). On a Mac, this database can be opened within the iPhoto application in order to view the photos within.

Prior to the iPhone 3GS, videos could not be taken from the device without first downloading an app that would record video. A standard camera came on the device, but recording videos was not an option. The previous "tree" output was from an iPhone 3G device, therefore videos were not included. For iPhone 3GS and later, an on-board video camera exists. When a video is taken on the device, it is stored in the /DCIM/100APPLE folder along with the photos.

Music that was synced through iTunes is located in Media/iTunes_Control/Music, and the actual audio files are stored within the F00, F01, F02, etc. subfolders.

Downloaded apps

The final subdirectory within the "mobile" folder is Applications. Here, a unique directory is created for each application downloaded to the device. Let us take a look at the hierarchical structure of this folder before discussing further.

```
kstrzempka@linux-wks:/home/kstrzempka/Desktop/iPhoneapp-mount/
mobile# tree -L 2 Applications/
Applications/
├── 04DA17CB-0D8E-469F-83CD-B928DF15A64E
│   ├── Documents
│   ├── foursquare.app
│   ├── iTunesArtwork
│   ├── iTunesMetadata.plist
│   ├── Library
│   └── tmp
├── 2FDA6380-1869-4797-B999-0B59359C4288
```

```
|    ├── Documents
|    ├── Groupon.app
|    ├── iTunesArtwork
|    ├── iTunesMetadata.plist
|    ├── Library
|    └── tmp
├── 59FA89C0-FC51-45F6-8270-93B624473CD9
|    ├── AroundMe.app
|    ├── Documents
|    ├── iTunesArtwork
|    ├── iTunesMetadata.plist
|    ├── Library
|    └── tmp
├── 65E4725B-3E7F-4AB1-B539-5F46FCCF3D27
|    ├── Documents
|    ├── iTunesArtwork
|    ├── iTunesMetadata.plist
|    ├── Library
|    ├── Taxi_Magic.app
|    └── tmp
├── 974F6DC6-BD41-445C-838E-4DA64C4FB158
|    ├── Documents
|    ├── golfputtpro.app
|    ├── iTunesArtwork
|    ├── iTunesMetadata.plist
|    ├── Library
|    └── tmp
└── CEBBA659-F8BC-4C71-9DBD-2CCDB74D4B4F
     ├── Documents
     ├── Facebook.app
     ├── iTunesArtwork
     ├── iTunesMetadata.plist
     ├── Library
     └── tmp
```

When an app is downloaded, a directory is created in the Applications folder, which contains the application executable, documents, and other files needed for the app to run. On the phone from which the sample output was extracted, there were six third-party applications downloaded on the device: Foursquare, Groupon, AroundMe, Taxi Magic, Golf Putt Pro, and Facebook.

A general hierarchy of folders (and some files) is consistent across all applications. In this section, the standard folders and files are discussed; however, the "iPhone Application Analysis and Reference" section will contain a detailed analysis of many of the popular apps available for download.

First, the application itself is installed in the root of its unique application folder. This file is a bundle that contains several files needed for the application to run. The following text is a listing of the files contained within the "AroundMe" app.

While many of the files are unique to that application, some common files are found across most third-party applications including Info.plist, ResourceRules.plist, and others (however, the content within these files will always be unique to each app).

```
kstrzempka@linux-wks:/home/kstrzempka/Desktop/iPhoneapp-
mount/mobile/Applications/59FA89C0-FC51-45F6-8270-93B624473CD9/AroundMe.app# ls
100000.png 120001.png  122200.png  320102.png 330011.png  333000.png
dist.plist      Italian.lproj            ruby
110000.png 120002.png  122201.png  320200.png 330012.png  333001.png
email.png       ja.lproj             SC_Info
110001.png 120010.png  122202.png  320201.png 330020.png  333002.png
emptylocation.png   loginbackground.png    searchit.png
110002.png 120011.png  123000.png  320202.png 330021.png  333300.png
English.lproj      MainWindow.nib         SearchLocationView.nib
110010.png 120012.png  123001.png  320300.png 330022.png  333301.png
FacebookView.nib    mapcompassarrow@2x.png   SearchView.nib
110011.png 120020.png  123002.png  320301.png 330030.png  333302.png   fancy
mapcompassarrow.png setting.png
110012.png 120021.png  23300.png   320302.png 330031.png  applestores.db
FavoriteView.nib    mapcompassdial@2x.png   settings@2x.png
110030.png 120022.png  123301.png  321000.png 330032.png  arcompassglass.png
FBConnect.bundle    mapcompassdial.png     settings.png
110031.png 120030.png  123302.png  321001.png 330100.png  arfunnel.png
forward@2x.png     mapcompassglass@2x.png   SettingsView.nib
110032.png 120031.png  300002.png  321002.png 330101.png  ARItemBackground.png
forward.png     mapcompassglass.png    simulator.plist
110100.png 120032.png  300003.png  321100.png 330102.png  ARItem.nib
frameimage.png     mark1.png          Spanish.lproj
110101.png 120100.png  300004.png  321101.png 330200.png  AroundMe
French.lproj      mark2.png          symbol-backgroundbw.png
110102.png 120101.png  300005.png  321102.png 330201.png  AroundMe_114.png
German.lproj      mark3.png          symbol-background.png
110300.png 120102.png  300006.png  322000.png 330202.png  AroundMe_72.png
globeIcon@2x.png    mark4.png          touchlocallogo.png
110301.png 120200.png  300204.png  322001.png 330300.png  AroundMeBeta_114.png
globeIcon.png      ModalWaitView.nib      transportuk.db
110302.png 120201.png  320000.png  322002.png 330301.png  AroundMeBeta_72.png
googleads-bw-de.png more@2x.png        turnlandscape.png
111000.png 120202.png  320001.png  322200.png 330302.png  AroundMeBeta.png
googleads-bw-en.png moreArrow@2x.png      warburgbg.png
111001.png 120300.png  320002.png  322201.png 331000.png  AroundMe.png
googleads-bw-es.png moreArrow.png       WarburgDetail.nib
111002.png 120301.png  320010.png  322202.png 331001.png  black
googleads-bw-fr.png more.png          warburgicon.png
111100.png 120302.png  320011.png  323000.png 331002.png  CategoryView.nib
googleads-bw-it.png NewTweetViewController.nib Warburg.nib
111101.png 121000.png  320012.png  323001.png 331100.png  classic
googleads-de.png    phone@2x.png        warburg.png
111102.png 121001.png  320020.png  323002.png 331101.png  CodeResources
googleads-en.png    phone.png          weatherbackgroundbw.png
113000.png 121002.png  320021.png  323300.png 331102.png  _CodeSignature
googleads-es.png    PhotoDetailView.nib    weatherbackground.png
113001.png 121100.png  320022.png  323301.png 332000.png  coffeebreak.png
googleads-fr.png    PhotoView.nib        WeatherView.nib
```

```
113002.png 121101.png  320030.png  323302.png  332001.png  Default@2x.png
googleads-il.png      PkgInfo                WikipediaView.nib
113300.png 121102.png  320031.png  330000.png 332002.png  Default.png
google.png            PrivacyView.nib        WikipediaWebview.nib
113301.png 122000.png  320032.png  330001.png 332200.png  DetailTextView.nib
imageplaceholder.png ResourceRules.plist
113302.png 122001.png  320100.png  330002.png 332201.png  DetailView.nib
Info.plist            RetailStoresView.nib
120000.png 122002.png  320101.png  330010.png 332202.png  directionarrow.png
Info.png              RootViewController.nib
```

Each application also contains a Documents, Library, and tmp folder. The files within those folders will vary depending on the application. As an example, Foursquare is an application that allows users to "check-in" to various businesses in order to notify their friends (possibly through Facebook) about where they are. As a Foursquare user, an individual can search for nearby businesses and check into that location. Foursquare's Documents folder contains an archive file containing the locations where the user had previously checked in. On the other hand, the Facebook application's Documents folder contains a "Friends" database, which contains a listing of the user's Facebook friends.

The Library folder contains many other subdirectories as well, including Caches, Cookies, and Preferences (though additional folders/files may be included depending on the application). The Preferences folder typically contains a plist file, such as com.ApplicatoinName.plist. This plist often times will have the username (and sometimes password) which is used to login to that application. Other general application data can also be recovered from this file such as version, application description, and even GPS info.

Finally, the tmp folder is typically empty since the device is not imaged while an application is running. If an iPhone was jailbroken and physically imaged while an application transaction was in progress, it is possible that temporary files would be stored in this folder.

Other

Besides the default applications that arrive on the iPhone as well as those downloaded through the iTunes store, other relevant data can also be recovered from the device, which can be very important in an investigation.

Geographical location data

Various applications will either ask the user if they wish to cache their current location, or the apps will store GPS data behind the scenes depending on the functionality of the app. For example, both the iPhone's camera and video camera will store latitude and longitude coordinates which describe where the device was at the time the photo or video was taken. The Google Maps application that arrives on the device by default also stores the user's current location as well as any other location that was searched within the application.

On top of these standard applications, there are countless apps available for download that will track GPS coordinates.

The consolidated.db file is new in iOS 4, and there is not a significant amount of documented information on the topic. This file stores GPS and Wi-Fi data in one central location, presumably to improve device efficiency since it now only has to access one file in order to send or retrieve location data. The database contains the following tables. The two that have been found to be the most beneficial are the WifiLocation and CellLocation tables.

```
Katie-Strzempkas-MacBook:~ kstrzemp$ sqlite3 ~/Desktop/
consolidated.db
SQLite version 3.6.12
Enter ".help" for instructions
Enter SQL statements terminated with a ";"

sqlite> .tables
Cell                       Fences
CellLocation               Location
CellLocationBoxes          LocationHarvest
CellLocationBoxes_node     LocationHarvestCounts
CellLocationBoxes_parent   Wifi
CellLocationBoxes_rowid    WifiLocation
CellLocationCounts         WifiLocationCounts
CellLocationHarvest        WifiLocationHarvest
CellLocationHarvestCounts  WifiLocationHarvestCounts
CompassSettings
sqlite>
```

The WifiLocation table contains the MAC address, timestamp, latitude and longitude coordinates, and other fields that can determine which wireless locations the device was connected to at a certain point in time. As an example, let us analyze the first row of the table shown in Figure 6.5.

First, we will need to translate the timestamp displayed in the first column (306439818.409918). Using the CFAbsoluteTimeConvert (as these times are in OS X Epoch format), the time converts to Friday, September 17, 2010, at 01:10:18 p.m.

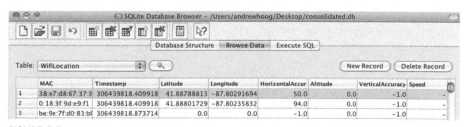

FIGURE 6.5

Consolidated.db – WifiLocation Table.

Next, we will need to look up the latitude and longitude coordinates provided in order to determine the actual location. There are various websites available that will translate these coordinates into an address; however, an easy way is to simply go to Google Maps (http://maps.google.com). Here, you will need to enter in the coordinates in the following format: +latitude, −longitude (see Figure 6.6).

A similar conversion can be done using the CellLocation table. Instead of Wi-Fi locations, this table contains cell tower logs, timestamps, and GPS coordinates (see Figure 6.7). The cell tower logs are displayed as MCC, MNC, LAC, and CI:

- MCC: Mobile Country Code
- MNC: Mobile Network Code
- LAC: Location Area Code
- CI: Cell ID

Using the timestamp and GPS coordinates within this table, a similar conversion can be done to determine which cellular tower the device was connected to at a certain point in time.

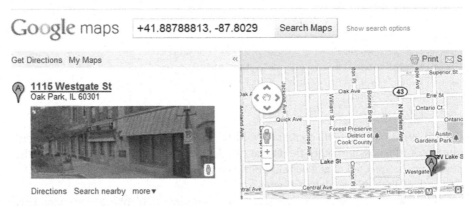

FIGURE 6.6

Googls Maps – Latitude and Longitude Conversion.

FIGURE 6.7

Consolidated.db – CellLocation Table.

Using these resources, we can determine that the device was possibly in Oak Park, IL, on Friday, September 17, 2010, at 01:10:18 p.m. You might be wondering why this is not definitive. With this file, it is understood that several different coordinates are populated into the database at one time. So, according to the timestamps and location, the device could be in several different areas at the same time (however, these areas are typically within a few miles of one another). This could be because the database is not constantly being updated as a new location is populated therefore, there might be 3, 4, or even 20 locations updated into the table at one time. For this reason, it is important not to rely solely on the timestamps until the consolidated.db file is researched further and better understood.

WARNING

Do not rely solely on the timestamps within the consolidated.db file. Several different records can be populated into the database at the same time. If the timestamps within all records were converted, this would show that the device was in multiple locations at one time. The information in this database should be used as a general guideline.

In the WiFiLocation table, there were 404 records on a lightly used iPhone 3GS. Imagine having to manually convert the timestamp and GPS coordinates for each record in order to find the right one. It has been mentioned that a script was developed that would parse the data into Google Earth, but there is no word on its release (iPhone GPS Data..., 2011). Until this file is better understood and tools developed to extract and convert the data, the information in this database should be used cautiously.

Within the file system, another area that contains geographical information on the device and its apps is the "locationd" folder. This folder is located in /private/var/root/Library/Caches/locationd. The locationd folder contains many different files:

```
kstrzempka@linux-wks:/home/kstrzempka/Desktop/iPhoneapp-mount/
root/Library/Caches# tree locationd/
locationd/
├── cache.plist
├── cells-local.plist
├── cells.plist
├── clients-b.plist
├── ephemeris
├── h-cells.plist
├── lto2.dat
├── stats.plist
└── wifi
    ├── B894C7D_1281764032.dat
    ├── B894CA7_1281764031.dat
    ├── B894CB0_1281764031.dat
    ├── B894CB1_1281764031.dat
    ├── B894CB4_1281764030.dat
    ├── B894CB5_1281764030.dat
    ├── B894D8F_1281764025.dat
```

```
├── B894D9D_1281764021.dat
├── B894DC3_1281764019.dat
└── B894DC7_1281764019.dat
2 directories, 17 files
```

One file worth mentioning is "cache.plist." This file contains the Core Location's last GPS fix, or where the device was last located on the basis of identified wireless signals. This portion of the file is shown in the beginning and looks similar to what is shown in the following code:

```xml
<?xml version="1.0" encoding="UTF-8"?>
<!DOCTYPE plist PUBLIC "-//Apple//DTD PLIST 1.0//EN"
"http://www.apple.com/DTDs/PropertyList-1.0.dtd">
<plist version="1.0">
<dict>
    <key>CLLocationCore::kLastFix</key>
        <dict>
            <key>Altitude</key>
            <real>0.0</real>
            <key>HorizontalAccuracy</key>
            <real>500</real>
            <key>Latitude</key>
            <real>41.873892060000003</real>
            <key>Lifespan</key>
            <real>-1</real>
            <key>Longitude</key>
            <real>-87.794191889999993</real>
            <key>Suitability</key>
            <integer>65534</integer>
            <key>SupportInfo</key>
        <dict>
```

Latitude and longitude coordinates are provided, which will translate to an approximate geographical location. While timestamps within the cache.plist file are not provided, an examiner can look at the day and time on which this particular file was last modified in order to get an approximate time the device was at this particular location.

Another file in the locationd folder that may be of use is cells.plist. This file contains numerous records of cell tower locations, similar to the CellLocations table found in consolidated.db. A snapshot of this file is shown in the following code:

```xml
<?xml version="1.0" encoding="UTF-8"?>
<!DOCTYPE plist PUBLIC "-//Apple//DTD PLIST 1.0//EN"
"http://www.apple.com/DTDs/PropertyList-1.0.dtd">
<plist version="1.0">
    <dict>
        <key>310,410,0x1e7a</key>
        <string>2,+41.88355916,-87.62691020,8000.000000,240,304557710.
        149</string>
```

```
<key>310,410,0x1e94</key>
<string>2,+41.93214869,-87.64807087,8000.000000,240,304557710.
149</string>
<key>310,410,0x52d3</key>
<string>2,+41.95102542,-87.92777836,13030.000000,240,304557710.
149</string>
<key>310,410,0x52d4</key>
<string>2,+41.87647861,-87.62853527,8000.000000,240,304557710.
149</string>
<key>310,410,0x52d5</key>
<string>2,+41.84576398,-87.84617710,12400.000000,240,304557710.
149</string>
...
</dict>
```

The numbers shown in the "key" correspond with the same numbers displayed in the consolidated.db CellLocations table: MCC, MNC, and LAC. So, in the example above, 310 is the MCC, 410 is the MNC, and 0x1e7a (in decimal this is 7802) is the LAC. The "string" listed directly below these numbers contains latitude and longitude coordinates as well as a timestamp shown in OS X Epoch (304.557710.149). This is very similar to the data we saw in the CellLocations table of the consolidated.db file. This is because all of the cell tower and GPS data was consolidated into one database with the release of iOS 4. Nevertheless, it is important for an examiner to understand that this data can be found in both locations. This way, regardless of whether the device is running iOS 4 or earlier, geographical location data can be recovered.

User names and passwords

Many applications, both default and downloaded, leverage Apple's Keychain database for user name and password management. The keychain-2.db file is stored on the root of the device in /private/var/Keychains. This database consists of six tables: genp, sqlite_sequence, inet, cert, keys, and tversion. The two main tables that are known to contain the most evidentiary data are genp and inet (however, it is never a bad idea to analyze all the tables in the database to ensure that important data are not missed).

The "genp" table contains a list of accounts that the device has been logged into at one point. Included in this table are wireless access points the device was connected to, voicemail login, device login (passcode), and any downloaded applications that elected to use the keychain database to store login credentials. The account name (username) and a description of that account are provided along with a "data" field, which contains an encrypted password for each account. This data is shown in Figure 6.8.

The "inet" table contains any e-mail accounts the device has been synced to through the default Mail application. The following information can be found about each account:

- Account (e-mail address or domain/username)
- E-mail server that the device was connected to

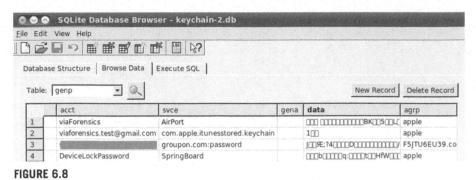

FIGURE 6.8

keychain-2.db: genp.

- Protocol used to connect to the server (imap, smtp, https, etc.)
- Port number (143, 25, 443, etc.)
- Data (encrypted password)

While the passwords in both tables are in an encrypted format, there are ways to decrypt this data. As pointed out in Chapter 5, with the release of iOS 4, encryption is now done at the device level. When an unencrypted backed-up device is initiated, the keychain file is encrypted using hardware keys stored on the device. When the database is opened, much of the information can be seen, but the passwords remain encrypted (as shown previously in this section). If an encrypted backup is generated, the keychain file is now encrypted using software keys generated from the backup password. Using Elcomsoft's iPhone Password Breaker, the passwords within the keychain file can be unencrypted and viewed in clear text. This technique is successful only on devices running firmware version 4.0 or higher. For detailed procedures on the use of Elcomsoft's software to crack the keychain file, see the section in Chapter 5 that discusses encrypted backups.

Another technique was able to reveal the keychain passwords without the use of purchased software. This attack requires possession of the phone as well as knowledge on jailbreaking the device. Once the device is jailbroken, an SSH server is installed on the device in order to allow software to run on the iPhone. Next, a keychain access script is copied to the device which is able to communicate with the keychain database and extract data, including passwords. This works because, with iOS 4, a key can be generated from within the device, without having to know the device passcode.

Snapshots

When the user selects the "Home" button to exit an application and go back to the main screen on the device, a screen shot is sometimes taken of the app prior to exiting, depending on the options selected by that particular application's developer. If enabled, these snapshots are stored on the device, and can later be recovered.

The images taken of the default apps can be found in /private/var/mobile/Library/ Caches/Snapshots, and the filename will be something like com.apple.mobilemail-Default.jpg, com.apple.mobilenotes-Default.jpg, or com.apple.mobilesafari-Default. jpg. Since these screen shots are taken at random points throughout the use of an application, they will often contain useful data. For example, if a user selected the "Home" button after reading an e-mail, it is possible that a snapshot of the e-mail content would be taken and stored on the device. The same goes for third-party applications that have been downloaded by the user. If the developer enabled this option, snapshots for a downloaded application would be stored in that particular Application folder.

For the recovery of these snapshots, data carving techniques are typically required. While a few snapshots may be stored in the /Caches/Snapshots folder, the remaining images are unallocated. Most of these images, however, can be recovered by running Scalpel (or another file carving utility) on the disk image, and they will be stored in one of the "jpg" folders.

Paired devices

Often times, it is necessary to prove that a device belonged to a certain individual. While this can be a difficult task, using the pairing records is one way to achieve this. Whenever an iPhone is synced with a computer, a key is stored on both the phone and the workstation in order to allow the two devices to share data. If the certificate on the phone matches the certificate on the computer, then it can be concluded that those two devices were paired at one point.

This information on the iPhone is stored within a plist file, which is named after the desktop's unique identifier. There will be one file per device, and they can be found at /var/root/Library/Lockdown/pair_records/ (refer to Table 6.5). Below, you can see that this particular iPhone was paired with five unique devices (not necessarily all computers).

```
Insert Tree Pair_records
```

Several files are listed, and the examiner will need to look at the modification date and time to determine which device to look at. Once the plist is open, the information is displayed in XML format. The "DeviceCertificate" is the key we are looking for. As it is, this key is base64 encoded. Once decoded, the certificate can be found within a file on the workstation. To decode the base64 certificate, any websites and tools are available on the Internet. Go to one of these websites, copy and paste the certificate in the field, click decode (or whatever the program specifies), and the resulting output will be the certificate you need.

Next, the examiner must look at the certificate contained on the workstation. The location of these files will depend on the operating system running on this machine. Refer to Table 6.5 for locations in both Windows and Mac environments as well as on the iPhone itself (Zdziarski, 2008).

In this example, a Mac workstation was used. So after navigating to the Lockdown directory, a series of plist files were found. In this case, the file names referred

Table 6.5 Pairing Record File Locations

Operating System	Location
Mac OS X	/Users/username/Library/Lockdown/
Windows XP	C:\Documents and Settings\username\Local Settings\Application Data\Apple Computer\Lockdown
Windows Vista	C:\Users\username\AppData\Roaming\Apple Computer\Lockdown
iPhone	/var/root/Library/Lockdown/pair_records/

to the Unique Identifier of the device was synced to the computer, not necessarily all iPhones. The certificates in the plist files on the iPhone must be compared with the certificates in the plist files on the computer. Manually, this could be a time-consuming process. It is suggested that comparison tools be utilized, such as "diff." This utility will compare two files, and the output will show only the differences between the two files. When using "diff" to compare the certificates, if there are two keys that do not result in any differences, it can be determined that those two devices were paired.

iPHONE APPLICATION ANALYSIS AND REFERENCE

In this section, each of the default applications as well as a select sample of popular third-party apps is analyzed. Each app is broken down to show where the files are located on the iPhone's file system, or in other words the full path to where that particular app's data is stored. Also within this subsection is a list of the files an examiner can expect to find for that particular app. Next, for every app that contains a database or plist full of important information, the structure of these files are shown, including the database schema as well as the type of data that can be found in that specific file. Finally, for every application there is an "Analysis Notes" section. Here, the reader is instructed where to look for the most significant data for that app. Methods on viewing the data in these files are also covered.

Default applications

The subsections that follow describe the various applications that arrive by default on the iPhone. For each app, the file system layout is described, including all the files that are commonly recovered for that app. The database or plist files that contain significant data is broken down and discussed in detail. Finally, there is an analysis notes section, which explains how each of these files can be read to show where the important data resides.

SMS

Text messages are one of the most significant data items to be recovered from an iPhone. The following sections outline the files that can be found on the device as well as where the most important information resides.

File system layout
/private/var/mobile/Library/SMS:

- Drafts: contains draft SMS messages in the form of "messages.plist"
- Parts: Contains attachments to MMS or SMS messages, mostly .jpg files, but they can also be .mov or other files.
- sms.db: The SMS/MMS database.

Databases/plists
sms.db The sms.db is the most important file in this directory. It contains the text and multimedia messages and can also contain deleted text messages. Here is a listing of the tables contained within this database:

```
_SqliteDatabaseProperties
message
sqlite_sequence
msg_group
group_member
msg_pieces
```

Analyst notes
The "message" and "msg_pieces" tables are the two areas that should be the main focus when analyzing the sms.db.

The messages table contains each of the text messages, including the phone number from or to which the message was sent, date and time of the message, the message content, a "flags" column (specifies whether the message was sent or received), and other data. The following is a breakdown of each of the columns within this table and a definition of each:

- ROWID: A sequential, unique number assigned to each message. The "sqlite_sequence" table tracks the last assigned ROWID for the message table as well as the other tables in the database.
- address: The phone number from or to which the message was sent. If this field is blank, the message is most likely a multimedia message (and the phone number is displayed in the "recipients" field).
- date: Unix Epoch timestamp. When translated, this is the date and time at which the message was sent or received.
- text: Message content. If it is an MMS message, this field will be blank.
- flags: Shows whether the message was sent or received: a "3" signifies a sent message, a "2" signifies a received one.
- replace: Unknown. This field is always zero.
- svc_center: Unknown. This field is always null.
- group_id: An integer assigned to each unique phone number. All messages sent to or from a particular number are considered one group and, therefore, assigned their own group_id.
- association_id: Unknown. This field sometimes contains a zero, and at other times will contain the same Unix Epoch timestamp as displayed in the "date" field.

- height: Always a zero.
- UIFlags: Unknown. Typically a zero; however, sometimes there are other one-digit integers found here.
- version: Unknown. This field is always zero.
- subject: Unknown. This field is always null.
- country: The country code is shown here ("us").
- recipients: For a text message, this field will be empty. If the message is a multimedia message, this field will contain the phone number from or to which the message was sent. The phone number will be encoded in XML format.
- read: This field shows whether the message was read by the user. There will be a "1" if it was read.

The msg_pieces table contains the text content that is sent along with an MMS message. The following is a breakdown of the meaningful columns within this table and a definition of each:

- ROWID: A sequential, unique number assigned to each row in the msg_pieces table (not necessarily unique to each message). The "sqlite_sequence" table tracks the last assigned ROWID for the msg_pieces table as well as the other tables in the database.
- message_id: A unique ID assigned to each message. Typically, an MMS record will contain three rows in the msg_pieces database: the first row has blank/zero/null data, the second row contains the message within a text/plain document, and the third row is the actual image that was attached. All three of these rows comprise one MMS message, and will all have the same message_id. A message ID in the msg_pieces table matches up with the ROWID in the message table.
- data: The text content that was sent along with the MMS attachment.
- content_type: This field will be null, text (plain), image (jpeg), video (3gpp), or application (smil).
- height: This field always contains a zero.
- version: This field contains a 0 or 1, possibly referring to the plist version displayed in the recipients field of the message table.
- content_loc: This field will either be null or show as text_####.txt or IMG_####.jpg. The IMG name is not the actual name of the image that is stored on the iPhone (such as IMG_0001, IMG_0002, etc.). Typically in this field, there will be one of two.jpg names shown: IMG_6807 or IMG_5249 (however, it is not uncommon to see others as well). It is unknown what these filenames signify.
- headers: This field is null.

Calendar

Calendar events that have been manually entered by the user or synced using a mail app or other program are stored on the device.

File system layout
/private/var/mobile/Library/Calendar:

- Calendar.sqlitedb: This is the only file that is stored for the Calendar app.

Databases/plists
Calendar.sqlitedb This database file contains each calendar event that was stored on the device as well as the metadata for each event. The database can be more deeply analyzed to potentially recover deleted events. Here is a listing of the tables contained within this database:

```
sqlite> .tables
Alarm                   OccurrenceCache
AlarmChanges            OccurrenceCacheDays
Attendee                Participant
AttendeeChanges         Recurrence
Calendar                RecurrenceChanges
CalendarChanges         Store
Event                   Task
EventChanges            TaskChanges
EventExceptionDate      _Sqlite
```

Analyst notes
The "Event" table is the one that examiners should focus on; however, other tables can also be analyzed as needed. The Event table contains information relevant to the calendar events that were manually entered by the user or possibly synced up with their e-mail account, MobileMe account, or another tool. The following is a breakdown of each of the columns that contain relevant information and a definition of each. Many of the columns have been omitted as they do not contain useful information.

- ROWID: A sequential, unique number assigned to each calendar event. The "sqlite_sequence" table tracks the last assigned ROWID for the event table as well as the Store and Calendar tables.
- summary: The actual text content of the calendar event.
- location: An optional field where the user can enter the location of the event.
- description: An option field where the user can enter a description for the event.
- start_date: The start date and time of the event, displayed in OS X Epoch time (described earlier in this chapter).
- start_tz: The time zone in which the device is set.
- end_date: The end date and time of the event, displayed in OS X Epoch time.
- calendar_id: The ID assigned to the calendar in which this event is stored. The user may have synced up multiple calendars, and these will be shown in the "Calendar" table. The "ROWID" that is assigned to each calendar is also its calendar_id in the Events table.

Call History

Phone calls placed by the user or placed to the user are stored on the device, along with other metadata that could be of interest to an examiner.

File system layout
/private/var/mobile/Library/CallHistory/:

- call_history.db: This table contains the call logs that have been stored on the device.

Databases/plists
call_history.db The call_history database contains each of the missed, placed, and received calls on the device. The database can be more thoroughly analyzed to potentially recover deleted call logs. Here is a listing of the tables contained within this database:

```
_SqliteDatabaseProperties
call
sqlite_sequence
data
```

Analyst notes
The "call" table is where most of the information is going to be found; however, as with the other database files, the "sqlite_sequence" table tracks the most recently used row ID for certain tables in the database. The following is a breakdown of each of the columns within the call table that contain relevant information and a definition of each.

- ROWID: A sequential, unique number assigned to each call record in the table. The "sqlite_sequence" table tracks the last assigned ROWID for the call table as well as the data table.
- address: The phone number from or to which the call was placed. If this field is blank, it was most likely an unknown number.
- date: Unix Epoch timestamp. When translated, this is the date and time at which the call was placed or received.
- duration: This field displays the duration of the call (in seconds). A value of zero signifies a missed call.
- flags: Shows whether the call was incoming (flag set to 4) or outgoing (flag set to 5).
- id: If an outgoing call was placed to a contact within the user's address book, the id represents the individual's contact id (or ROWID assigned to that contact).
- name: This field is null.
- country_code: This is the MCC described earlier in the geographical data section. For the United States, the MCC is 310.

On the iPhone, there is a call history limit of 100 logs. Any calls placed or received above 100 will be stored in the database, but the oldest record will be removed. Therefore, upon viewing the call_history.db file in a SQLite database browser, an examiner will not see more than 100 records in the call table. However, using the advanced analysis techniques described earlier in this chapter (strings, hex editor, etc.), it is possible to recover the old call logs that were replaced.

User dictionary/keyboard

Whenever a user manually types a word into the iPhone, the device generates a dynamic dictionary file that stores words unique to that user. For example, anything entered into a text message, e-mail, note, or other form of text entry would be stored in this file.

File system layout

/private/var/mobile/Library/Keyboard:

- dynamic-text.dat

Analyst notes

While this is not a database or plist, the user's dynamic dictionary file can contain interesting artifacts. A .dat file is a "data" file, and the way it is viewed depends on its contents. Because it is known that this particular file stores text, it can be opened in any text editor. However, when opened in this manner, all the words run together and the analysis is difficult.

```
DynamicDictionary-4[testmailtesttestgolfclubsheywhattypeofclubs
wouldyour
firstchoicecallowaymailhowamsupposedtogetintothestoreafterhours
checkouts
ureisnicedayoutwhat'reyoudoingtodaydinneratgreatmayneedtoheadout
aroundbu
tthatshouldgiveusplentyoftimeoakcoakparkoakparkillakeoakparkil
pieceofcak
ecan'twaittotryoutonsundaytesttobradtesttobradwillyougogetme
coffeeguessy
ou'llneverknowviaforensicsgmailgolfsmithtaylormadesbcglobals
arpinosmccal
isterem
```

It is much more efficient to use the "strings" command and either redirect the output into a text file or display the output through the "less" command (see Chapter 1 on how to use basic Linux commands).

```
Katie-Strzempkas-MacBook:Keyboard kstrzemp$ strings dynamic-text.
dat | less

DynamicDictionary-4
[test
mail
test
test
golf
```

```
clubs
what
type
clubs
would
your
first
choice
calloway
mail
supposed
into
store
after
hours
check
sure
```

Oftentimes, full text messages and e-mail content are found in this file; however, it is impossible to determine any other information about the source, such as date and time or the individual who sent or received the message.

Many examiners want to know whether passwords are stored in this file, and the technical answer is no. If a user enters a password (or PIN) into a password field on the device, such as when he or she logs into his or her e-mail account, the device knows not to store that information. However, if the user decides to enter their password into a note, document, or e-mail on the device, it is possible that it would be stored in the dynamic text file.

Mail

When a user syncs their e-mail account(s) to a device, account information as well as e-mail content is stored within the device.

File system layout

/private/var/Keychain/:

- keychain-2.db: Contains e-mail account information.

/private/var/mobile/Library/Mail/:

- Mail Folder for each e-mail account synced to the device (containing.emlx and emlxpart files: see "Analysis Notes" section).
- AutoFetchEnabled
- Envelope Index

/private/var/mobile/Library/Webkit/Databases:

- Databases.db: Contains a list of the webkit database files on the device.
- mail.yahoo.com folder with .db file: Contains data related to the Yahoo! mail account.

- mail.google.com folder with .db file: Contains data related to the Google mail account.
- Any other mail accounts that may have been synced to the device.

Databases/plists

keychain-2.db This database stores user login credentials and other metadata related to those accounts. Wi-Fi accounts, application logins, e-mail accounts, and more can be found here. The following tables can be found in this database:

```
cert
genp
inet
keys
sqlite_sequence
tversion
```

The "inet" table is where e-mail account data can be found. The "acct" column contains the e-mail address, or for an Exchange account, the domain and username. The "srvr" column includes the mail server that the device is retrieving content from, the "ptcl" and "port" columns list the protocol and port used to connect to that mail server, and the "data" column contains the encrypted password for that account.

Databases.db This databases contains three tables:

```
Databases
Origins
sqlite_sequence
```

The "Databases" table is the only one containing unique data, and here the examiner can view the various webkit database files on the device. For example, if the user synced both Yahoo and Gmail, the folder containing each database is listed in the "origins" column. For the databases listed below, the origins are: http_m.mg. mail.yahoo.com_0 and https_mail.google.com_0 >. These are subfolders, which also contain the database file. In the "Databases" table, the examiner can also see the e-mail address for the user.

http_m.mg.mail.yahoo.com_0 > 0000000000000004.db The database within the Yahoo mail folder contains a significant amount of important data, including the e-mail addresses of the senders and the recipients of the e-mail, e-mail subjects, timestamps, and even partial e-mail content. The following is a listing of the tables contained within this database:

```
_WebKitDatabaseInfoTable_
action
message
folder
vfolder
contact
```

The two tables worth looking at are the "folder" and "message" tables.

The message table contains the full e-mail subject, partial e-mail content (in the "snippet" column), the e-mail addresses of both the sender and receiver, and finally the Unix Epoch timestamp. When converted, this is the date and time when the e-mail was received. There is also a column called "hasAttachment," which, as expected, will have a "1" if there was a file attached to that particular e-mail (otherwise it will have a "0").

The folder table shows a list of all of the folders within that e-mail account. The standard folders, such as Inbox, Sent, Trash, etc., may not be of importance, but this table also contains a list of the personal folders created by the user. Along with the folder names, also included as part of this table is the total number of messages within each folder and the number of messages:

https_mail.google.com_0 > 0000000000000001.db The database within the Google mail folder also contains the e-mail addresses of the senders and the recipients of the e-mail, e-mail subjects, timestamps, and partial e-mail content. The following is a listing of the tables contained within this database:

```
__WebKitDatabaseInfoTable__
action_queue_11_crf
cached_queries
hit_to_data
cached_conversation_headers
cached_messages
cached_labels
cached_contacts
config_table
log_store
```

The two main tables to focus on in this database are "cached_conversation_ headers" and "cached_messages." While some of the contents between these two tables overlap, there are some differences making it worthwhile to take a look at both.

The following is a breakdown of each of the columns within the cached_ conversation_headers table that contain relevant information and a definition of each:

- isInbox/isSpam/isTrash/etc.: These columns are flagged with a "1" if true. For example, if the "isInbox" column contains a "1," then the e-mail message in that row was recovered from the user's Inbox.
- subject: Contains the message Subject.
- snippetHtml: Contains a portion of the message body.
- senderListHtml: Contains the name assigned to the sender in the e-mail contacts (not necessarily the e-mail address).
- dateMs: The date and time the message was received in Unix Epoch (milliseconds). To convert manually, the examiner will need to remove the last three digits; otherwise, it can be converted through a website or other tool.

- modifyDateMs: The date and time the message was modified in Unix Epoch (milliseconds). This is typically the same timestamp as the dateMs.
- hasAttachment: If the message has an attachment, this field will be flagged with a "1" (otherwise it will be a "0").

The following is a breakdown of each of the columns within the cached_messages table that contain relevant information and a definition of each.

- messageID: A unique ID assigned to each message.
- conversationId: An ID assigned for each conversation (group of messages for each sender). This ID might be the same as the message.
- isInbox/isSpam/isTrash/etc.: These columns are flagged with a "1" if true. For example, if the "isInbox" column contains a "1," then the e-mail message in that row was recovered from the user's Inbox.
- subject: Contains the message Subject.
- snippetHtml: Contains a portion of the message body.
- address_from: Contains the e-mail address of the sender.
- address_to/address_cc/address_bcc: Contains the e-mail address that the message was sent to. If an individual was cc'd or bcc'd, that e-mail address would be listed in the appropriate columns.
- receivedDateMs: dateMs: The date and time the message was received in Unix Epoch (milliseconds). To convert manually, the examiner will need to remove the last three digits; otherwise, it can be converted through a website or other tool.

Analyst notes

From the files described in the previous sections, one can see that there are various locations within the iPhone file system where e-mail remnants can be found: the "Mail" folder and the "WebKit" folder. The databases within the WebKit folder have been thoroughly discussed as they contain allocated files. Next, the contents of the Mail folder are discussed.

As mentioned earlier, there is a specific folder assigned to each Mail account synced to the device, and these files can be viewed with a physical image of the device. For an exchange mail account, the folder will begin with "ExchangeActiveSync...," whereas a Gmail or Yahoo account might begin with "IMAP-email@address.com". Within this folder, the following folders can be seen:

```
23K241-39E2-AP09-A284-B39T02955E.mbox  (User's Inbox - random
string of characters)
Deleted Items.mbox
Drafts.mbox
Junk E-mail.mbox
Outbox.mbox
Sent Items.mbox
```

Within these folders are some of the actual e-mail messages in the form of a ".emlx" extension. These files can be viewed in a text editor, or by importing them into the Mail program on a Mac. In addition to e-mail messages, there are also files with a ".emlxpart" extension. This contains files that have been attached to one or more of the e-mails. Let us assume that this file extension is unknown. The following command can be run on a Linux machine to determine what type of file this is, and thus understand what tool is needed to view it. First, we will list out the files in the "Messages" folder and then determine the file type.

```
root@linux-001:~/mount/mobile/Library/Mail/ExchangeActiveSync-
[Mail-ID].mbox/Messages# ls -l
total 1428
-rw-r--r-- 1 501 501 721191 2010-08-05 13:53 14.1.2.emlxpart
-rw-r--r-- 1 501 501 148142 2010-08-05 13:05 16.emlx
-rw-r--r-- 1 501 501 178494 2010-08-05 13:05 17.emlx
-rw-r--r-- 1 501 501 403407 2010-08-05 13:05 20.emlx

root@linux-001:~/mount/mobile/Library/Mail/ExchangeActiveSync-
[Mail-ID].mbox/Messages# file 14.1.2.emlxpart
14.1.2.emlxpart: Zip archive data, at least v2.0 to extract

root@linux-001:~/mount/mobile/Library/Mail/ExchangeActiveSync-
[Mail-ID].mbox/Messages# file 16.emlx
16.emlx: RFC 822 mail text
```

From the output of the "file" command, it can be seen that the .emlx file is text and the .emlxpart file is a compressed archive, which must be unzipped. This file can be copied to another location on the examiner's machine (since the iPhone dmg should be mounted as read-only) and unzipped to view the file contents and attachments.

While messages in the user's "Deleted" mail folder can be recovered, those that have been fully deleted or emptied from trash cannot be found in the Mail folder. A file carving utility can be used to extract e-mails from a disk image (see the "File Carving" section earlier in this chapter). Here, e-mails can be recovered, including those that have been deleted. The examiner can then use the "grep" command to search through all the e-mail files for specific keywords. In the following example, all the e-mail files (*.email) are searched for the viaForensics e-mail address shown.

```
$ cd scalpel-output/email-10-0
$ grep "test@viaforensics.com" *.email
```

With the ability to perform file carving on a full physical disk image, a significant amount of e-mail content can be recovered from a device. Unfortunately, a physical acquisition is not always possible. In the event that only a logical or backup acquisition is possible, the WebKit is a good place for an examiner to start, and at the very least, e-mail account information can always be found in the keychain database. Refer back to Chapter 5 for details on how passwords stored in this database can be decrypted!

Maps

The Maps app allows the user to search for specific locations and directions using Google Maps. This application will often times store the user's current location (see the section on "Geographical Info" later in this chapter).

File system layout

/private/var/mobile/Library/Maps/:

- Bookmarks.plist: Contains locations bookmarked by the user.
- Directions.plist: Contains directions searched by the user.
- History.plist: Contains map history searched by the user.

Analyst notes

Each of these plists is in binary format. When hitting the space bar to open one of these files in Preview (on a Mac), some of the data appears to be encrypted, or otherwise unreadable. However, when opening it in a text editor, the directions, bookmarks, and history can be read. In this instance, converting from binary to XML is not necessary. As an example, here is what Directions.plist looks like when it is converted to XML and opened in a text editor:

```
<?xml version="1.0" encoding="UTF-8"?>
<!DOCTYPE plist PUBLIC "-//Apple//DTD PLIST 1.0//EN"
"http://www.apple.com/DTDs/PropertyList-1.0.dtd">
<plist version="1.0">
<dict>
    <key>DirectionsFileVersion</key>
    <integer>2</integer>
    <key>DirectionsMode</key>
    <integer>2</integer>
    <key>EndSearchProto</key>
    <data>
    CAAQABgAIAA1AAAAAJoBDk4gQ2x5Ym91cm4gQXZlogEWVy1SZmlwNUti
    cDJXaEhwNVBm
    bFBkQagB16n/E7ABnMmY1v//////AbgB/////wfAAQDIAQDYDAA=
    </data>
    <key>Responses</key>
    <array>
        <dict>
            <key>Mode</key>
            <integer>2</integer>
            <key>ResponseData</key>
            <data>
            CAAQACswADovCgtOIE1hcmlvbiBTdBIOCAVyCgiqxvknEOOM31Ma
            DkZaVXhmd01kemp6RS1nIAAsKzAAOjIKDk4gQ2x5Ym91cm4gQXZl
            Eg4IBXIKCK7T/icQx+3OUxoORmRmVWZ3SWRuQ1RHLWcgACxDSp4F
```

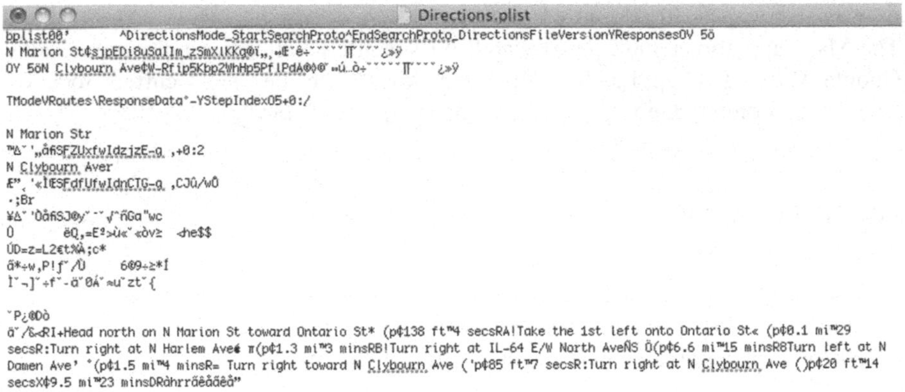

FIGURE 6.9

Directions.plist (Binary).

When the same file is left as a binary plist and opened in a text editor, the data is difficult to decipher, but the directions are legible (see Figure 6.9).

Notes

This application allows the user to create notes, and stores the date and time when the note was created.

File system layout

/private/var/mobile/Library/Notes:

- notes.db: Stores the note contents and other metadata.
- notes.idx: An index file which also contains note fragments.

Databases/plists

notes.db This database contains all allocated notes as well as creation and modification timestamps. The following tables are contained in the notes.db file:

```
Note
NoteChanges
_SqliteDatabaseProperties
note_bodies
sqlite_sequence
```

Analyst notes

This app is pretty straightforward. There is one file that needs to be analyzed: notes. db. Upon opening it in a database browser, the "Note" table is where an examiner should focus his or her attention. The "note_bodies" table also contains note content; however, this same data is available in the Note table. The following is a breakdown of each of the columns within the Note table that contain relevant information and a definition of each:

- ROWID: A sequential, unique number assigned to each note. The "sqlite_sequence" table tracks the last assigned ROWID for the Note table.
- creation_date: Timestamp in OS X Epoch; when converted, this will show the date and time the note was created (see "Advanced Forensic Analysis" section for details on converted timestamps).
- title: Note content.
- modification_date: Timestamp in OS X Epoch; when converted, this will show the date and time the note was modified (see "Advanced Forensic Analysis" section for details on converted timestamps).

Web browsing

The Safari web application is used on an Apple device to allow web browsing. Various types of data can be found within this application.

File system layout

/private/var/mobile/Library/Safari:

- Bookmarks.plist or Bookmarks.db: Contains locations bookmarked by the user (with iOS 4, bookmarks are stored in a database).
- History.plist: Contains the URL visited by the user; also stored is the last visited URL and the date and time it was accessed.
- SuspendState.plist: May contain deleted web history, Google search terms, and the last visited URL.

Databasess/plists

Bookmarks.plist or Bookmarks.db These files contain information related to websites that were bookmarked by the user. When looking at the XML plist in a text editor, the data is organized as follows, with the URL and website title shown within the <string> tags:

```
<?xml version="1.0" encoding="UTF-8"?>
<!DOCTYPE plist PUBLIC "-//Apple//DTD PLIST 1.0//EN"
"http://www.apple.com/DTDs/PropertyList-1.0.dtd">
<plist version="1.0">
<dict>
    <key>Children</key>
    <array>
      <dict>
        <key>URIDictionary</key>
        <dict>
          <key></key>
          <string>http://chicago.cubs.mlb.com/schedule/index.
          jsp?c_id=chc</string>
          <key>title</key>
```

```
        <string>2010 Cubs Schedule | cubs.com: Schedule</string>
    </dict>
    <key>URLString</key>
    <string>http://chicago.cubs.mlb.com/schedule/index.jsp?
    c_id=chc</string>
    <key>WebBookmarkType</key>
    <string>WebBookmarkTypeLeaf</string>
    <key>WebBookmarkUUID</key>
    <string>1CAFF247-95A0-4D99-8DF8-3EC5377798A7</string>
</dict>
```

For devices running iOS 4.0 or higher, bookmarks are stored in bookmarks.db file. The database contains the following tables:

```
bookmark_title_words
bookmarks
generations
sync_properties
```

The "bookmarks" table contains the most significant data, including the title of the website and URL, similar to that shown in the plist. The database is, however, a bit easier to read, as it is organized into rows and columns as opposed to XML format.

History.plist The user's visited websites are stored in the History.plist file as well as the last visited URL and the date and time it was accessed. In the example that follows, there is one history item shown, which includes the URL as well as the OS X Epoch timestamp for the last time this site was visited. To convert this timestamp, see the "Advanced Forensic Analysis" section earlier in this chapter.

```
<dict>
    <key></key>
    <string>http://chicagocubs.com/</string>
    <key>D</key>
    <array>
        <integer>1</integer>
    </array>
    <key>WebViewportArguments</key>
    <dict>
        <key>height</key>
        -1
        <key>initial-scale</key>
        -1
        <key>maximum-scale</key>
        -1
        <key>minimum-scale</key>
        -1
        <key>user-scalable</key>
        -1
```

```
    <key>width</key>
    <real>-1</real>
</dict>
<key>lastVisitedDate</key>
<string>304450956.3</string>
<key>redirectURLs</key>
<array>
    <string>http://chicago.cubs.mlb.com/index.jsp?c_id=chc</
    string>
</array>
<key>title</key>
<string>The Official Site of The Chicago Cubs | cubs.com:
Homepage</string>
<key>visitCount</key>
<integer>1</integer>
</dict>
```

SuspendState.plist This file contains additional web history, some of which can also be found in History.plist. However, deleted web history is also found in this file which is not the case for History.plist. The data structure is similar for both files; however, only the URL and website title is shown in Suspend State.

Analyst notes

Each of the Safari data files (Bookmarks, History, and Suspend State) by default are in binary plist format, just as the files within the Maps directory. In this instance, however, the data can be easily viewed and examined by opening the file with the space bar on a Mac. When attempting to open the Safari binary plists in a text editor, the data is not formatted appropriately. Using plutil, or another utility to convert the binary plists to XML, the information is displayed in a more organized manner (as shown in the examples for each plist).

Allocated web history will be stored in History.plist, but in order to access deleted web browsing data, the SuspendState.plist must be analyzed. The only downside to SuspendState.plist is that timestamps are not shown as they are in History.plist.

Voicemail

The Voicemail app stores messages that have been left for the user on the device.

File system layout

/private/var/mobile/Library/Voicemail:

- voicemail.db: Contains information about each of the allocated voicemail files.
- _subscribed: This is typically an empty file.
- .amr files: These are the actual voicemail files that can be listened to using a media player.

Databases/plists

voicemail.db This database contains information about the voicemails stored on the device. The following tables are contained in this file:

```
_SqliteDatabaseProperties
sqlite_sequence
voicemail
```

The "voicemail" table should be the main focus for an examiner. The following is a breakdown of each of the columns within the voicemail table that contain relevant information and a definition of each:

- ROWID: A sequential, unique number assigned to each voicemail. The "sqlite_sequence" table tracks the last assigned ROWID for the voicemail table.
- date: The date and time that the voicemail was created in Unix Epoch timestamp.
- sender: The phone number of the user who left the voicemail.
- callback_num: The phone number of the user who left the voicemail.
- duration: The duration of the voicemail message.
- expiration: The date and timestamp when the voicemail expires (1 month after the creation date).
- trashed_date: If applicable, this is the date and time that the user placed the voicemail in the "Deleted" folder.

Analyst notes

The database contains details about each of the voicemails; however, to actually listen to the messages, the examiner must open the ".amr" files using a media player. These files are named after the ROWID in the database. For example, for ROWID "6," the equivalent voicemail will be "6.amr".

The iPhone contains a feature known as visual voicemail. This allows the user to visually see the different voicemails contained on their device. If they wish to delete a voicemail, they can select that option on the touch screen. However, from a forensic standpoint, it is important to understand that when deleted, the voicemail first goes to a "Deleted" folder that can actually be seen in the Voicemail application on the device. The user can then go into this folder and either restore that voicemail or permanently delete it (think of this as a Windows Recycle Bin). Oftentimes, a logical acquisition tool will report a voicemail as "Deleted" when in fact it is simply sitting in the "recycle bin" on the device.

It is easy to determine from the voicemail database whether any records have been permanently deleted by taking a look at the ROWIDs. Since they increment by 1, if there is a missing number, it can be assumed that the missing record was deleted by the user. SQLite analysis techniques can be used to try and recover these deleted rows.

YouTube

The YouTube mobile application can be used to search for and view videos on the Internet.

File system layout
/private/var/mobile/Library/Preferences/:

- com.apple.youtube.plist: Contains YouTube video Bookmarks, History, and most recent search terms.

Databases/plists
com.apple.youtube.plist This plist contains data related to the YouTube mobile application on the device. When a user watched a video using this app, it is stored as a history item. The user also has the ability to add videos to his or her "Favorites," which show up as bookmarks in the plist that follows:

```
<dict>
    <key>Bookmarks</key>
    <array>
        <string>t1yPhNZ1B1Q</string>
    <array/>
    <key>History</key>
    <array>
        <string>t1yPhNZ1B1Q</string>
        <string>KxaOmnDjObs</string>
        <string>qla13aWrNP4</string>
        <string>L_zRDchkDXg</string>
    </array>
    <key>lastSearch</key>
    <string>golf swing tips</string>
    <key>selectedCategory</key>
    <string>YTSearchCategoryController</string>
</dict>
```

Analyst notes
At first glance, the bookmarks and history items appear to be encrypted data. However, the characters within the <string> tags are actually a YouTube ID. This ID can be copied into a URL in order to view the actual video. For example, here is the URL for a random YouTube video: http://www.youtube.com/watch?v=1yk8bC6QDYo. The string of characters following the "=" sign is the ID. By replacing this ID with one shown in the plist, the YouTube bookmarks and history can easily be viewed.

The most recent YouTube search performed by the user is also in this file, and is shown under the "last Search" key. In this example, the most recent search was "golf swing tips."

Photos/videos
Photos and videos that have been taken from or synced to the device are also stored within the file system. The original iPhone model as well as the generation following it (3G) did not originally contain an on-board application that allowed recording videos from the device. For this reason, users turned to the App Store for applications

that would allow them to perform this function. However, this changed with the later models, and the "Camera" could be used for both pictures and videos. Videos recording from the on-board camera could then be recovered from the device.

File system layout
/private/var/mobile/Media/:

- /DCIM/100APPLE: Contains the photos and videos that have been taken from the device.
- /DCIM/999APPLE: Contains screen shots of the device taken by the user.
- /PhotoData/Photos.sqlite (iOS 4 only): Contains metadata for photos and videos on the device.

Databases/plists
photos.sqlite This table stores information about the allocated photos and videos within the device. Photos.sqlite contains the following tables:

```
Globals
Keyword
Photo
PhotoAlbum
PhotoAlbumToPhotoJoin
PhotoExtras
sqlite_sequence
```

The "Photo" table is where an examiner should focus his or her analysis in this database. The following is a breakdown of the columns that contain important information as well as a definition of each:

- title: The name of the file (minus the extension).
- captureTime: The OS X Epoch timestamp for when the photo or video was taken.
- width: The width of the photo; this field will show a "0" if the file is a video.
- height: The height of the photo; this field will show a "0" if the file is a video.
- directory: The path to where the file is stored within the file system. This field will typically say "DCIM/100APPLE."
- filename: The name of the file, including the extension (usually .jpg or .mov).
- recordModDate: The OS X Epoch timestamp for when the photo or video was modified.

Analyst notes
Most examiners will want to see not only the photos that were stored on the device but also information about these photos. By using the information retrieved from the photos.sqlite database in combination with the actual photos or videos stored in the 100APPLE or 999APPLE folder, the examiner can determine information such as when those photos were taken or modified. Some of the advanced techniques discussed earlier, such as using a hex editor or the "strings" command, can help to

locate deleted files within the database as well. While deleted videos are extremely difficult to recover (and sometimes impossible), deleted photos can be recovered through file carving. Unfortunately, at this time the metadata cannot be paired up with the recovered file because the photo no longer has its original file name, timestamps, etc.

User account info
User account and other login data are stored in the device's Keychain file.

File system layout
/private/var/Keychains:

- keychain-2.db: Contains e-mail account information.

Databases/plists
keychain-2.db The keychain database contains various tables that store user login information for various accounts and applications within the device. These may include wireless access points, iTunes store logins, user credentials for any third-party applications, voicemail accounts, and more. Here is a listing of the tables contained within this database:

```
cert
genp
inet
keys
sqlite_sequence
tversion
```

Analyst notes
The "inet" table is where e-mail account data can be found, and the "genp" table is where the remaining login data can be located. As the "inet" table has been elaborated on in the Mail section, we will discuss only the "genp" table here. The following is a breakdown of each of the columns within the genp table that contain relevant information and a definition of each:

- acct: Name of the account (i.e., username, Wi-Fi connection, e-mail address).
- svce: Description of the account (i.e., AirPort, Enhanced Voicemail, com.apple. itunesstored.keychain, <third-party-application>).
- data: This field typically contains the password in encrypted format.
- agrp: The name of the Keychain access group (these are used to share data between applications).

In Chapter 5, we discussed the possibility of using Elcomsoft's iPhone Password Breaker to decrypt an encrypted backup file, and therefore gain access to passwords within the keychain file. This method is successful only with a device running iOS 4 or higher, and the backup file must be encrypted.

Another option is available on jailbroken devices only. The "keychain_dumper" utility, developed by Patrick Toomey, is run from the device and can decrypt Keychain passwords on the fly. To acquire and use this tool, the following instructions should be followed:

1. Download keychain_dumper from: https://github.com/ptoomey3/Keychain-Dumper.
2. Look at the README files for details on how to install. The developer steps the user through the installation process.
3. Make sure ldid is installed on the jailbroken iPhone. To do this, download the "Aptbackup" package from Cydia, then run the following command on the device (this can be done through the Mobile Terminal application from Cydia, or the command can be run through a remote connection): $ apt-get install ldid (Hint: for details on how to remotely connect to a jailbroken device, refer to Chapter 5 – "Acquisition – Jailbroken Device").
4. Upload keychain_dumper to iPhone /usr/bin using scp (again, refer to Chapter 5).
5. Dump "entitlements" (aka access groups) from the keychain database using the following command: ./keychain_dumper -e > /var/tmp/entitlements.xml.
6. Sign the entitlements into keychain_dumper using the following command (NO space between S and /var): ldid -S/var/tmp/entitlements.xml keychain_dumper.
7. Dump contents to screen or output to a text keychain_ dumper > keychainresults. txt.

Assuming that the application developer was leveraging the Keychain file and was not using an alternative form of encryption, the passwords should be available in clear text and displayed in a format similar to the following:

```
Service: Facebook
Account: via@viaforensics.com
Entitlement Group: AB92F8A1L.*
Label: Generic
Field: data
Keychain Data: fbpassword987
```

Geographical info

Many apps, both default and third party, store GPS data on the iPhone. As an example, both the Camera and Google Maps application prompts the user to store their current GPS location prior to taking a picture or searching directions. This type of data is stored within the iPhone's file system and can be recovered.

File system layout

/private/var/root/Library/Caches/locationd: Some of the following files may or may not appear in the locationd folder, depending on the firmware version running on the device. Listed here are the files that contain significant data, and a couple of these are discussed in further detail in the "Databases/plists" section that follows.

- cache.plist: Contains the device's last GPS fix.
- cells.plist: Contains information related to the cell towers the device was connected to and the date and time of connection.
- clients-b.plist: Contains a list of "blacklisted" or unauthorized applications.
- h-cells.plist: Contains additional information on cell tower logs, including GPS coordinates and timestamps.
- consolidated.db: Contains cell tower logs, GPS coordinates, and wireless connections specific to the device as well as timestamps for each of these occurrences.

Databases/plists

consolidated.db The files contained in the locationd folder will vary depending on the iOS version. iOS 4 devices now contain the "consolidated.db" file. It contains a wealth of GPS data, cell tower logs, and Wi-Fi connection information. This database has been discussed in the "iPhone Data Storage Locations" section earlier in this chapter; however, its contents are summarized here as well. The following is a listing of the tables contained within this database:

```
Cell                          Fences
CellLocation                  Location
CellLocationBoxes             LocationHarvest
CellLocationBoxes_node        LocationHarvestCounts
CellLocationBoxes_parent      Wifi
CellLocationBoxes_rowid       WifiLocation
CellLocationCounts            WifiLocationCounts
CellLocationHarvest           WifiLocationHarvest
CellLocationHarvestCounts     WifiLocationHarvestCounts
CompassSettings
```

The main tables on which an examiner should focus his or her analysis are CellLocation and WifiLocation; however, the other tables should also be reviewed to ensure that no information is missed. For complete details related to the interpretation of the information contained in the CellLocation and WifiLocation tables, refer to the earlier section on "Geographical Location Data."

cache.plist This file contains what is referred to as the last GPS fix on the device. More specifically, it contains the most recent GPS location that the device was connected prior to being powered off or disconnected from Wi-Fi/cellular networks. At the beginning of this file, the following data is displayed:

```
<key>CLLocationCore::kLastFix</key>
<dict>
    <key>Altitude</key>
    <real>0.0</real>
    <key>HorizontalAccuracy</key>
    <real>500</real>
    <key>Latitude</key>
    <real>41.873892060000003</real>
    <key>Lifespan</key>
```

```
<real>-1</real>
<key>Longitude</key>
<real>-87.794191889999993</real>
<key>Suitability</key>
<integer>65534</integer>
<key>SupportInfo</key>
<dict>
    <key>kCLSupportInfoCell</key>
    <dict>
        <key>kCLSupportInfoCell_CI</key>
        <integer>12781</integer>
        <key>kCLSupportInfoCell_Index</key>
        <integer>0</integer>
        <key>kCLSupportInfoCell_LAC</key>
        <integer>21205</integer>
        <key>kCLSupportInfoCell_MCC</key>
        <integer>310</integer>
        <key>kCLSupportInfoCell_MNC</key>
        <integer>410</integer>
        <key>kCLSupportInfoCell_RSSI</key>
        <integer>-105</integer>
        <key>kCLSupportInfoCell_TA</key>
        <integer>-1</integer>
        <key>kCLSupportInfoCell_TATime</key>
        <real>0.0</real>
    </dict>
    <key>kCLSupportInfoCell_Mineable</key>
    <true/>
    <key>kCLSupportInfoPos_Technology</key>
    <string>kCLSupportInfoPos_Technology_Cell</string>
</dict>
<key>Timestamp</key>
<real>304616134.30302697</real>
<key>VerticalAccuracy</key>
<real>-1</real>
```

In the very first line, the "LastFix" key is displayed, followed by a long list of data. The latitude and longitude coordinates are displayed, which must be converted in order to recover the actual address of that location (Google Maps can be used for this purpose as well as for performing a search within a web browser for "GPS coordinates converter"). Cell tower logs are also listed as well as a Timestamp is shown in OS X Epoch time.

cells.plist This file contains information on the cell towers that the device was connected to. The following is an example of the data structure within cells.plist:

```
<key>310,410,0x1e7a</key>
<string>2,+41.88355916,-87.62691020,8000.000000,240,304557710.
149</string>
```

```
<key>310,410,0x1e94</key>
<string>2,+41.93214869,-87.64807087,8000.000000,240,304557710.
149</string>

<key>310,410,0x52d3</key>
<string>2,+41.95102542,-87.92777836,13030.000000,240,304557710.
149</string>

<key>310,410,0x52d4</key>
<string>2,+41.87647861,-87.62853527,8000.000000,240,304557710.
149</string>
```

Within the "key" tags is the MCC, the MNC, and the LAC in hex. To convert from hex to decimal, an examiner can use a calculator or a web search for "hex to decimal converter."

Within the "string" tags are latitude and longitude coordinates as well as a time-stamp in OS X Epoch time. Information within this file is very similar to that shown in the "CellLocation" table of the consolidated.db file.

Analyst notes

While these files appear to contain very important information on where the device was, what cell towers it was connected to, and the specific dates and times of these occurrences, it is also important to note that there has not been much research on these files. Oftentimes, the data in these files place the device at multiple geographic locations at the same time. Therefore, this information should be used as a guideline only when performing an investigation.

Third-party (downloaded) applications

A few of the popular applications that can be downloaded on an iPhone are discussed in this section. Of course, maintaining a complete reference would be nearly impossible due to the sheer number of applications. Just as with the default applications, there is a standard location where much of the important data can be recovered. Third-party apps are most commonly stored within the /private/var/mobile/Applications folder, and the following sections highlight the specific files that can be recovered for each of the listed apps as well as the techniques for viewing these files.

For each application, the following is provided:

- App information
- A list of important files and directories
- Database or property list files that contain meaningful data
- Analyst notes

Facebook

With the Facebook iPhone application, individuals can send messages to their friends, upload and view photos, and even check into their favorite restaurant or store to let their friends know where they are. When this app is used, much of this information is stored within the device and can easily be recovered with a basic understanding of the file system.

File system layout
/private/var/mobile/Applications/<Facebook Application Identifier>/:

- /Documents/friends.db: Contains a list of all the user's Facebook friends as well as a link to their profile pictures.
- Library/Preferences/com.facebook.Facebook.plist: Contains the user's Facebook login (which is also an e-mail address).

Databases/plists
friends.db This file contains two tables: "friend" and "meta". The "friend" table stores full details related to the user's Facebook friends, including their first and last names, links to their profile pictures, and phone/cell/email fields, which are encrypted or formatted in a way that is not readable by the examiner.

Analyst notes
In addition to the allocated files recovered from the Application folder, much more app data can be recovered through additional techniques. After running the "strings" command on the entire disk image (refer to the earlier section on "Analysis Techniques" for details on running strings), simply doing a search for the user's Facebook login will recover additional data. Some of this data includes status updates, messages written on the user's wall, and actual messages that were sent to or from the user.

Groupon
Groupon is a service that provides local deals and coupons, allowing users to purchase gift certificates for various businesses at a large discount. The Groupon iPhone application allows the user to purchase, manage, and redeem these coupons through their mobile device. Some of the user's personal information, which is needed for this application, is stored on the device.

File system layout
/private/var/mobile/Applications/<Application   Identifier>/Documents/v1/users/<username>/groupons:

- myGroupons.plist: Contains a list of the Groupons purchased by the user and when they were purchased.
- userInfo.plist: Contains the user's personal information, including full name, address, e-mail address, and more.

/private/var/mobile/Applications/<Application Identifier>/Preferences/:

- com.groupon.grouponapp.plist: Contains user ID and user login (e-mail address).

Databases/plists

myGroupons.plist This file contains a list of the Groupons that were purchased by the user as well as when they were purchased, and the price of the Groupons. The following is an example of the type of data that might be seen for each purchased item:

```
<dict>
    <key>available_quantity</key>
    <real>1</real>
    <key>deal_id</key>
    <string>gap-inc-chicago</string>
    <key>deal_title</key>
    <string>$50 Groupon to Gap</string>
    <key>expires_at</key>
    <string>2010-11-20T05:59:00Z</string>
    <key>price</key>
    <string>25.00USD</string>
    <key>purchased_at</key>
    <string>2010-08-19T18:48:44Z</string>
    <key>total_quantity</key>
    <real>1</real>
    <key>unused_quantity</key>
    <real>1</real>
    <key>updated_at</key>
    <string>2010-08-19T18:48:44Z</string>
    <key>vendor_name</key>
    <string>Gap</string>
</dict>
```

userInfo.plist This file contains a significant amount of personal user information. In order to purchase the Groupons, a user typically sets up a credit card within their account. In this userInfo file, data such as the name, address, expiration date, and last four digits of the credit card number can be recovered (in the following example, the actual credit card numbers were replaced with "1111" for security reasons). The user's personal e-mail address is also stored here.

```
<key>user</key>
<dict>
    <key>billing_records</key>
    <array>
        <dict>
            <key>city</key>
            <string>Oak Park</string>
            <key>country</key>
            <string>United States</string>
            <key>expires_at</key>
            <string>8/2012</string>
            <key>first_name</key>
```

```
                        <string>Katie</string>
                        <key>id</key>
                        <real>2618317</real>
                        <key>last_name</key>
                        <string>Strzempka</string>
                        <key>number</key>
                        <string>****-1111</string>
                        <key>postal_code</key>
                        <string>60301</string>
                        <key>state</key>
                        <string>IL</string>
                        <key>street_address_1</key>
                        <string>1000 Lake Street</string>
                        <key>street_address_2</key>
                        <string></string>
                        <key>type</key>
                        <string>visa</string>
            </dict>
        </array>
        <key>credits_available</key>
        <real>0.0</real>
        <key>email</key>
        <string>test@viaforensics.com</string>
        <key>email_addresses</key>
        <array>
            <string>test@viaforensics.com</string>
        </array>
        <key>first_name</key>
        <string>Katie</string>
        <key>id</key>
        <string>katie-strzempka</string>
        <key>last_name</key>
        <string>Strzempka</string>
        <key>referral_code</key>
        <string>uu2198074</string>
        <key>reward_points_available</key>
        <real>0.0</real>
    </dict>
```

Analyst notes

The information within these files is fairly straightforward. To view the property lists, they have to be first converted from binary to XML using plutil (or another utility). The date and time do not need to be converted. When this app is being analyzed, the plists in the "dealLocations" and "deals" folders should not be confused with those listed under the specific user name. The Groupons listed in those two folders are simply coupons that were available, but the user did not actually purchase them.

Kik Messenger

Kik Messenger is an application downloaded by users in order to replace the existing text messaging application on their device. It is intended to provide a faster, more reliable interface for exchanging messages as well as a replacement for expensive text messaging plans. Just as the SMS App Stores its content, Kik's data is also stored in various locations on the device.

File system layout

/private/var/mobile/Applications/<Application Identifier>/:

- /Documents/kik.sqlite: Stores message content, and user names and display names for all contacts within the app.
- /Library/Preferences/com.kik.chat.plist: Stores user name, password, and e-mail address.

Databases/plists

kik.sqlite Much of the data specific to the applications is stored in the kik.sqlite database. The following lists out the tables within:

```
ZKIKMESSAGE
ZKIKUSER
Z_METADATA
Z_PRIMARYKEY
```

The ZKIKMESSAGE table contains the message content. The following is a listing of the significant columns within this table as well as a description of each:

- ZTIMESTAMP: This is the timestamp (OS X Epoch) that translates to the date and time when the message was sent or received.
- ZBODY: This field contains the message body.

The ZKIKUSER table stores all the contacts within the app. Within this table is each individual's user name, kik.com address ("ZJID"), and display name.

com.kik.chat.plist This file stores a significant amount of sensitive login information, including e-mail address, first and last name, username, and password. An example of the data that can be seen within this plist is as follows:

```
<dict>
    <key>deviceToken</key>
    <string>f32dd7c4ff4644ce2d0f8562a8b4f272a3df3c4a1066e443df2
    ed91bfb0df969</string>
    <key>deviceTokenUpdated</key>
    <false/>
    <key>doAddressBookMatching</key>
    <false/>
    <key>email</key>
    <string>test@viaforensics.com</string>
    <key>emailConfirmed</key>
```

```
        <key>firstName</key>
        <string>Via</string>
        <key>has_asked_to_rate_app</key>
        <key>install_date</key>
        <date>2010-11-09T17:33:50Z</date>
        <key>lastName</key>
        <string>Forensics</string>
        <key>username</key>
        <string>viaForensics</string>
        <key>wipeCoreData</key>
        <key>xmppIsRegistered</key>
        <key>xmppPassword</key>
        <string>789kik123</string>
        <key>xmppUsername</key>
        <string>viaForensics_dvy</string>
    </dict>
```

Analyst notes

The files described in this section contain a significant amount of data; however, this is data that has not been deleted from within the app. To recover deleted information, it is suggested that an examiner use some of the additional analysis techniques described earlier in this chapter. For example, looking at the disk image in a hex editor and searching for a unique user name should recover messages sent to or from that user, including some deleted data.

DropBox

The DropBox iPhone app allows the capability to upload and download files to be stored in the cloud. With this app, users can download or upload files for offline viewing, such as documents, photos, or videos.

File system layout

/private/var/mobile/Applications/<DropBox Application Identifier>/:

- /Documents/Dropbox.sqlite: Contains names of files stored within DropBox for those that have been viewed.
- /Library/Preferences/com.getdropbox.Dropbox.plist: Contains the DropBox username (which is an e-mail address) as well as DropBox favorites.
- /Library/Caches/Dropbox: Contains actual documents.
- /Library/Caches/Three20: Contains JPG images that were uploaded or downloaded to or from DropBox.
- /Library/Caches/Dropbox/FavoriteFiles.plist: Contains files marked by the user as favorites.

Databases/plists

Dropbox.sqlite This database contains the following three tables:

```
ZCACHEDFILE
Z_METADATA
Z_PRIMARYKEY
```

The ZCACHEDFILE table stores files that were viewed by the user as well as the metadata associated with those files. The "ZPATH" column stores the file name, including the full path from DropBox. It also contains an OS X Epoch timestamp for each file in the "ZLASTVIEWED" column, which tells when the user last viewed that particular file.

com.getdropbox.Dropbox.plist This file lists all the files that the user has marked as favorites, as well as other metadata related to those files. The Dropbox user name is also stored here. An example of the data that can be viewed is as follows:

```
<key>Dropbox Favorites</key>
<array>
    <dict>
        <key>bytes</key>
        <integer>289688</integer>
        <key>icon</key>
        <string>page_white_acrobat</string>
        <key>is_deleted</key>
        <false/>
        <key>is_dir</key>
        <false/>
        <key>modified</key>
        <string>Sat, 20 Nov 2010 18:12:13 -0500</string>
        <key>path</key>
        <string>/iPhoneBook/Physical-Acquisition.docx</string>
        <key>revision</key>
        <integer>142384111</integer>
        <key>size</key>
        <string>282.9KB</string>
        <key>thumb_exists</key>
        <false/>
    </dict>
</array>
<key>Dropbox Username</key>
<string>test@viaforensics.com</string>
<key>DropboxBrowseState</key>
```

Analyst notes

In addition to the allocated files described in this section, data carving methods can also be performed on the iPhone.dmg file to recover the actual files that were stored within DropBox, including deleted files. As data carving extracts .doc, .pdf, .jpg, and more, this method can be very useful.

If the iPhone user's computer is also available, be sure to look for a DropBox folder on their machine in order to recover additional files.

Mint.com

Mint.com allows an individual to collectively manage his or her finances in one central location. All bank accounts, investments, loans, and more are synced to this app, allowing users to budget and manage their money accordingly. This particular app also tends to store much of this information on the device.

File system layout

/private/var/mobile/Applications/<Mint.com Application Identifier>/Documents:

*   mint_gala.db: Stores all transactions within the app, including account name, balance information, and a description of the transaction.

Databases/plists

mint_gala.db This database contains several different tables, with many of these tables storing sensitive application data. The following contains a list of the tables within mint_gala.db:

```
account
alert
attributes
budget
budget_overall
category
fi_login
investment
refresh
spending
transaction_bankcc
transaction_usertag
user
user_tag
version
```

The account table stores a list of the accounts synced within the app. Here, an examiner can view the name of the account and the user's balance for each account.

The alert table contains details on the alerts sent to the user. Within the app, there is a setting to allow mint.com to notify the user when a bill is due, or the amount he or she spent within a certain category, or when a deposit went through. Within this table, an examiner can view the details of that particular alert, a Unix Epoch timestamp for when the alert was sent, and the alert "Type" (such as Bill, Overbudget, or Large Deposit).

The transaction_bankcc table stores a detailed description of each transaction completed for each of the accounts. These transactions do not need to be done within the app on the device. For example, for every purchase a user makes on his or her credit card, details related to these purchases will be shown within this table. The following columns within this table contain important data:

- description: A description of the transaction (i.e., Chipotle, Best Buy, Transfer to Chase Checking).
- amount: The amount of money credited or debited for that transaction.
- categoryID: The category this transaction falls under; the category number shown in this field corresponds with the category name shown in the "category" table.
- datePostedString: The date on which the transaction occurred.
- yodDesc: This field contains more details related to the transaction, and depending on the account used, may even contain account numbers.

> **NOTE**
>
> The date shown within the "transaction_bankcc" table does not need to be converted. It is the actual date (i.e., 20101109 = Nov. 9, 2010).

Analyst notes

While only a few of the tables have been discussed, there is additional data in the remaining tables. If an examiner is required to analyze the mint.com mobile app, he or she should be sure to review all the data meticulously so as not to miss any data.

With this particular app, the user has the option to log out of the app. If this is done, no data will be found in the mint_gala.db file. All of this information is still stored on the device, but advanced techniques (such as those discussed earlier in the chapter) are required to recover the data.

Windows Live Messenger

The Windows Live Messenger app allows a user to use instant message, check e-mail, and use certain features within Windows Live, Facebook, and MySpace. When used regularly, some of this data can potentially be recovered from the device.

File system layout

/private/var/mobile/Applications/<Windows Live Messenger Application Identifier>:

- /Documents/CurrentUserName.tmp: Contains the current user's hotmail e-mail address used within the application.

Databases/plists

The CurrentUserName.tmp file is actually a plist, and when analyzed contains the user's hotmail address. This is a binary plist and would typically require a tool such as plutil to be converted to XML; however, as the file contains only the user name, viewing the binary plist to retrieve this data works just as well.

Analyst notes

Aside from the user name (or hotmail e-mail address in this case), Windows Live Messenger did not appear to store specific app data. Keep in mind that version 1.1.1 was analyzed for this example, and future versions may store additional data.

SUMMARY

In this chapter, data and application analysis techniques were covered as well as where data is stored within the iPhone's file system. The task of mounting a disk image on various platforms was mentioned, followed by file carving and other data extraction techniques. Since many files on an iOS device have timestamps associated with them, timeline creation and analysis was mentioned as a key component to any investigation. The reader was walked through the process of installing a timeline analysis kit, running the tool, and finally analyzing the data. Advanced forensic techniques were also covered, specifically using a hex editor to analyze the disk image.

In the next section, the iPhone's file system hierarchy was stepped through in order to point out where common data was stored. The location of data files for default applications as well as downloaded third-party applications was outlined within this section, in addition to other important files that can be crucial to an investigation but are otherwise buried deep within the file system's folder structure.

The chapter is wrapped up with the iPhone application analysis and reference section. Here, a list of popular applications (including those that are incorporated by default on the device) is parsed in order to demonstrate to the reader where important data and files can be found. Also included is a detailed "Analysis Notes" section to describe the recovered files and, more importantly, the interpretation of this data.

References

Apple Inc. (2007, August 23). Time utilities reference. Mac OSX Reference Library. Retrieved February 17, 2011, from http://developer.apple.com/library/mac/# documentation/CoreFoundation/Reference/CFTimeUtils/Reference/reference.html

Carrier, B. (2009, May 18). Mactime output – SleuthKitWiki. Main Page – SleuthKitWiki. Retrieved February 13, 2011, from http://wiki.sleuthkit.org/index.php?title=Mactime_output

Dartmouth College. (n.d.). UNIX file permissions tutorial. Dartmouth College. Retrieved February 17, 2011, from http://www.dartmouth.edu/~rc/help/faq/permissions.html

Digital Assembly: Adroit Photo Forensics – SmartCarving™. (n.d.). Digital assembly – A smart choice for photo forensics. Retrieved February 13, 2011, from http://digital-assembly.com/products/adroit-photo-forensics/features/smartcarving.html

International Data Group. (2011, February 10). iPhone attack reveals passwords in six minutes – Software, security, Phones, operating systems, Mac OS, iPhone, Fraunhofer Institute for

Secure Information Technology, Exploits/vulnerabilities, encryption, consumer electronics. Techworld. Retrieved February 11, 2011, from http://www.techworld.com.au/article/376245/iphone_attack_reveals_passwords_six_minutes/

iPhone GPS Data UPDATE. (2011, February 16). Cellular.Sherlock. Retrieved February 18, 2011, from http://blog.csvance.com/?p=71

Kessler, G. (2011, February 10). File signatures. GaryKessler.net Home Page. Retrieved February 13, 2011, from http://www.garykessler.net/library/file_sigs.html

Kubasiak, R. (n.d.). The Sleuth Kit and Mac OS X. The Apple examiner. Retrieved February 14, 2011, from http://www.appleexaminer.com/MacsAndOS/Analysis/TSK/TSK.html

Richard, G. G.III, (2006, December 8). Scalpel: A frugal, high performance file carver. Digital Forensics Solutions. Retrieved February 9, 2011, from www.digitalforensicssolutions.com/Scalpel/

Zdziarski, J. (2008). *iPhone Forensics: Recovering evidence, personal data & corporate assets (1st ed.).* Beijing/Sebastopol, CA: O'Reilly.

Commercial tool testing

7

CHAPTER POINTS:

- Data Population
- Analysis Methodology
- CelleBrite UFED (Universal Forensics Extraction Device)
- iXAM
- Oxygen Forensic Suite 2010
- XRY
- Lantern
- MacLock Pick
- Mobilyze
- Zdziarski Technique
- Paraben Device Seizure
- MobileSyncBrowser
- CellDEK
- EnCase Neutrino
- iPhone Analyzer

INTRODUCTION

This chapter reviews forensic tools available for the iPhone and walks the reader through a forensic analysis with each tool with a discussion of the installation, acquisition, reporting, and accuracy. The 3G iPhone (firmware version 3.1.3) was used for these tests, as many of the tools did not support iOS 4 at the time of testing. The overall process involves populating the device, performing a logical acquisition with each of the tools, and then analyzing the image to determine the specific data that each piece of software was able to acquire.

DATA POPULATION

The device was first wiped to ensure that it had no data on it prior to the testing of the software. The device was extensively used to simulate the type of data that would be on a typical iPhone, such as the following:

- E-mail, contacts, and calendar (Microsoft Exchange Active Sync with Exchange 2007)
- Web browsing (news, Gmail accounts, Google, etc.)
- Phone calls, voicemail, text messages (some deleted), multimedia messages
- App Store (Facebook, Google Earth, Twitter, Wi-Fi Plus, TripAdvisor, iCamcorder, etc.)
- Wi-Fi network
- Pictures (some deleted)
- YouTube movies
- Google Maps
- Notes
- GPS

Table 7.1 contains details related to the data that was populated on the test device, including expectations regarding the data that should be acquired by each of the tools.

Table 7.1 Test Scenarios

Scenario	Description	Outcome
Call Logs	Determine whether the tool can find call log information on the phone. iPhone contained full populated Call Log, no entries were deleted.	Expect that the tool can connect, acquire, and report on full call log containing 100 records. Expect that remnants of purged logs can be recovered and reported.
Short Message Service (SMS)	Determine whether the tool can find SMS information on the phone. iPhone contained seven SMS conversations, each with multiple messages. Total messages were 49. Deleted two conversations (with three messages) resulting in 46 total messages.	Expect that the tool can connect, acquire, and report on 46 undeleted SMS messages. Expect that remnants of deleted SMS messages can be recovered and reported.
Multimedia Message Service (MMS)	Determine whether the tool can find MMS information on the phone. iPhone contained two MMS messages; neither was deleted.	Expect that the tool can connect, acquire and report on two undeleted MMS messages.
Contacts	Determine whether the tool can find contact information on the phone. iPhone contained 2486	Expect that the tool can connect, acquire, and report on 2483 undeleted contacts. Expect that remnants of three deleted

Table 7.1 Test Scenarios—cont'd

Scenario	Description	Outcome
	contacts. Deleted three contacts resulting in a total of 2483.	contacts can be recovered and reported.
E-mail	Determine whether the tool can find email messages on the phone. iPhone was synchronized with Exchange 2007 and contained thousands of e-mails.	Expect that the tool can connect, acquire, and report on several hundred e-mail messages. Expect that remnants of deleted or purged e-mail messages can be recovered and reported.
Calendar	Determine whether the tool can find calendar information on the phone. Calendar contained four appointments and no entries were intentionally deleted; however, during normal usage some appointments were likely deleted.	Expect that the tool can connect, acquire and report on four calendar items. Expect that remnants of deleted or purged Calendar items can be recovered and reported.
Notes	Determine whether the tool can find notes information on the phone. iPhone contained one note and one note was deleted.	Expect that the tool can connect, acquire, and report on one undeleted note. Expect that remnants of the deleted note can be recovered and reported.
Pictures	Determine whether the tool can find image files on the phone. iPhone contained seven pictures taken with the on-board camera and two were deleted.	Expect that the tool can connect, acquire, and report on five remaining undeleted pictures. Expect that remnants of deleted pictures can be recovered and reported. Expect that pictures downloaded by various iPhone applications including Safari web browser, Facebook application, and more can be recovered and reported
Songs	Determine whether the tool can find music files on the phone. iPhone contained 654 songs synchronized via iTunes from a host PC. No song was deleted.	Expect that the tool can connect, acquire, and report on 654 undeleted music files.
Web History	Determine whether the tool can find web browser history information on the phone.	Expect that the tool can connect, acquire, and report on browser history entries. Expect that remnants of deleted browser history can be recovered and reported.
Bookmarks	Determine whether the tool can find bookmarks from the Safari web browser on the phone. iPhone contained three Safari bookmarks and one was deleted.	Expect that the tool can connect, acquire, and report on two undeleted user bookmarks. Expect that remnants of deleted bookmark messages can be recovered and reported.

Continued

Table 7.1 Test Scenarios—cont'd

Scenario	Description	Outcome
Cookies	Determine whether the tool can find web browser cookie information on the phone. iPhone contained numerous cookie files from web browsing via Safari and other applications.	Expect that the tool can connect, acquire, and, report on Safari cookie files. Expect that cookie files of other applications can be recovered and reported.
Applications	Determine whether the tool can find Application information on the phone. iPhone contained nine Applications and two that were deleted.	Expect that the tool can connect, acquire, and report on seven undeleted applications and their associated information. Expect that remnants of deleted applications can be recovered and reported.
Google Maps	Determine whether the tool can find Google Maps information on the phone. iPhone contained the Google Maps application and it was used for location information and directions. No information was deleted from this application.	Expect that the tool can connect, acquire, and report on Google Maps information including history of location information and directions. Expect that remnants of map tiles (images) can be recovered and reported.
Voicemail	Determine whether the tool can find Voicemail information on the phone. iPhone contained five voice mail messages on the phone and one that was deleted.	Expect that the tool can connect, acquire, and report on four undeleted voice mail messages. Expect that remnants of deleted voicemail can be recovered and reported.
Passwords	Determine whether the tool can find various application and network password information on the phone. iPhone contained various passwords from Applications and network resources such as Wi-Fi, Apple iTunes ID, and more.	Expect that the tool can connect, acquire, and report on application and network passwords. Expect that remnants of deleted passwords can be recovered and reported.
Configuration files	Determine whether the tool can find phone and application configuration files in the XML and Plist formats on the phone. iPhone contained many XML and Plist configuration files. In the course of normal usage, some configuration information would have been deleted	Expect that the tool can connect, acquire, and report on many XML and Plist configuration files. Expect that remnants of deleted configuration files can be recovered and reported.
Phone Information	Determine whether the tool can report on basic phone information. iPhone is a GSM device and contains basic identification information such as	Expect that the tool can connect, acquire, and report on basic phone information listed above.

Table 7.1 Test Scenarios—cont'd

Scenario	Description	Outcome
	IMSI, IMEI, ICCID, MSISDN (phone number), serial number, phone name, Wi-Fi MAC address, and Bluetooth MAC address.	
Video	Determine whether the tool can find video information on the phone. iPhone contained six videos and one deleted video. Two were created using the iCamcorder app and four were imported via iTunes.	Expect that the tool can connect, acquire, and report on five undeleted video files. Expect that remnants of one deleted video file can be recovered and reported.
Speed Dials	Determine whether the tool can find Speed Dial information on the phone. iPhone contained two speed dial (Favorites) and one speed dial was deleted.	Expect that the tool can connect, acquire, and report on one Speed Dial favorite.
GPS	Determine whether the tool can find GPS information on the phone. iPhone contains GPS device and software and many applications use this information.	Expect that the tool can connect, acquire, and report on GPS information including coordinate and date/time from various application usage.
File Hashes	Determine whether the tool creates MD5 or SHA1 hashes for information on the phone.	Expect that the tool will create MD5 hashes for files extracted from the iPhone.
YouTube	Determine whether the tool can find YouTube video information on the phone. iPhone was used to watch YouTube videos via the YouTube application.	Expect that the tool can connect, acquire, and report on YouTube videos viewed.
HTML	Determine whether the tool can find cached HTML files on the phone. iPhone was used to browse many web sites and cached files from this activity are located on the phone.	Expect that the tool can connect, acquire, and report on HTML files on the phone from Safari and other applications.
Office Documents	Determine whether the tool can find Office Documents (PDF, Word, Spreadsheets, and PowerPoint) on the phone. iPhone contained Office Documents that were downloaded through e-mail or the Safari web browser.	Expect that the tool can connect, acquire, and report on Office Documents located on the phone.
Wi-Fi	Determine whether the tool can find Wi-Fi connection information on the phone. iPhone was connected to one Wi-Fi connection; none was deleted.	Expect that the tool can connect, acquire, and report on one Wi-Fi connection.

Table 7.2 Expected Results

Scenario	Description
Call Logs	100
SMS	5 threads/46 total messages (deleted 2 threads/3 total messages)
MMS	2
Contacts	2483 (deleted 3)
E-mail	Synced with Microsoft Exchange and Gmail accounts
Calendar	4 events
Notes	1 (deleted 1)
Pictures	5 (deleted 2)
Songs	654
Web History	No history was deleted
Bookmarks	2 (deleted 1)
Cookies	Unknown
Applications	7 (deleted 2)
Google Maps	Yes
Voicemail	4 (deleted 1)
Passwords	Wi-Fi password
Plists/XML	Unknown
Phone Information	Yes
Video	5: 4 iTunes/1 recorded from device (deleted 1)
Speed Dials	1 (deleted 1)
GPS	Unknown
File Hashes	N/A
YouTube	Unknown
HTML	Unknown
Office Documents	Unknown
Wi-Fi	1 connection

As a result of the data test scenarios, there were certain expectations regarding the type of data that should be acquired. For example, all contacts, call logs, short messaging service (SMS) messages, pictures, etc. that still remained on the device were expected to be acquired regardless of the tool being used. Deleted data may not necessarily be expected from some of the tools as they only support logical acquisitions. Table 7.2 outlines in detail what was expected from each test scenario.

ANALYSIS METHODOLOGY

Once the device was populated, the SIM (subscriber identity module) card was removed and the device placed in airplane mode to prevent further network communication. Prior to the phone being imaged, each piece of software needed to be downloaded and installed. In this chapter, the reader is stepped through the process of examining the iPhone from start to finish. Detailed documentation of the installation process is covered, as are any issues that occurred during the acquisition of the device. If the tool provided reporting capabilities, these are also included. At the end of each section, each piece of software is analyzed for accuracy.

To determine the accuracy of a forensic tool, the results of the acquisition were compared with the expected results outlined in the previous section. Each test scenario was assigned a quantitative number between 0 and 5. If a tool failed to recover any data in a particular area, it was given a rating of 0 for that category. A rating of 1, 2, or 3 indicated that some information was recovered, but it did not meet the expected result. A rating of 4 indicated that the tool met the expected results. A rating of 5 indicated that the tool exceeded the expected result including recovery of deleted data and/or more information than the other tools were able to recover. For readability, the following text description of each rating is also included:

- 0: miss
- 1–3: below
- 4: meet
- 5: above

If a forensic tool provided multiple methods of acquiring information from the iPhone and the analysis took place separately, each method was analyzed on an individual basis and the accuracy determined based on the overall tool.

The goal of this testing was to simply note the differences between the available tools and, most importantly, the data they were capable of acquiring. It was also intended to show other examiners the steps that were involved in the installation and usage of many of the different forensic tools. This analysis is in no way an endorsement of any forensic tool or technique reviewed. Each examiner is strongly encouraged to personally test the forensic tools himself or herself (many offer a demo version) and form his or her own opinions of each product.

In addition, some of these tools have also been tested by the National Institute of Standards and Technology (NIST), a forensic technology agency. In order to develop standards and verify and validate mobile forensic tools, the NIST has started the Computer Forensics Tool Testing (CFTT) Project. For each type of forensic investigation, such as mobile forensics, a test methodology has been developed. This methodology is followed to systematically test each tool based on relevant test cases (NIST, 2010). A report is created, reviewed, and published on the National Institute of Justice (NIJ) website: http://nij.ncjrs.gov/App/publications/Pub_search.aspx? searchtype=basic&category=99&location=top&PSID=55. Table 7.3 provides a list of each tool tested in this paper, and also shows whether this particular software has been tested by the NIST. If the software has not yet been tested, it does not mean the tool should not be used, but just that it has not yet gone through the review process. In addition to the tools displayed in Table 7.3, MOBILedit was also tested by NIST, but it has not been analyzed in this chapter. At the time of testing, MOBILedit did not support the firmware version running on the test device, but it

Table 7.3 Mobile Forensic Tools Tested

Software	Company	Tested by NIST
CelleBrite UFED	Cellebrite	Yes
iXAM	Forensic Telecommunications Services Ltd. (FTS)	Yes
Oxygen Forensic Suite 2010 PRO	Oxygen Software Company	No
XRY	Micro Systemation	Yes
Lantern	Katana Forensics	No
MacLock Pick	SubRosaSoft	No
Mobilyze	Black Bag Technology	Yes
Zdziarski Technique	Jonathan Zdziarski	Yes
Paraben Device Seizure	Paraben Corporation	Yes
MobileSyncBrowser (MSB)	Vaughn S. Cordero	No
CellDEK	Logicube	No
EnCase Neutrino	Guidance Software, Inc.	Yes
iPhone Analyzer	Leo Crawford, Mat Proud	No

has since released updates that support more recent versions. Any mobile forensic tool not listed in the table either did not support the model and firmware version, or the company did not provide a demo version for testing.

CELLEBRITE UFED

The following overview of Cellebrite was provided by the vendor:

- The CelleBrite UFED is a stand-alone, self-contained, fast, and reliable system that provides data extraction of content stored in mobile phones. It can quickly extract critical evidence from over 2500 verified, up-to-date, supported Mobile Devices, that is, Phonebook, Images, Videos, SMS, and Call History, and much more. With little to no set-up time and no PC or frustrating drivers to install for extraction, a first responder can easily and reliably preserve and acquire on-scene evidence in real time.
- CelleBrite works exclusively with over 140 carriers worldwide including Verizon Wireless, AT&T, Sprint/Nextel, T-Mobile, Alltel, US Cellular, Cricket, Rogers, Bell Mobility, Orange France, Telstra Australia, Orange, Vodafone, SFR, and O2.
- The CelleBrite UFED also has a built-in SIM card reader and cloner. The ability to clone a SIM card is a powerful feature, as one can create and insert a clone of the original SIM to make the phone function normally. However, it will not register on the mobile carrier's network, eliminating the need for Faraday bags and the

possibility that the data on the phone might be updated (or erased). The UFED package ships with about 72 cables for connecting to most mobile devices available today. Connection protocols include serial, USB, infrared, and Bluetooth.

- Data is extracted onto a USB Flash drive or SD card and is organized in clear and concise reports. CelleBrite also distributes the UFED Report Manager, which provides an intuitive reporting interface and allows the user to export data/reports into Excel, MS Outlook, Outlook Express, and CSV, or to simply print the report. The UFED device fully supports Unicode and thus can process phones enabled with any language. The following data types are also extracted:

  ○ Phonebook Extraction (~95% of all cellular handsets on the market today)
  ○ Multimedia Extraction (~75% of all CDMA and 95% of all GSM handsets) – Pictures, Video, Text messages, and Audio
  ○ Additional extractions: Missed/Dialed/Received, ESN/IMEI, Deleted SMS Messages (SIM/USIM only), Deleted Call History (SIM/USIM only), Deleted Contacts
  ○ Additional Features: PC reporting tool (MD5 Hash & SHA256 Signature), SIM ID Cloning
  ○ System Files Dump/ Hierarchical "tree" (Beta- ~800 devices supported)
  ○ New Apple iPhone Support (2G, 3G/3GS, and iPhone 4 versions jailbroken and non-jailbroken)
  ○ # Multi-Language User Interface

Installation

The UFED package should contain the UFED device, manuals/CD, USB Bluetooth radio (Cambridge Silicon Radio Ltd.), 250 MB USB drive, and roughly 72 cables for connecting to supported devices. The manual was sparse but sufficient and very straightforward.

To start things off, the UFED software version should be checked to ensure that it was up to date. There are options to update via a PC, USB, or SD card, or via the Internet.

For this update, the online upgrade feature is utilized. When the UFED is first powered on, the date/time must be set. Next, the device is connected via an Ethernet cable to a switch running DHCP. To begin the upgrade, Services → Upgrade → Upgrade Application Now should be selected as well as HTTP Server as the source.

> **WARNING:**
> If the download freezes prior to completion, try connecting to a different switch.

A few minutes later, the device should be upgraded to the latest application software that supplies the UFED application and support for the various phones. CelleBrite seems to add new phone support often, and a forensic examiner should check for updates frequently. The version used for this test was 1.1.4.4.

The UFED contains two other pieces of software termed "Images." One dubbed "Tiny" contains the core system software. The other image named "Full" contains additional core system software. Both were up to date (1.0.2.1 and 1.0.2.4, respectively). The update process for the Image software is under a separate menu in Services and the updates are performed independently.

Forensic acquisition

The acquisition of the 3G iPhone was simple and fast on the UFED (with the exception of acquiring audio files). After powering the device on, the following was selected: Extract Phone Data, Apple, iPhone 2G/3G, USB disk drive (destination), Content types (F2 was pressed to select all including Call Logs, Phonebook, SMS, Pictures, Videos, and Audio/Music) and was then instructed to connect the iPhone to the source port with Connect cable 110 and the USB disk drive into the target port. After entering the passcode, the extraction began. The total estimated time was approximately 4 h. Since most of this time was allotted to the "Audio/Music" files, it was decided that all other categories would be extracted first. After removing the "Audio/Music" files, the extraction took 5 min, and the files were copied into an automatically created folder on the attached USB drive.

Next, Audio/Music files were extracted, which was estimated to take just under 4 h. Throughout this process, the examiner is prompted to enter the passcode and click "continue" every so often. This requires sitting next to the device the whole time for the acquisition to continue. If Audio/Music files are not necessary for your investigation, you may want to skip them. However, the extraction took 1 h and 30 min, which was much less than the estimated time.

Also performed was a File System dump of the iPhone using UFED's Physical Analyzer. This software provides physical extraction support, and in this case, provided file system dump capabilities. The Physical Analyzer installation CD was used to quickly and easily install this software on the PC used for testing. The File System Dump option extracts all accessible files using a logical process. To do this, File System Dump was selected, then Apple, iPhone 2G/3G, and PC (destination). The user is then prompted to click "Read Data from UFED" within Physical Analyzer, and then "Start" to begin the process. The File System Dump took a couple of hours, and a .zip file was automatically created in the specified destination folder. Also in this folder is a "UFED Dump" file which can be opened and viewed as a report in the UFED Physical Analyzer software.

Results and reporting

> **NOTE:**
> Since UFED has both a "standard" acquisition process and a File System Dump option, please note there are two sections detailing the results.

Standard acquisition results

The standard acquisition resulted in a roughly 160 MB folder containing the extracted audio and images, proprietary files with extensions such as .SMS and .PBB, and reports in both HTML and XML containing the following sections: Contacts, SMS, Call Logs, Images, Ringtones (Not Supported), Audio, and Video. The files can be easily viewed by opening the UFED Content Manager file into the UFED Report Manager for a user-friendly interface. Another option is to also view the "Report. htm" file which is created on the USB by default.

When you run UFED Report Manager, you can import the data from the USB drive by clicking on File → Open Extraction (from folder). You can then add Optional Information including case, examiner, and other investigation information.

Along the left-hand side, you can see the major areas of focus, including Optional Information, Report, Contacts, SMS, Call Log, Images, Videos, Audio, and Ringtones. Figure 7.1 shows some basic information included in the Report section.

The Images section previews all the images found, as shown in Figure 7.2. You can also open the Image files from the Report Manager. EXIF data in an image can be viewed by looking at the properties of the file in Windows.

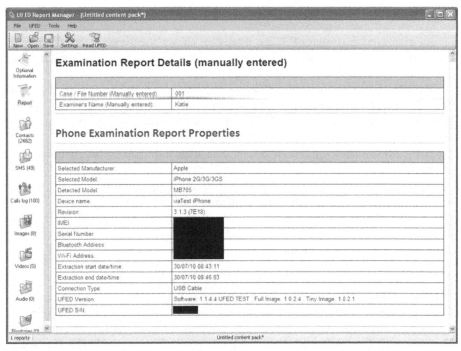

FIGURE 7.1

UFED Report.

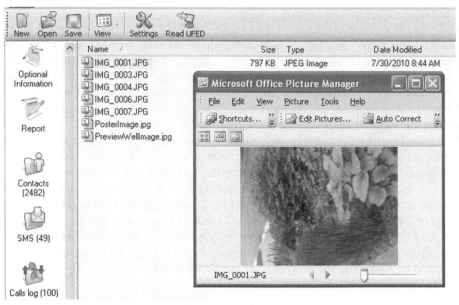

FIGURE 7.2

UFED Images.

As displayed in Figure 7.3, the Call Log shows the type of call (Outgoing, Incoming, or Missed) as well as the Name (if found in Contacts), phone number, date/time, and duration.

The SMS section shows the full set of messages and a detailed message window (see Figure 7.4). The details include Number, Name, Message, date/time, SMSC, Status (Sent, Read, Unsent, etc.), Folder where it was stored, and the type (Incoming or Outgoing).

The Audio section contains all the audio (iTunes) .mp3 files. Voicemails were not included in this section.

Figure 7.5 displays the user's contacts information, including name, various numbers, and text fields including company name, e-mail address, notes, etc.

The data can be extracted into Excel (or CSV) as well as imported directly into Outlook or Outlook Express. While this is an interesting feature, importing the information into Outlook would not be needed in most situations.

Physical Analyzer (File System Dump) results

The File System Dump acquisition was 3.76 GB. The top level folder included the following three subfolders: AFC Service, Backup Service, and Lockdown Service. The majority of the data were songs under the AFC Service $\rightarrow$ iTunes_Control $\rightarrow$ Music directory. The Backup directory contains important database, Plist, and other files allowing a more complete recovery of data from the iPhone.

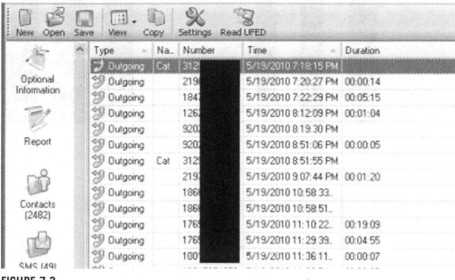

FIGURE 7.3

UFED Call Log.

FIGURE 7.4

UFED SMS.

When imported into Physical Analyzer, the software provided a summary of the data acquired, as shown in Figure 7.6.

The File System Dump got several more items than the standard extraction, including additional Call Logs, MMS, Notes, Web History, Bookmarks, Cookies, Applications, Voicemails, and more. Figure 7.7 displays two deleted call logs that were retrieved.

Also retrieved was an additional "deleted" SMS message; however, this was most likely a draft, as the Status reads "Unsent." This message also did not contain a phone number or any text content.

The keychain-2.db SQLite database contained information about the networks the user attached to, including Wi-Fi, VPN, Bluetooth, and the Apple iTunes store ID.

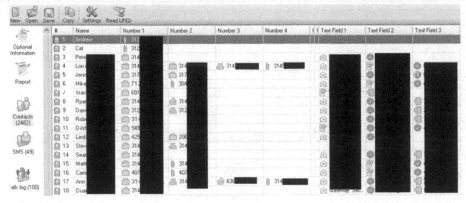

FIGURE 7.5

Contacts.

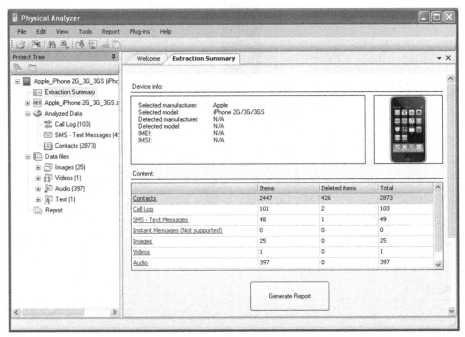

FIGURE 7.6

Physical Analyzer – File System Dump Summary.

Outgoing Calls

Number of entries: 89

#	Type	Number	Name	Date & Time	Duration	Deleted
1	Outgoing	3124939636		5/19/2010 3:40:07 PM	00:00:03	Yes
2	Outgoing	18664365709		5/19/2010 2:50:55 AM	00:00:00	Yes
3	Outgoing	3129334567		5/19/2010 7:18:15 PM	00:00:00	No
4	Outgoing	2196806986		5/19/2010 7:20:27 PM	00:00:14	No

FIGURE 7.7

Physical Analyzer – Deleted Call Logs.

In addition, other SQLite databases under the Documents folder contained information from some App Store programs such as Pinch Media (used to take video on the device) and Facebook and could provide valuable information to the investigator. All this was done without jailbreaking the phone, a major plus for any forensic investigation. By analyzing the SQLite databases and Plist files, an investigator can recover deleted information as well as important configuration and usage information.

A report was then generated that contained all of the acquired data. The report is first generated within the Physical Analyzer application; then the user has the option to export it to HTML, PDF, XML, or just open it in a browser. In this example, an html report was created, with the "Summary" section of the report shown in Figure 7.8.

The report includes the following sections: Summary, Device Information, Geotags, Contacts, SMS – Text Messages, Call Logs, Images, Videos, Audio, and Text. All the information is displayed in an easy-to-read format. For the sections that contain actual files (such as videos, music files, pictures, or voicemails), there is a link allowing the examiner to access the file itself. This is helpful because videos can be viewed and voicemails listened to.

One of the sections within the report is "Geotags" on Google Earth. Once you click the "Open Externally" link, information on the Google Maps locations is displayed within XML format. The data includes the camera make and model (in this case Apple iPhone 3G), the Google Maps link, and latitude and longitude information, as shown in Figure 7.9.

A summary of the accuracy results is shown in Figure 7.10.

Extraction Summary

Selected manufacturer:	Apple
Selected model:	iPhone 2G/3G/3GS
Extraction start date/time:	7/20/2010 5:20:20 PM
Extraction end date/time:	7/21/2010 9:26:09 AM
UFED S/N:	███████████
UFED version:	1.1.4.4
UFED Physical Analyzer version:	1.9.0.4957
Connection type:	Cable No. 110
Image #1:	File name: Apple_iPhone 2G_3G_3GS.zip
Case/File number:	001
Examiner name:	Katie
Department:	
Location:	
Notes:	

Device Information

Detected manufacturer:	N/A
Detected model:	N/A

FIGURE 7.8

Generated HTML Report.

```
- <description>
  - <![CDATA[
      <br/><table><tr><td colspan="2"><img src='../Images/IMG_0007.JPG' width='640'
      height='480'></td></tr>
      <tr><td width="300">Resolution:</td><td>72x72 (Unit: Inch)</td></tr>
      <tr><td width="300">Pixel resolution:</td><td>1600x1200</td></tr>
      <tr><td width="300">Bits per pixel:</td><td>24</td></tr>
      <tr><td width="300">Camera Make:</td><td>Apple</td></tr>
      <tr><td width="300">Camera Model:</td><td>iPhone 3G</td></tr>
      <tr><td width="300">Lat/Lon:</td><td>41.88867 / -87.80267</td></tr>
      <tr><td width="300">Google Maps Link:</td><td><a target="_blank" href="http://maps.google.com/
      <tr><td width="300">Latitude:</td><td>41.88867</td></tr>
      <tr><td width="300">Longitude:</td><td>-87.80267</td></tr>
      <tr><td width="300">Camera Make:</td><td>Apple</td></tr>
      <tr><td width="300">Camera Model:</td><td>iPhone 3G</td></tr>
      <tr><td width="300">Orientation:</td><td>6</td></tr>
      <tr><td width="300">X Resolution:</td><td>72</td></tr>
      <tr><td width="300">Y Resolution:</td><td>72</td></tr>
      <tr><td width="300">Resolution Unit:</td><td>Inches</td></tr>
```

FIGURE 7.9

XML Geotags Information.

Scenario	Cellebrite - Direct	Ranking	Cellebrite - File System Dump	Ranking	UFED Total	Results
Call Logs	100	4	103	5	5	Above
SMS (allocated)	46	5	46	5	5	Above
SMS (unallocated)	0	0	0	0	0	Miss
MMS	Messages, but no pictures	1	2	4	4	Meet
Contacts	2482	4	2873 (some are duplicates)	4	4	Meet
Email	0	0	0	0	0	Miss
Calendar	0	0	4	4	4	Meet
Notes	0	0	2 (1 deleted)	5	5	Above
Pictures (allocated)	5	5	5	5	5	Above
Pictures (unallocated)	0	0	0	0	0	Miss
Screenshots	0	0	0	0	0	Miss
Songs	392	2	392	2	2	Below
Web History	0	0	Yes	4	4	Meet
Bookmarks	0	0	2	4	4	Meet
Cookies	0	0	Yes	4	4	Meet
Applications	0	0	7 (found in plist)	4	4	Meet
Google Maps	0	0	2 histories	4	4	Meet
Voicemail	0	0	5	4	4	Meet
Passwords	No	0	No	0	0	Miss
Plists/XML	0	0	152	5	5	Above
Phone Information	Yes	4	Yes	4	4	Meet
Video	0	0	1 (no iTunes videos)	2	2	Below
Speed Dials	0	0	1	4	4	Meet
GPS	0	0	Yes	4	4	Meet
File Hashes	Yes	4	Yes	4	4	Meet
YouTube	0	0	Searches and history	4	4	Meet
HTML	0	0	0	0	0	Miss
Office Documents	0	0	0	0	0	Miss
Wifi	No	0	Yes	4	4	Meet

FIGURE 7.10

CelleBrite UFED Matrix of Results.

iXAM

The following overview of iXAM was provided by the vendor:

- Zero-Footprint Forensic Acquisition for Apple iPhone™ and iPod Touch™
- iXAM® is able to provide comprehensive noninvasive data recovery from the Apple iPhone™ and iPod Touch™.

- iXAM® has been proven to deliver a range of information potentially vital to law enforcement investigation, providing anything from a stored contact or text message to an e-mail, photograph, or specific map location. The forensic read is a byte-level physical data copy which can be set to target specific data sets or the entire file system.
- Our secure extraction technique creates a full forensic image of the device via USB download, which can be retained for additional investigations in the future. An evidential report can then be produced along with an XML audit trail covering the data extraction process.
- iXAM® has recently been tested and verified by the NIST.

> **NOTE**
> iXAM® has recently been tested and verified by the National Institute of Standards and Technology (NIST)

Installation

The iXAM package arrived with a dongle, USB drive with software files and installation guide, and registration information. iXAM hosts an FTP site to which users can connect and get updated software. In this case, the site was accessed and recent updates downloaded. With the instructions provided, this was a simple task. Prior to installation, the "provisioning" process must be completed on an Internet-connected machine. This step needs to be performed only once per USB media device. The manual provides a much more detailed description of this process. After the provisioning process was complete, which took about 5 min, the installation was started via the setup.exe file provided. Prerequisites were first installed, which involved several prompts the user had to accept in order to continue with the process. Once the software was installed, a postinstallation sequence was performed to purge all existing Apple Device drivers. The entire installation process, including provisioning and postinstallation, took approximately 20 min.

Forensic acquisition

After first installing iXAM, the user is prompted to configure the software. In other words, the examiner is asked to set a standard directory in which they want all case files to be created. The instructions in the manual take the user through each of the settings and explain what they mean. Once this step is complete, the device is ready to be acquired.

The acquisition of the 3G iPhone was a complex process, partially because it was being done through a virtual machine. iXAM immediately found the connected device and proceeded to walk through the instructions on the method of acquiring data off the device. The iPhone was first powered off and then placed in DFU mode (refer to Chapter 2 for more information on the various operating modes) with the help of a timer in the upper right-hand corner.

The next step involved installing drivers. Because a virtual machine was being used for testing, the device had to be manually connected each time a driver needed to be installed; otherwise, the driver-installed wizard would not be displayed. It is assumed that this would not be an issue when using a physical machine.

Following this step, the Stage 1 bootloader had to be sent to the device. Next, the user was asked to verify the hardware (Figure 7.11) after which Stage 2 and Stage 3 bootloaders were sent to the iPhone. Again, there were issues because the device kept getting disconnected from the virtual machine and had to be reconnected; but after getting past this, all stages completed successfully. The phone was then ready for imaging.

The "Forensic Image" option was chosen as opposed to a logical download. Next, the Case information was completed, and "Begin Download" selected. The total acquisition time was estimated to take about 85 h, so the imaging was run over the weekend. The imaging was started on a Friday evening and completed the following Tuesday morning at 4:53 a.m. (see Figure 7.12); however, the use of a virtual machine in testing could have been one reason for the excessive amount of time. The next release of iXAM is expected to decrease the acquisition time by 75%.

Results and reporting

The standard acquisition resulted in a 14.6 GB DMG file. To view this image, it was first mounted as read-only on a Macintosh. Here, the directory structure could be browsed through in order to find a majority of the items. Most of the standard data

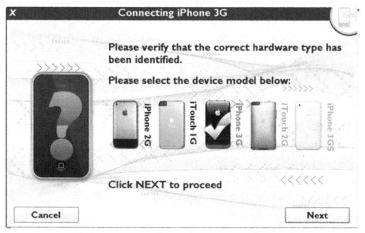

FIGURE 7.11

Verify Hardware.

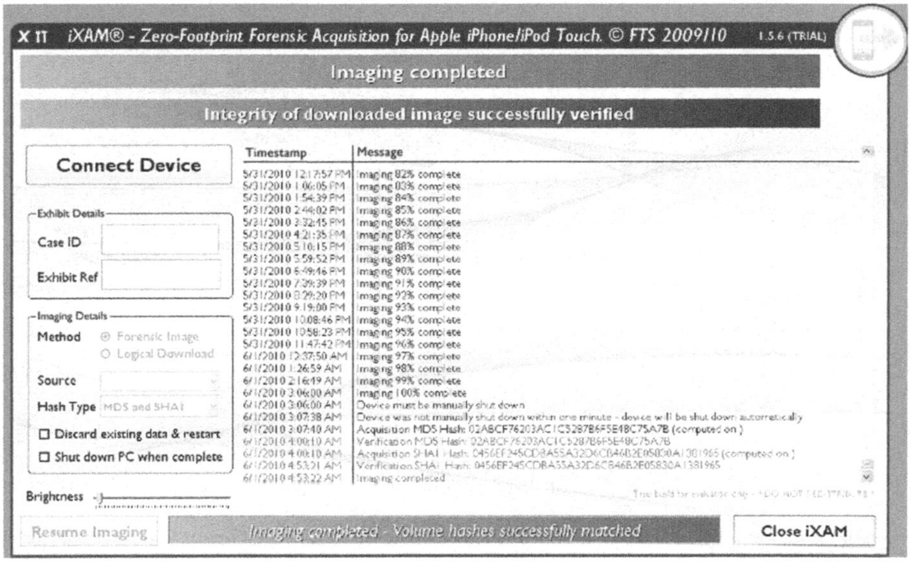

FIGURE 7.12

Forensic Image – Acquisition Complete.

could be viewed by looking at the database and plist files, including Call Logs, Contacts, SMS, Calendar Events, Pictures, etc.

Following the initial browsing, iXAMiner, which is iXAM's reporting tool, was used. The log file or backup files can be used as a data source. During an attempt to choose the log file, an HFS Driver error popped up, which said "There is either no HFS file system driver installed, or the driver is not working correctly. Please ensure that one is installed and functions." The manual states that this error message is received because iXAMiner requires the installation of Macdrive software in order to parse the image file. When iXAM was contacted, it was explained that future releases will include a native HFS reader to remove the reliance on third-party software.

Next, the backup files were chosen as the data source, and the user had the option to select from the categories shown in Figure 7.13 in order to create the report.

All options were selected first, and then "Analyze Data." This process took about 5 min, and the results were exported into an Excel file, with a different tab for each category. All logical data was parsed, with an example of the speed dials shown in Figure 7.14. One nice feature of this tool is that it also shows the filename and path of the data source. For example, below, the speed dial information was gathered from the com.apple.mobilephone.speeddial.plist file. This is helpful for an examiner to explain where the data originated.

With the reporting tool, only allocated files could be viewed. Having the .dmg file is beneficial, because various Linux tools could be run in order to parse out

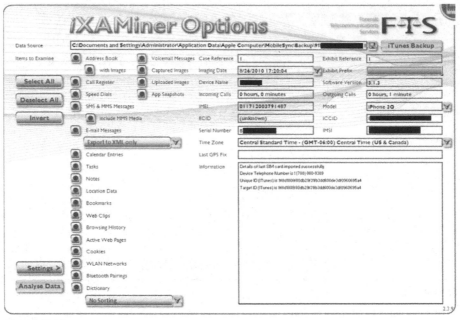

FIGURE 7.13

iXAMiner Main Screen.

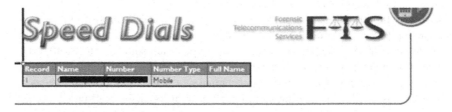

FIGURE 7.14

Speed Dials/Favorites.

unallocated data. Scalpel was first used to perform file carving on the dmg file to see whether deleted items could be recovered. The data within these files could easily be viewed by opening each file with the appropriate application (in this case, SQLite Database Browser v1.3 was used for the .db files, and textedit for the .plist files).

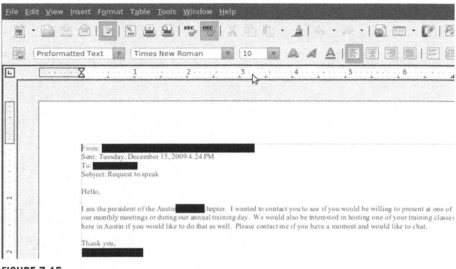

FIGURE 7.15

Recovered E-mails.

E-mails were significant pieces of information that were recovered. In the mounted image, only mailbox information and contacts could be viewed, not the message content itself. With scalpel, each e-mail file could be opened using a text editor and all the content viewed. Specific keywords known to be on sent, received, or deleted e-mails on the device were searched. Each of these keywords was able to be located as well as the e-mail content surrounding them (Figure 7.15).

The resulting scalpel files also included hundreds of .jpg, .gif, and .png images. Looking through these, one of the two photos that were deleted from the iPhone was able to be recovered. Also among these files were snapshots of the iPhone at random points in time. When a user switches between applications, the iPhone automatically takes a screen shot of the device prior to changing. Because of this, many images of this nature were recovered.

The next item looked at was potential deleted SMS messages. To do this, the "strings" command was run on the entire image to search for specific keywords. All SMS messages were located, including the three known deleted messages. An example of the command and output is shown in Figure 7.16.

A summary of the accuracy results is shown in Figure 7.17.

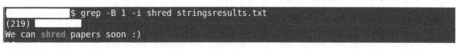

FIGURE 7.16

Strings Output – Deleted SMS.

Scenario	iXAM Results	Ranking	Results
Call Logs	100	4	Meet
SMS (allocated)	46	5	Above
SMS (unallocated)	3	5	Above
MMS	2	4	Meet
Contacts	2483	4	Meet
Email	250 e-mail files from scalpel	5	Above
Calendar	4	4	Meet
Notes	2 (1 deleted)	5	Above
Pictures (allocated)	5	5	Above
Pictures (unallocated)	6 taken from phone (1 deleted) + 21 gif, 251 jpg, and 1,291 png	5	Above
Screenshots	Yes (images recovered in scalpel)	5	Above
Songs	654	4	Meet
Web History	Yes + screenshots of web browsing	5	Above
Bookmarks	2	4	Meet
Cookies	Yes	4	Meet
Applications	7 (plus screen shots of 2 deleted apps)	5	Above
Google Maps	2 histories + map tiles	5	Above
Voicemail	5	4	Meet
Passwords	0	0	Miss
Plists/XML	Yes, 2,711 plists	5	Above
Phone Information	Yes	4	Meet
Video	5 (4 iTunes videos)	5	Above
Speed Dials	1	4	Meet
GPS	Yes	4	Meet
File Hashes	Yes	4	Meet
YouTube	Searches and history	4	Meet
HTML	47 files (including some emails)	5	Above
Office Documents	Screenshot of excel file	2	Below
Wifi	Yes	4	Meet

FIGURE 7.17

iXAM Matrix of Results.

OXYGEN FORENSIC SUITE 2010

The following overview of Oxygen Forensic Suite 2010 was provided by the vendor:

- Oxygen Forensic Suite 2010 is mobile forensic software that goes beyond standard logical analysis of cell phones, smart phones, and PDAs. Use of advanced proprietary protocols and phone APIs makes it possible to pull much more data than can be extracted by forensic tools utilizing standard logical protocols, especially for smart phones.

- Oxygen Forensic Suite 2010 helps you to extract most of the information from a great majority of mobile devices for investigation purposes. This program has played a significant role in criminal and other investigations all over the world and is used by Law Enforcement units, Police Departments, army, customs and tax services, and other government authorities.
- Current software version provides access to the following sections: Phonebook, Calendar, Tasks, Messages, Event Log, File Browser and Extras (Life Blog, Phone Activity, Wi-Fi Connections, Skype, and Web Cache analyzer). It is to be noted that the number of sections and list of extractable data fields depends on the device model.

You can examine:

- Common phone information
- Contact list (including mobile, wire line, fax numbers, postal addresses, e-mails, contact photos and other contact information)
- Missed/outgoing/incoming calls
- Caller Groups information
- Organizer data
- SMS messages (messages, log, folders, deleted messages with some restrictions)
- Multimedia messages with attachments
- E-mail messages with attachments and folders
- GPRS, EDGE, CSD, HSCSD, Wi-Fi session log and traffic amount
- Photos and gallery images
- Video clips and films
- Voice records and audio clips
- All files from internal phone memory
- GPS and XMP coordinates stored in camera snapshots
- Web browsers bookmarks and cache files
- iPhone password-protected backups
- Skype information
- Wi-Fi connections

- Oxygen Forensic Suite 2010 offers an easy and convenient management of all examined devices in one window: phone properties, case details and status, the person in charge of it, etc.
- Mobile device information analysis can be done from the program directly or with the help of advanced export function. You can create reports in the most popular file formats (XLS, RTF, PDF, XML, CSV, TSV) and either print or send them to remote departments and experts.
- The program has a powerful built-in search engine. You can easily find the necessary information in all the sections with few mouse clicks in Oxygen Forensic Suite 2010. What is important, the search results are saved between

sessions and can be either exported or printed. Besides, a contextual filter in every section helps you to sort out the data the way you need it.

- Oxygen Forensic Suite 2010 contains two viewers that can open database as well as .plist files.
- Moreover, the software allows you to save extracted data to a file and then load it into the program on another computer. Thus you need to connect a phone and extract data only once and then send the extracted information outside, for example for analysis by remote experts.
- Current version works with more than 1600 mobile devices from Nokia, Apple (iPhone 2G, 3G, 3GS), RIM (Blackberry), Google (based on Android OS), Samsung, Sony Ericsson, Motorola, Panasonic, LG, HTC, Asus, HP, and other manufacturers.
- Oxygen Forensic Suite 2010 has a strong support for Symbian OS and Windows Mobile 5/6 smart phones and communicators (ActiveSync is not required). Upcoming versions will have support for Android devices too. The list of supported models is rapidly growing. Oxygen Forensic Suite 2010 supports USB cable connection, Bluetooth (Microsoft, Widcomm, BlueSoleil) connection, infrared connection using IrDA stack. Support for different types of connection depends on the phone series and model.
- The software works under 32-bit or 64-bit versions of Windows 7, Windows Vista, Windows XP, Windows Server 2003 and Windows 2000.

Installation

Oxygen Forensic Suite 2010 PRO was downloaded from Oxygen's website, and minutes later an automated e-mail was received with a registration code, activation key, and contact information. The registration code was updated using the instructions provided, and the setup.exe file initiated. The software was installed and ready to go within minutes. Oxygen Forensic Suite does not require a dongle, but the activation key (which was attached to the automated e-mail) had to be entered prior to use. The version used at the time of testing was 2.7.0.232.

Forensic acquisition

The acquisition of the iPhone was simple and straightforward. After selecting the "Connect new device" link, the user is prompted to choose a connection type. Since the device was physically connected to the workstation, the "connect via Cable" option was chosen, rather than Bluetooth or Infrared. There were some minor issues getting the software to "see" the device. After several unsuccessful connection attempts, the error message conveniently provides a link that allows the examiner to e-mail the error to Oxygen technical support. Tech support responded to all queries within 24 h (however, it is important to note that tech support is overseas, so most e-mail responses arrive overnight in the United States). The solution was to install the latest version of iTunes. The device could then be connected after the software was restarted.

When prompted to select the data types to be extracted from the device, the option to do a full file structure reading and acquire all data from the device was selected.

The entire acquisition took approximately 10 min. When it is complete, the user has the option to open the device and analyze, or create a report. In this test, the device was immediately analyzed, and the report created at a later time.

Results and reporting

The standard acquisition resulted in the following categories along the left-hand side: Device Info, Phonebook, Calendar, Notes, Messages, Event Log, File Browser, and Extras (see Figure 7.18).

The Device Info section includes model number, software revision, and serial number, also showing whether the device has been jailbroken. On the left-hand side, there is also "device extended information," which provides more details than many

FIGURE 7.18

Device Info.

of the other tools. Wi-Fi and bluetooth MAC addresses are given, along with SIM status and other information.

Also included in this section is information on the acquisition, namely extraction time and hash algorithm.

The Phonebook contains contact info, e-mail address, address, notes, and MD5 Hash value for each contact, provided this information was entered in the device. Calendar events are parsed out and displayed one at a time on each row, including start and end time, alarm (if set), and the text content of the appointment.

Notes can also be viewed within the software, as shown in Figure 7.19. While the tool did not display the one note that was deleted from the phone, this note was later found in the "notes.idx" file (located in the "Extras" section discussed below).

The Messages section includes all SMS and MMS messages that were sent or received, the phone number of both parties, a timestamp, the content of the message, and MD5 Hash value. Also included is the location: whether the message was recovered from the SMS "Inbox" or "Sent" folder, indicating whether it was outgoing or incoming.

The Event Log contains all call logs including the phone number, call duration, timestamp, and MD5 Hash value. Separate tabs are also provided if you wish to look only at answered, received, or missed calls.

File Browser is the next section, and this is where images, songs, videos, and other documents and files can be found (see Figure 7.20). GPS coordinates are provided for each image (if available). An "Applications" tab is also included in this section, but it was empty and did not contain any of the applications downloaded on the iPhone used for testing. Nonetheless, a full directory structure is provided, allowing an examiner to look at each and every file on the device and, from there, determine the significance of that file. Within this directory was the "Applications" folder containing each of the applications on the device.

Oxygen Forensic Suite also provides a Search functionality. You can search for either text or contact activity. The search for text function simply finds all occurrences of the specified text in all phones, or just those that are selected. The "Search for contact" feature allows you to enter only part of any contact data – name, phone number, or other fields. If the program finds a contact satisfying the search criteria, it analyzes all phone numbers, e-mails, and other fields of this contact and starts searching for any of this information through all sections of specified mobile devices. By double-clicking on the entry, you can switch to the corresponding section of the relevant phone for more detailed analysis. All search results can then be saved, printed, or exported, and reused later.

Time ▲	Text	MD5 Hash
5/19/2010 01:36	Check on loans	7294fc14693f17e1b3a24cda688eb426

FIGURE 7.19

Notes.

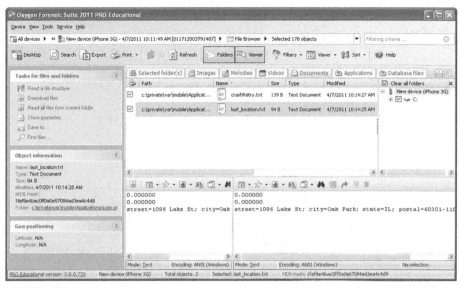

FIGURE 7.20

File Browser.

The final section is Extras (see Figure 7.21), which includes information related to any Wi-Fi connections, Internet history cache files, Skype information (if applicable), and an "Activity" link that allows the examiner to sort all phone activity according to date, remote party, or contact. The Wi-Fi connection information extracted from the test device contained a lot of important information. Geo location data was provided for this particular SSID as well as the last time the device joined automatically and the last time a user initiated the joint. This is vital information that could be used to determine where a person was at a certain point in time.

Figure 7.22 contains the results from the Oxygen Forensic Suite 2010 PRO.

XRY

The following overview of XRY was provided by the vendor:

- XRY is a dedicated mobile device forensic tool developed by Micro Systemation (MSAB) based in Stockholm.
- XRY has been available since 2002 and "XRY Complete" is a package containing both software and hardware to allow both Logical and Physical analysis of mobile devices. The product comes shipped in a handy portable case with bespoke interior and all the necessary hardware included:

  ○ XRY Forensic Pack Software License Key
  ○ Communication Hub for USB, Bluetooth, and Infrared connectivity

FIGURE 7.21

Extras (Browser Cache Files).

- ○ SIM Id Cloner Device
- ○ Pack of SIM Clone Cards
- ○ Write-Protected Universal Memory Card Reader
- ○ Complete set of Cables for Logical and Physical acquisition
- ○ XACT Hex Viewer Software Application
- ○ XRY Reader Tool for distribution to third parties

- XRY was designed and refined with the input of forensic investigators and a wizard guides you through the entire process to assist the examination. The new unified Logical/Physical extraction Wizard and the resulting reports help to show the examiner the full contents of the device in a neat, clean, and professional manner.

Scenario	Oxygen Results	Ranking	Results
Call Logs	100	4	Meet
SMS (allocated)	46	5	Above
SMS (unallocated)	0	0	Miss
MMS	2	4	Meet
Contacts	2483	4	Meet
Email	Content in Webkit database	3	Below
Calendar	4	4	Meet
Notes	2 (1 deleted)	5	Above
Pictures (allocated)	5	5	Above
Pictures (unallocated)	0	0	Miss
Screenshots	0	0	Miss
Songs	604	2	Below
Web History	Yes	4	Meet
Bookmarks	2	4	Meet
Cookies	Yes	4	Meet
Applications	7	4	Meet
Google Maps	2 histories	4	Meet
Voicemail	5	4	Meet
Passwords	0	0	Miss
Plists/XML	Yes, 83 plists	4	Meet
Phone Information	Yes	4	Meet
Video	1 (no iTunes videos)	2	Below
Speed Dials	1	4	Meet
GPS	Yes (Geo location provided for each image)	4	Meet
File Hashes	Yes	4	Meet
YouTube	Searches and history	4	Meet
HTML	0	0	Miss
Office Documents	0	0	Miss
Wifi	Yes, in Extras	4	Meet

FIGURE 7.22

Oxygen Matrix of Results.

- One of the unique features of XRY is the Device Manual containing a complete and detailed list of the available support for each device: identifying the data that can be retrieved, and also what cannot be recovered which is sometimes just as relevant to investigators.
- All extractions, Logical or Physical, are saved in a XRY file, which remains unaltered, for forensic security purposes. From this file, one can create reports as required in Word, Excel, Open Office, or PDF. Case data and references can be included, data that is included in the report, or otherwise, can be chosen, and then it can be distributed to other parties involved in the investigation: lawyers, prosecutors, or other investigators. MSAB offers a free XRY reader and this can be provided to third parties to allow them to make notes on the report while maintaining the original forensic integrity of the data.

- Within the package is the XACT Hex Viewer application to undertake more detailed examination of the raw data recovered and assist with searching and manual decoding to supplement the automatic decoding available in XRY Physical.

> Version 5.1 of the XRY Forensic Pack was released on June 28, 2010 with additional support for the Apple iPad.

Installation

XRY was installed via the setup.exe file. The installation wizard walked the user through everything step by step, and the entire process took approximately 15 min. Also received was a software update, which was downloaded and run as an executable, and the updated patch was applied within seconds. An activation/registration key was not needed, but a USB dongle was required to run the software.

Forensic acquisition

Once XRY was running, the option to start an acquisition was selected. The user is prompted to select a type of examination from the following options: Logical, Physical (Dump + Decode), Dump, Import, or Finish. The Logical examination was selected, as the Physical Dump requires the device to be jailbroken. For our testing purposes, a jailbroken device was not utilized, but the XRY user manual provides instructions on how it can be done. The data shown in Figure 7.23 shows what would be acquired from a Logical examination.

Clicking "Next" began the acquisition process, which took approximately 30 min. A ".xry" file was created in the specified destination folder, which could then be opened within the application at a later time for analysis.

Results and reporting

Upon opening the .xry file, the main screen displayed a summary of the report, with the data explorer on the left-hand side including the following categories: Summary, Case Data, General Information, Contacts, Calls, Calendar, Notes, SMS, MMS, Pictures, Videos, Audio, Documents, Files, and Log.

In the SMS, Calls, Voicemail, and Notes categories, there is a "Deleted" column at the end of the row, which is set if the data is found to be deleted.

First, the "General Information" icon was selected to see the type of data it was able to acquire about the device (see Figure 7.24).

The Contacts were selected next. Once a contact is chosen, detailed information related to the individual is shown on the right-hand side, including name, phone number, and the location where the contact is stored: on the device, SIM card, or

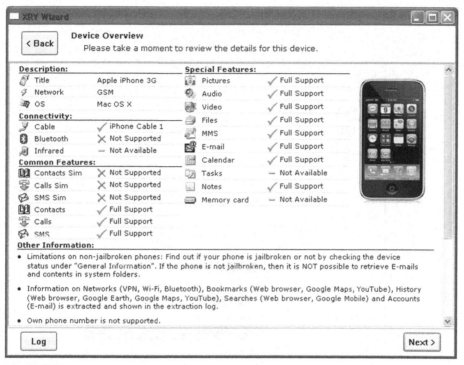

FIGURE 7.23

Device Overview.

removable media (for other device types). It was also noted that there was a check box next to each contact, allowing the user to export selected items into a report. Only those items that were "checked" would be included in the final report.

The "Calls" section displays outgoing, incoming, and missed calls. Voicemails are also included at the bottom of the list, as well as in the Audio section – where each file can be listened to within the application. This is discussed in more detail later in this section.

The calendar events are displayed as shown in Figure 7.25.

XRY is the only software program that was tested, which actually extracted the deleted Note and incorporated it into its reporting tool. While many of the remaining tools found the "notes.idx" file containing the scrambled, deleted data, the user would have to know what the note content was to recognize it as deleted data. Figure 7.26 displays both the undeleted and deleted Notes recovered from the device.

The SMS and MMS messages were split into two sections, both containing the phone number, contact name (if available), and message. Selecting a specific message provides more details, including date and time, and whether the message had been read. For the MMS messages, XRY offers the capability to save or launch the file directly from the software, but in an attempt to open it in Windows Media

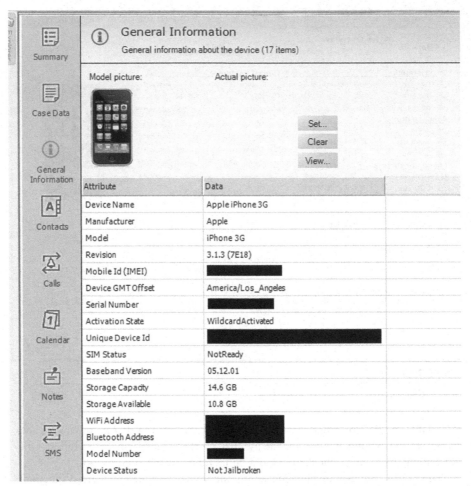

FIGURE 7.24

General Information.

Player, the picture could not be viewed in either message. On contacting tech support, it was learned that this is because XRY allows the user to use external players instead of the built-in player. To resolve this issue, the user is instructed to go into the options menu (in the top-right corner), select the "File Types" tab, and add a new line telling the app to open all .mms files using Quicktime (refer to Figure 7.27). From there, both MMS messages were able to be viewed.

Pictures and Videos were also stored in separate sections and contained each of the photos/videos taken or saved on the iPhone, including those sent via an MMS message. Upon clicking on a particular file, the examiner can view the name, type, size, metadata, and path. The metadata includes EXIF data such as the equipment make and model, date and time the photo was taken, and dimensions.

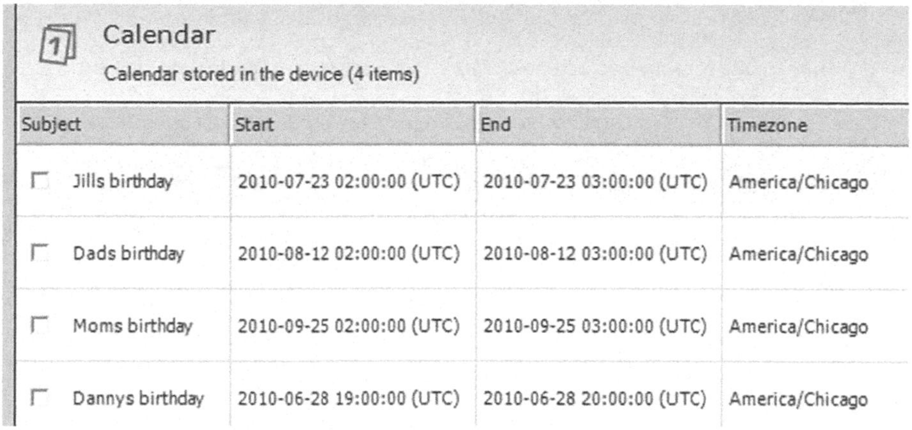

Calendar
Calendar stored in the device (4 items)

Subject	Start	End	Timezone
Jills birthday	2010-07-23 02:00:00 (UTC)	2010-07-23 03:00:00 (UTC)	America/Chicago
Dads birthday	2010-08-12 02:00:00 (UTC)	2010-08-12 03:00:00 (UTC)	America/Chicago
Moms birthday	2010-09-25 02:00:00 (UTC)	2010-09-25 03:00:00 (UTC)	America/Chicago
Dannys birthday	2010-06-28 19:00:00 (UTC)	2010-06-28 20:00:00 (UTC)	America/Chicago

FIGURE 7.25

Calendar.

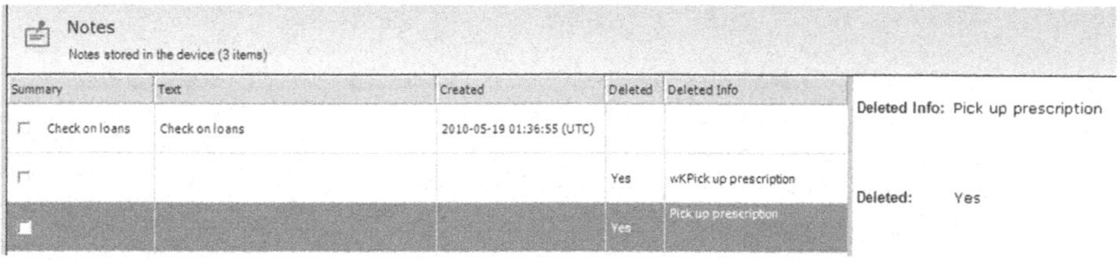

Notes
Notes stored in the device (3 items)

Summary	Text	Created	Deleted	Deleted Info
Check on loans	Check on loans	2010-05-19 01:36:55 (UTC)		
			Yes	wKPick up prescription
			Yes	Pick up prescription

Deleted Info: Pick up prescription
Deleted: Yes

FIGURE 7.26

Notes.

The remaining sections, Documents, Files, and Log, contain plist files, database files, and log activity. Within the .plist and .db files, additional data that was not extracted into its own category can be found, such as Wireless networks that were connected to, browser history, bookmarks, and more. The "Log" section is also significant. It provides not only the status of the extraction process but also information related to Networks, Bookmarks, History, Searches, and Accounts; more specifically, the YouTube application's browsing history was located within the log file, as well as the two applications that were deleted from the device (see Figure 7.28).

Figure 7.29 contains the results from XRY.

LANTERN

The following overview of Lantern was provided by the vendor:

- Katana Forensics' goal is to design affordable, intuitive tools for extracting data and artifacts from Smartphone devices without altering the evidence. Katana

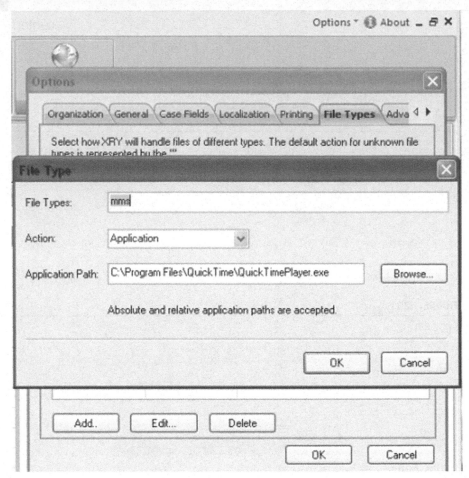

FIGURE 7.27

Options – File Type.

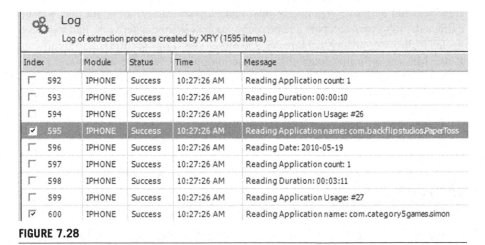

FIGURE 7.28

Log File – Deleted Applications.

Scenario	XRY Results	Ranking	Results
Call Logs	100	4	Meet
SMS (allocated)	46	5	Above
SMS (unallocated)	0	0	Miss
MMS	2	4	Meet
Contacts	2483	4	Meet
Email	Content in Webkit database	3	Below
Calendar	4	4	Meet
Notes	2 (1 deleted)	5	Above
Pictures (allocated)	5	5	Above
Pictures (unallocated)	0	0	Miss
Screenshots	0	0	Miss
Songs	654	4	Meet
Web History	Yes	4	Meet
Bookmarks	2	4	Meet
Cookies	Yes	4	Meet
Applications	9 (names only)	3	Below
Google Maps	2 histories	4	Meet
Voicemail	5	4	Meet
Passwords	No	0	Miss
Plists/XML	77 plists	4	Meet
Phone Information	Yes	4	Meet
Video	5 (4 iTunes/1 from phone)	4	Meet
Speed Dials	1	4	Meet
GPS	Yes	4	Meet
File Hashes	Yes	4	Meet
YouTube	Searches and History	4	Meet
HTML	0	0	Miss
Office Documents	0	0	Miss
Wifi	Yes	4	Meet

FIGURE 7.29

XRY Matrix of Results.

Forensics is a US-based company with an extensive background in law enforcement and computer forensics. Unlike similar products, our software does not require extensive training or costly service agreements and everchanging hardware devices. With a wide distribution in North America, Australia, and Europe, Lantern is rapidly growing to be the tool of choice of Law Enforcement agencies, Fortune 500 Companies, and e-Discovery firms around the world.

- Lantern 2.0 was also released in early 2011, a major improvement on the already successful 1.x version. Added tools include SQLite Deleted data and Blackberry monitoring programs for law enforcement.

Installation

To install Lantern, a Disk Image file was sent via e-mail. This image was mounted on a Macintosh system (Mac is required for this software) and, when the file was dragged into the "applications" folder, it installed right away. On opening the software, one can find a "Register" button. Here, license information, which was also included in the e-mail, was entered. The installation process was the fastest and easiest of all the software tested.

Forensic acquisition

To begin the acquisition, Lantern was started and a New Case created. The examiner has the option to select a Full Acquisition or only certain data, such as Audio, Video, or Photos. For this test, the Full Acquisition was selected. Clicking "Next" begins the acquisition, but it is important to note that the passcode on the device must first be entered. The software began to extract and transfer files from the device onto the workstation (see Figure 7.30). Acquiring data from the device took approximately 20–30 min, and the resulting case file was created and saved in the directory that had been selected earlier in the process.

Results and reporting

Lantern displays the results in a simple format, with the data categorized on the left-hand side and the rest of the screen acting as a viewing pane. The following types of data are categorized: Device Info, Calls, Voicemail, Contacts, Messages, Notes,

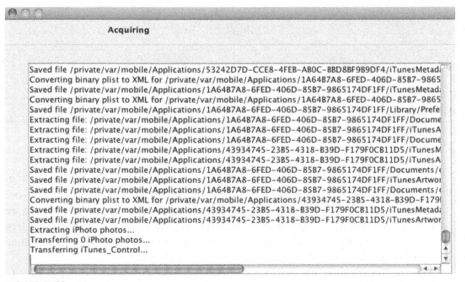

FIGURE 7.30

Acquisition Process.

Calendar, Internet, Media, Photos, Dictionary, Maps, and VoiceMemo. Examples of some of these sections can be found below. For data that do not fall within one of these categories, the investigator has the option to view the library directory, photo directory, applications directory, or just the overall artifact root directory. This option is located within the "Info" section, as shown in Figure 7.31.

Once one of the directories has been selected, the folder structure automatically opens up (in Figure 7.32 the Artifact Root Directory is shown). Here, the examiner has the option to analyze all the files located on the device, including SQLite database files, plists, pictures, and web history.

The remaining sections contain most of the standard data. "Calls" lists the entire call history including call time, number, duration, and status (outgoing/received/ missed). The "Voicemail" section goes one step further, and includes a link that allows the user to open and listen to the Voicemail (see Figure 7.33). There is a "Flags" column, which mentions whether the voicemail has already been listened to and whether it was deleted on the device. It is important to note the difference between the file being actually removed from the phone and being "deleted." On the iPhone, when a voicemail is deleted using visual voicemail, it is placed in a "Deleted" folder within the application. To actually delete the file from the device, the user would have to empty the Deleted folder. Within Lantern, when a voicemail

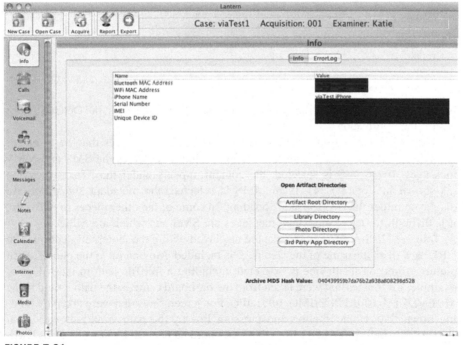

FIGURE 7.31

Lantern – Info.

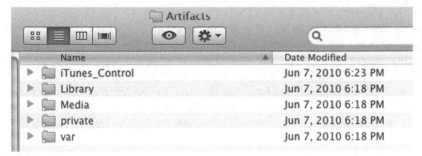

FIGURE 7.32

Artifact Root Directory.

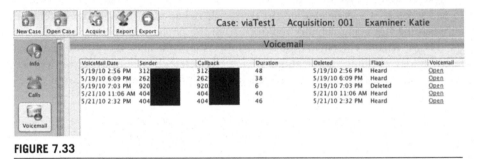

FIGURE 7.33

Voicemail.

is marked as "Deleted," it simply means that this file was placed in the Deleted folder within the application.

The Messages section includes all SMS and MMS messages that were sent or received. What is unique about this section is that it separates the SMS and MMS messages. If an SMS is selected, the content appears under the "Text": heading (as shown in Figure 7.34). If an MMS is selected, the metadata and photo are displayed under the "MMS Data": heading. In some of the other pieces of software, it is difficult to determine which messages are SMS and which are MMS.

Internet History and Bookmarks are displayed within the "Internet" section. The URL as well as the name of the web page is included. Moving on to the photos, each picture stored on the device is extracted, including a full file path to that file. For example, for images that were taken from the on-board camera, the path would show Media/DCIM/100APPLE/IMG_0001.JPG. For screen shots that were taken by holding down the "Home" button and pressing Power, the path would show Media/DCIM/999Apple/IMG_0002.JPG. For each photo recovered, Lantern contains EXIF data including file name, type, hash, etc. For most photos taken from the actual iPhone, GPS coordinates and timestamps are also included.

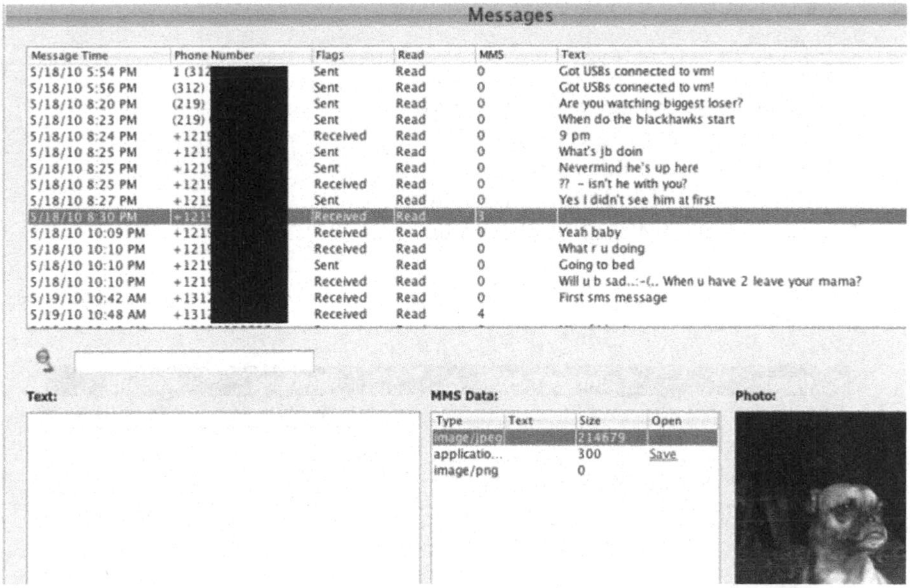

FIGURE 7.34

Messages.

Other features include the ability to export a file as well as create a report. To do this, the "Report" option at the top of the screen has to be selected; then the user can select the categories they wish to include in the report. The resulting report is in the form of a .PDF file.

The results from Lantern are shown in Figure 7.35.

MacLock Pick

The following overview of MacLock Pick was provided by the vendor:

- MacLockPick II (MLP) by SubRosaSoft (makers of MacForensicLab) adopts a unique approach to forensic acquisition. The goal of MLP is to provide a cross-platform forensic solution that performs a live acquisition of a suspect machine after inserting the USB device. The information is stored on the USB device and software is provided to analyze the results. The solution supports plug-ins for many acquisition types; however, only the iPhone plug-ins were tested.
- MLP does not work directly on the iPhone and instead targets the backup directory where the iPhone stored most files as MDBACKUP files. The following data is recoverable:

  - Call History (Received, Dialed, Missed)
  - Text messages (SMS)

- Phonebook
- Notes
- Photos
- Mail accounts setup for synchronization
- International roaming edge status
- Favorites – Speed dial entries
- Safari – State, History, and Bookmarks
- Phone details (IMEI/ESN, phone number, TMSI, IMSI)

Scenario	Lantern Results	Ranking	Results
Call Logs	100	4	Meet
SMS (allocated)	46	5	Above
SMS (unallocated)	0	0	Miss
MMS	2	4	Meet
Contacts	2483	4	Meet
Email	Content in webkit database	3	Below
Calendar	4	4	Meet
Notes	2 (1 deleted)	5	Above
Pictures (allocated)	5	5	Above
Pictures (unallocated)	0	0	Miss
Screenshots	0	0	Miss
Songs	654	4	Meet
Web History	Yes	4	Meet
Bookmarks	2	4	Meet
Cookies	Yes	4	Meet
Applications	7	4	Meet
Google Maps	2 histories	4	Meet
Voicemail	5	4	Meet
Passwords	0	0	Miss
Plists/XML	Yes, ~75	4	Meet
Phone Information	Yes	4	Meet
Video	5	4	Meet
Speed Dials	1	4	Meet
GPS	Yes	4	Meet
File Hashes	Yes	4	Meet
YouTube	Searches and history	4	Meet
HTML	0	0	Miss
Office Documents	0	0	Miss
Wifi	Yes	4	Meet

FIGURE 7.35

Lantern Matrix of Results.

Installation

After getting familiar with MLP's approach to forensic acquisition, the setup was quite simple. Initially, you must license the device by running a program to generate a key file and send to SubRosaSoft. An .inf file is then sent back, which must be placed at the root of the USB key. This process had to be followed at a later time after updating the MLP executables, but the device initially arrived licensed.

After the examiner inserts the device into a computer, he or she can explore the drive and run various programs. To configure the acquisition process, MacLockPick Setup (OS X) was run on a Mac 10.6.3 workstation. The program read the device configuration and allowed the examiner to select what type of data to acquire from the target device. Apple Mobile and Apple Mobile Pictures were selected (see Figure 7.36).

TIP

Quitting the application actually saved the settings, but that was not apparent from the interface.

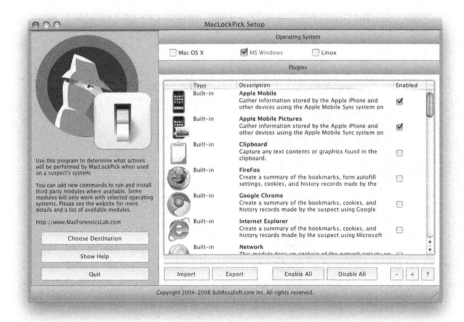

FIGURE 7.36

MacLockPick Setup.

The device was then ready to acquire data from target computers.

During testing, there were a few application updates received from SubRosaSoft and, as mentioned above, the licensing process had to eventually be completed by running MacLockPick Authenticator and following the steps. This process was intuitive. However, afterwards there were issues running the updated software on the original Windows XP target. After switching to a different computer, there were also several problems updating the software. Finally, the entire contents of the device were moved to an "old" folder and the contents of the updated zip file were extracted from a Mac instead of a Windows XP computer.

Forensic acquisition

With the device licensed and software updated, the acquisition process was quite simple. The iPhone had to be first connected to iTunes and a backup created. Once this was complete, the MLP dongle was inserted into the target Macintosh computer, the application started, and the acquisition began.

Results and reporting

The MacLockPick Reader was run on the Mac and the Log Database file opened (see Figure 7.37).

After selecting the file from the MLP device output directory, the examiner is presented with the main MLP window. Here, results can be examined, searched,

FIGURE 7.37

MacLockPick Reader.

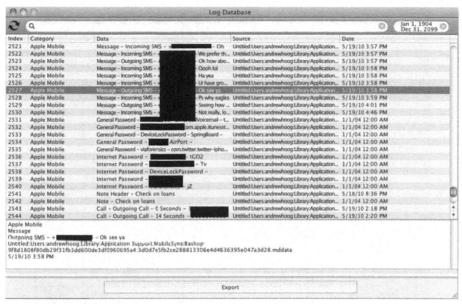

FIGURE 7.38

MacLockPick User Interface.

and exported into a report. The user interface, shown in Figure 7.38, is simple and allows quick searches, but access to more information such as the raw files recovered would have been helpful. The reports were generated quickly, but they were basically text file representations of the analysis window. There was an option to export to HTML as well, which would presumably contain much more data if a full computer acquisition was performed. The latest version extracted pictures found within the backup directory and placed them in a subdirectory for direct review.

The results from the MacLockPick tests are shown in Figure 7.39.

MOBILYZE

The following overview of Mobilyze was provided by the vendor:

- Mobilyze was specifically designed to forensically analyze iPhone, iPod Touch, and iPad devices. It runs natively in Mac OS X, offering examiners the most comprehensive means of accessing the most relevant data from heavily used applications such as text (SMS), camera (photos), and phone (calls and voicemails), as well as raw data from hundreds of apps. The product is capable of analyzing multiple devices simultaneously, reducing the time and effort spent in consolidating findings into one comprehensive report.

Scenario	MacLockPick Results	Ranking	Results
Call Logs	100	4	Meet
SMS (allocated)	46	5	Above
SMS (unallocated)	0	0	Miss
MMS	2	4	Meet
Contacts	2483	4	Meet
Email	0	0	Miss
Calendar	4	4	Meet
Notes	1	4	Meet
Pictures (allocated)	5	5	Above
Pictures (unallocated)	0	0	Miss
Screenshots	0	0	Miss
Songs	0	0	Miss
Web History	0	0	Miss
Bookmarks	0	0	Miss
Cookies	0	0	Miss
Applications	0	0	Miss
Google Maps	0	0	Miss
Voicemail	0	0	Miss
Passwords	0	0	Miss
Plists/XML	0	0	Miss
Phone Information	Yes	4	Meet
Video	0	0	Miss
Speed Dials	0	0	Miss
GPS	0	0	Miss
File Hashes	0	0	Miss
YouTube	0	0	Miss
HTML	0	0	Miss
Office Documents	0	0	Miss
Wifi	Yes	4	Meet

FIGURE 7.39

MacLockPick Matrix of Results.

- Mobilyze offers a set of rich features designed to efficiently force a forensic backup or point to an existing forensic image for analysis and case reporting. The benefits include the following:
  - *Flexibility:* Analyze data from iPhones, iPod Touch, and iPad devices using one seamless utility to search and report important case information.
  - *Comprehensive analysis:* Universally search across multiple devices and quickly access data from hundreds of apps.
  - *Reporting:* Tag important text, photos, phone calls, and pictures as you go, automatically incorporating them into a consolidated report.

Installation

Mobilyze arrives with two files: a Disk Image file and a license key. The .dmg file was downloaded onto a Macintosh workstation, the image mounted, and the application installed. Once open, the examiner is to browse the license file and select "OK," and the application is immediately ready for use.

Forensic acquisition

Once Mobilyze was running, the "Acquire Devices" button was selected. From there the user is prompted with two options: to acquire data from the device directly or through a backup file. The data was first acquired directly. Once this option was selected, the program began creating a backup file and acquiring/importing files from the device. The entire process took about 10 min. The acquisition was then run again using a backup file; however, the results appeared to be the same.

Results and reporting

Following the acquisition, an image file was created in the specified location. To view the results, this file was opened within the Mobilyze application, which displayed Device Info, Applications, Messages, Photos, Phone, and Contacts. The Device Info icon was first selected. Here, information about the device was displayed, as well as a convenient "overview" section, which gave a summary of the type of data required (see Figure 7.40). The examiner can click on the arrow next to each data type in order to view the specific files. For example, clicking the arrow next to "Movies: 6" opened the "Photos" icon, which displayed all images and videos.

The Applications icon was then selected, which lists out not only all downloaded applications but also any files related to that particular application. In figure 7.41, the "iCamcorder Lite" app is highlighted, and on the left-hand side the related .mov files are shown. The spotlight icon next to the file can be used to browse those files within a folder, in this case allowing the investigator to access and watch the .mov file.

The "Messages" section contains both SMS and MMS messages. Each row contains the type of messages, date and time sent, content of the message, and both the sender and recipient's phone numbers.

The photos and videos are displayed in the "Photos" section, and the examiner is able to adjust the size of the thumbnails (see Figure 7.42). Also contained within each section is a search function to locate specific files.

The call logs and voicemails are displayed in the "Phone" section. Information related to each of the calls is provided here. For the voicemails, an "expiration date" and a "deleted date" is also included. It was noticed that the year was incorrect for the deleted date, but the month and day were correct. Mobilyze tech support was contacted. They were aware of the issue and have since corrected it for the next

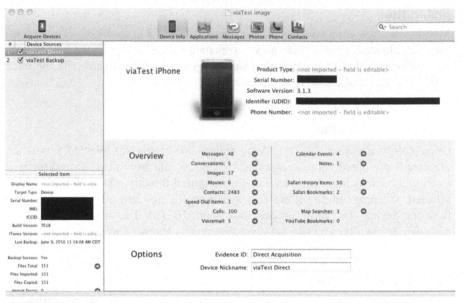

FIGURE 7.40

Device Info.

FIGURE 7.41

Applications.

release. The voicemails can also be played within the Mobilyze software itself. This is a convenient feature, as the investigator does not have to go searching through the folder structure to locate the .amr files.

Besides the categorized data, Mobilyze also allows the user to view the directory structure containing all the acquired data. Here, evidence can be found within plist and database files. To open all the files in a Finder, the arrow on the left-hand side of the screen next to "Backup Success/Files Total" must be selected (see Figure 7.43).

FIGURE 7.42

Photos/Videos.

FIGURE 7.43

All Acquired Data.

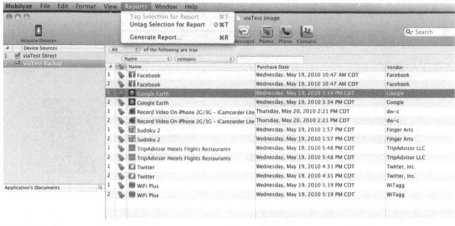

FIGURE 7.44

Tag Selection for Report.

Mobilyze also has an impressive reporting tool. However, it is important to select the items you want added to this report, because it does not add any files by default. To "tag" an item for the report, the appropriate item(s) have to be selected first. In this case, all the application files were selected. Once selection is done, click on "Reports" from the menu, and then "Tag Selection for Report" (see Figure 7.44). A red tag will appear next to each file that has been added to the report.

Once you have tagged all the files you need, select Reports > Generate Report. Here you will be prompted to create a Report Name (then click Choose Report). The next step is to fill out all the Report Information. When this is completed, the user has the option to Export and Display the report in html format, and the file is saved in the specified folder.

The results from Mobilyze are shown in Figure 7.45.

ZDZIARSKI TECHNIQUE

Jonathan Zdziarski is a former Research Scientist for McAfee, Inc. He is well known outside of work in the iPhone community as "NerveGas" and has contributed significantly to research into the iPhone and iPod Touch.

He has authored many utilities and devised many of the methods used to open the iPhone's platform to the open-source community. Zdziarski has written three books pertaining to the iPhone platform: *iPhone Open Application Development*, *iPhone SDK Applications*, and *iPhone Forensics: Recovering Evidence, Personal Data, and Corporate Assets*.

Prior to publishing *iPhone Forensics*, Zdziarski maintained an unofficial forensics guide for the iPhone distributed exclusively to law enforcement.

Scenario	Mobilyze Results	Ranking	Results
Call Logs	100	4	Meet
SMS (allocated)	46	5	Above
SMS (unallocated)	0	0	Miss
MMS	2	4	Meet
Contacts	2483	4	Meet
Email	Content from webkit database	3	Below
Calendar	4	4	Meet
Notes	2 (1 deleted)	5	Above
Pictures (allocated)	5	5	Above
Pictures (unallocated)	0	0	Miss
Screenshots	0	0	Miss
Songs	654	0	Miss
Web History	Yes	4	Meet
Bookmarks	2	4	Meet
Cookies	Yes	4	Meet
Applications	7	4	Meet
Google Maps	2 histories	4	Meet
Voicemail	5	4	Meet
Passwords	No	0	Miss
Plists/XML	Yes, 77 plists	4	Meet
Phone Information	Yes	4	Meet
Video	1 (no iTunes videos)	2	Below
Speed Dials	1	4	Meet
GPS	Yes	4	Meet
File Hashes	No	0	Miss
YouTube	Searches and history	4	Meet
HTML	0	0	Miss
Office Documents	0	0	Miss
Wifi	Yes	4	Meet

FIGURE 7.45

Mobilyze Matrix of Results.

The "holy grail" of any forensic acquisition is performing a bit-by-bit copy of the original media and retaining proof that the two are identical by comparing the unique cryptographic signatures of the original and the copy to ensure they match. While the processes and procedures for this are well established in traditional hard drive-based computer forensics, the process for mobile forensic devices proves to be quite a challenge. Unlike hard drives that can be removed or computers that can start in special read-only forensic environments, cell phones have a comparatively limited operating system, cannot boot into a forensic environment, and possess a typically nonremovable memory. Logical copies have been the only method of performing mobile forensics outside of imaging removed memory cards or reading SIM card data.

The uniqueness of Zdziarski's method is that it allows the examiner to perform a bit-by-bit copy of the iPhone's user partition and can provide an MD5 sum to prove that the copy was authentic. However, this ability does not exist in the standard iPhone operating system and requires modification of a read-only system partition to allow for this technique. Fortunately, this partition remains completely isolated from the partition containing user data and is intended to remain in a factory state throughout the life of the iPhone. This makes it an ideal and forensically sound location to perform the necessary payload installation, without violating user data.

Zdziarski recognized that the technique has obstacles that have to be overcome before it is fully understood and accepted, and addressed various concerns in the second page of his book. He explains that because his technique modifies only the system partition and preserves the user partition, the process is not only valid but also more reliable and complete than other "triage" approaches, as it provides access to the raw disk images and allows the examiner to bypass any security added onto the iPhone, such as a user passcode.

It is important to point out that, during the normal operation of the iPhone, the system partition remains in a factory state and is modified only during a firmware upgrade. As such, the likelihood of any user data or evidence existing in this system partition in highly unlikely; so modifying this system partition is not much different from modifying a desktop's boot sequence to boot a USB keychain or CD-ROM.

Another important point to note is the difference between Zdziarski's methods and the popular jailbreaking methods, and the forensic superiority of the former over the latter. The term jailbreaking refers to a hacking process by which the iPhone firmware is overwritten in order to install third-party application bundles or perform baseband unlocking. The jailbreaking process makes many modifications to the user data partition (as well as the baseband radio) to accomplish this, making it forensically unsound. Zdziarski's procedures, on the other hand, are more custom-tailored to forensic recovery and operate only on the read-only system partition. Unlike jailbreaking, they do not install any additional software or modify the user data partition in any way.

Zdziarski's procedure involves the creation of a custom forensic recovery RAM disk that is booted as if it were a firmware restore. Rather than actually restoring the iPhone, this bundle installs a recovery payload onto the iPhone's read-only system partition, granting the examiner SSH access to the device and bypassing any pass code security that might exist. The payload can also be optionally modified to disconnect the iPhone's user data from the system keychain, preventing the iPhone from logging into a suspect's e-mail account after it has been seized.

In a discussion with the author, he revealed that the concerns attorneys, law enforcement officers, judges, or juries might have are quickly alleviated when a simple explanation and overview of his technique is presented. He stressed the importance of explaining the difference between the jailbreaking hacking techniques and his own recovery techniques, and explained that some misconceptions about his procedures may have led some agencies to quickly discount his procedures based on incorrect assumptions.

Installation

As Zdziarski's technique is not an application but rather the installation of a forensic toolkit and the acquisition of a bit-by-bit copy (dd image), there is no single application to install. Rather, you must possess the tools and technical knowledge to follow his procedures.

The first step is to log into iPhoneinsecurity.com and download the "Automated Tools" to your system. In the test scenario, a Macintosh workstation was used. Once the tools were downloaded, the folder that was specific to the version on the test iPhone was copied to the desktop and renamed something meaningful. After verifying that there were no iTunes processes running in the background, the setup.sh command was run, which took approximately 5 min to install.

Forensic acquisition

With the help of the iPhone Forensics Cheat Sheet provided on the iPhoneinsecurity .com website under "Documentation," the acquisition was a simple process. The first command incorporated the forensic live recovery agent into the system partition of the device. The user is prompted to put the device in DFU mode prior to running the command (holding down power and the home key together for 10 s, then releasing the power button while still pressing the home key for another 10 s). The process was completed in less than a minute, and after disconnecting and reconnecting the device a couple of times (as prompted on the screen), the first part was complete. This entire process was also implemented for the "sh boot-kernel.sh" command, which booted the unsigned kernel from memory (Zdziarski compares this process to jump-starting a vehicle). The final command "sh recover.sh" began the process of recovering data off the device and onto the machine. The entire acquisition process took approximately 40 min.

Results and reporting

Unlike other tools that subsequently guide the examiner through analysis of the acquired data, Zdziarski's method produces a raw dd image and can thus be imported into many forensic tools or analyzed by command line. By simply renaming the file to a ".dmg", the image can be easily mounted on a Macintosh computer.

The image was not imported into any commercial forensic tools; instead, command line analysis was performed on a Linux forensic workstation and the mounted directory structure browsed.

Like any standard dd image analysis, the investigator will likely want to carve files from allocated and unallocated space as well as extract all strings. Zdziarski provides a scalpel configuration file in the sample code section of his website that is tailored to recovering important iPhone files such as images, XML files, SQLite database, Plist files, and more. When scalpel was run on the Linux workstation, it processed the image in just over 5 min and carved 11,150 files. Figure 7.46 shows the output from the command. This process was fast and produced many carved files, but the drawback is the potential for many false positives. However, using standard techniques such as the file command, scripts, image viewers, and more, you can whittle away the extraneous files quickly. The results were quite effective and provided many insights into iPhone usage.

Of the 1500+ images exported, many gave detailed information about the phone and the owner. One feature of the iPhone is that screens zoom in and out as you switch between applications. To achieve this, the iPhone takes a screenshot of the iPhone just prior to changing screen and then applies the transition. Because of this, the iPhone is full of images that show what the user was viewing when he or she switched screens. Figure 7.47 is an example of an image recovered from the iPhone, in particular, one of the photos that had been deleted.

Another useful technique is to run strings on the dd image. Below is the output from that command:

```
kstrzempka@linux-001: home/kstrzempka/iPhonePaper$ time strings
viaTest-iPhone-3G.dmg > stringsresults.txt
real 3m0.245s
user 2m40.950s
sys 0m9.230s
```

The resulting text file could be easily searched to locate important information.

As with other tools, analysis of the SQLite databases directly (using a hex editor, strings, and other techniques) revealed some deleted rows that were not yet purged from the file. Zdziarski's technique was able to recover the 1000+ e-mail messages on the system. This highlights the drawback to techniques that do not perform a bit-by-bit copy. In scenarios where a logical copy is made, the technique can only produce information that is presented by the operating system or transfer protocols, or that known only to the forensic vendors. It is assumed that most of the other products missed the e-mails because they were stored in nonstandard areas, downloaded as they were via Microsoft's Active Sync, or because the iPhone transfer protocol does not expose these files. Assuming some criminals are technically savvy and have some financial support, it would be quite simple to develop an application for the iPhone that stores the information they want in nonstandard ways, thus thwarting any logical data extractions.

Zdziarski's technique also recovered almost 4000 Plist files. Undoubtedly there are some repeats and false positives, but it is believed that a more thorough investigation of these files will result in even more detailed information being discovered.

The results from the Zdziarski tests are shown in Figure 7.48.

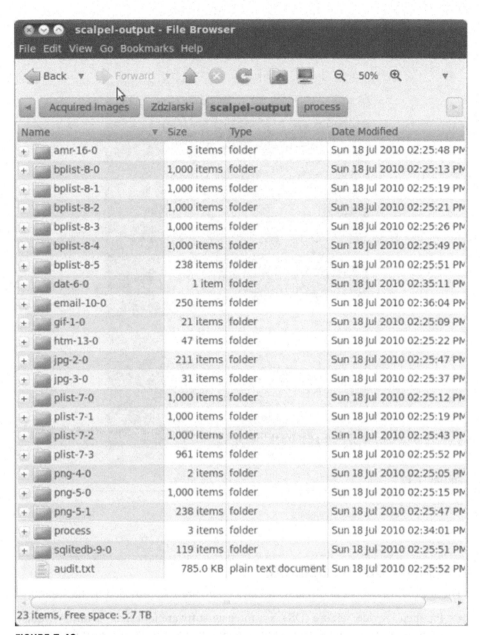

FIGURE 7.46

Scalpel Output.

FIGURE 7.47

Deleted Photo.

PARABEN DEVICE SEIZURE

The following overview of Paraben Device Seizure was provided by the vendor:

- Paraben Device Seizure (DS) is a forensic software tool that performs acquisitions on over 2200 handheld devices (including phones, PDAs, and GPS devices) and runs on Microsoft Windows. The package is designed to support the full acquisition and investigation process. Paraben emphasizes its potential to perform physical acquisition versus logical ones, as it provides the ability to recover deleted files and other important information. It has several packages, which include the DS software and various cables for phone acquisitions.

Scenario	Zdziarski Results	Ranking	Results
Call Logs	100	4	Meet
SMS (allocated)	46	5	Above
SMS (unallocated)	3	5	Above
MMS	2	4	Meet
Contacts	2483	4	Meet
Email	250 e-mail files from scalpel	5	Above
Calendar	4	4	Meet
Notes	2 (1 deleted)	5	Above
Pictures (allocated)	5	5	Above
Pictures (unallocated)	6 taken from phone (1 deleted) + 21 gif, 242 jpg, and 1,240 png	5	Above
Screenshots	Yes (pictures recovered in scalpel)	5	Above
Songs	654	4	Meet
Web History	Yes, plus screen shots of web browsing	5	Above
Bookmarks	2	4	Meet
Cookies	Yes	4	Meet
Applications	7 (plus screen shots of 2 deleted apps)	5	Above
Google Maps	2 histories + map tiles	5	Above
Voicemail	5	4	Meet
Passwords	0	0	Miss
Plists/XML	3,961 plists	5	Above
Phone Information	Yes	4	Meet
Video	5 (4 from iTunes)	5	Above
Speed Dials	1	4	Meet
GPS	Yes	4	Meet
File Hashes	Yes	4	Meet
YouTube	Searches and video history	4	Meet
HTML	47 files (including some e-mails)	5	Above
Office Documents	Screenshot of Excel file	2	Below
Wifi	Yes	4	Meet

FIGURE 7.48

Zdziarski Matrix of Results.

- The DS software allows an investigator to perform the acquisition, view data in various formats (ASCII, Hex, file and data viewers, etc.), bookmark important data, export data, and run various reports. Paraben states that DS can extract the following from cell phones (varies by model):
  - SMS history (text messages)
  - Deleted SMS (text messages)
  - Phonebook (both stored in the memory of the phone and on the SIM card)
  - Call history
  - Received calls
  - Dialed numbers
  - Missed calls

- ○ Call dates and durations
- ○ Date book
- ○ Scheduler
- ○ Calendar
- ○ To-do list
- ○ File system (Physical memory dumps)
- ○ System files
- ○ Multimedia files (images, videos, etc.)
- ○ Java files
- ○ Deleted data
- ○ Quicknotes
- ○ E-mail

Installation

In order to download and install Paraben DS, a user account must be created for the user to log-in and retrieve the files. First, the "Product," which consists of a Windows Installer Package and other files necessary for the setup, including a Microsoft Word document providing specific download/install instructions, must be downloaded. Once these files are downloaded, the DeviceSeizureSetup file needs to be run. Here, the examiner is prompted to install various programs, including Dongle Manager, as well as several drivers. Once the installation is complete, the "License" file must be downloaded from the website provided. The examiner is instructed to place this file in the root directory of the install (in this case, it was: C:\Program Files\Paraben Corporation\Device Seizure).

When initially running the software and trying to acquire the phone, an error was displayed saying that iTunes may need to be installed. To resolve this issue, the most recent version of iTunes was installed (v9.1.1).

Forensic acquisition

This review was based on Paraben Device Seizure 4.0, but more recent releases address the issue of not being able to analyze the phone directly (as described further in this section).

To acquire data from the iPhone, the user must select "Data Acquisition" and follow the steps for the Device Seizure Acquisition Wizard. There were two device type options for the iPhone: iPhone Advanced (logical) and iPhone Devices Only (logical). First, the Devices Only option was selected (all data types), and the acquisition began. The first time around, there was an error stating that the "iTunesMobileDevice.dll" had trouble loading. Tech support was contacted, who promptly responded saying that this error arrives with the installation of iTunes versions greater than 8.2. As the newer versions are not compatible with DS, iTunes v9.1.1 was uninstalled and replaced with 8.2.

When this did not resolve the issue, it was discovered that with DS 4.0, if the iPhone has firmware above 3.0, the iPhone Logical plugin would not work (as it is designed for firmware below 3.0 or for jailbroken iPhones only). Because the test phone had firmware v3.1.3 and it was not jailbroken, the only option available was to create a backup file via iTunes, and import that backup file into DS to view. To do this, iTunes v9.1.1 was reinstalled, a backup created, and the files imported by going to "Tools >> Import From.." and browsing for the backup. There were three main backup files (located in: C:\Documents and Settings\username\Application Data\ Apple Computer\MobileSync\Backup) that had to be imported on an individual basis: Info.plist, Manifest.plist, and Status.plist. Once imported, the examiner is able to navigate through the folder structure to view the acquired data.

Results and reporting

Device Seizure presents the investigator with a user interface consisting of the case and acquired elements in a left pane, and a window for the properties of the acquired data (MD5 and SHA1 hashes, category, and description). There is a large pane for viewing the contents of data elements. Above the viewer, when appropriate, there are tabs to view the data in text or hex.

Paraben acquired 3789 files from the backup files, and displayed this information in a directory structure. Because the acquisition was only of the backup file, the iPhone's common data was found within the "Parsed Data" folder. Here, one can view Notes, Calendar Events, SMS History, Call History, etc., as displayed in Figure 7.49.

Paraben extracted all 46 of the undeleted SMS messages. In the "Parsed Deleted Data" folder, it also showed three deleted SMS messages, but there was no content or phone number(s) in these files. The call history section included the phone number, date and time, duration of call, and whether it was outgoing or incoming. Once again, in the "Parsed Deleted Data" folder, two additional call logs were recovered, but the data included only the phone numbers dialed. There was no date and time, duration, or type of information. One of these numbers was not found in any of the 100 undeleted calls, so it is safe to conclude that Paraben extracted at least one, and probably two, deleted call history items (see Figure 7.50).

Other types of data outside of the "Parsed Data" categories can be found within the remaining folders contained in the backup. For example, images were located in /Media/DCIM/100APPLE/.MISC/. Metadata from this file can viewed in text or hex within Paraben. In the lower left-hand corner, both the MD5 and SHA1 hash values are displayed in the Properties window.

Also located were voicemails, videos, plists, database, and other important files; however, they could only be viewed as text or hex. DS does not provide a way to view these files. So, for example, while the voicemail.db file located each of the voicemail files, the actual voicemail messages could not be listened to because the .amr files were missing. Additionally, the video file names were located, but not the actual .mov or .wav files.

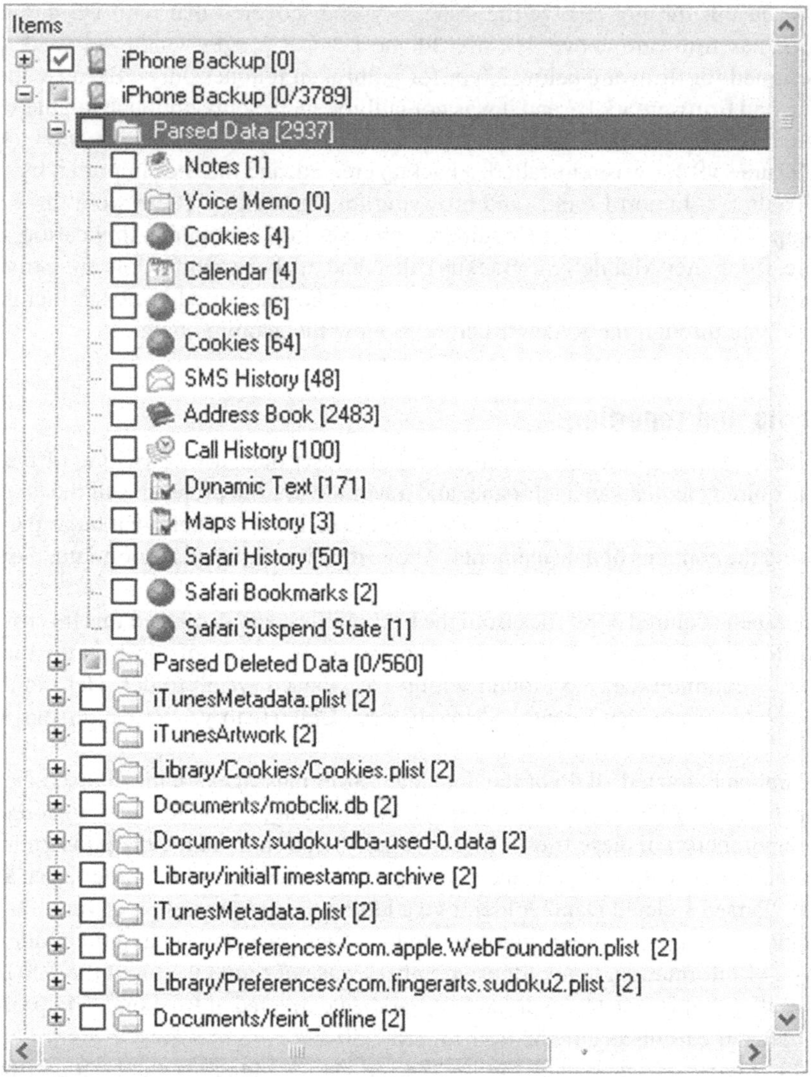

FIGURE 7.49

Paraben – Parsed Data.

One attractive feature that Paraben offers is that, while going through the investigation, one can check files that contain important data. At the end, Paraben will create a report containing only the data/files that the examiner has selected. This helps to eliminate some of the insignificant files and provide a more meaningful report. Figure 7.51 displays part of the report wizard, and Figure 7.52 is a preview of the resulting .pdf report (which can also be exported as a .csv, .html, .txt, or .xls file).

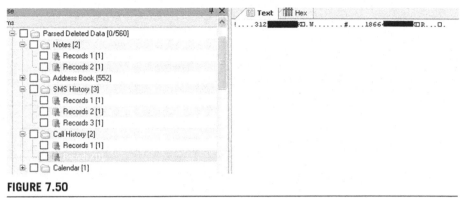

FIGURE 7.50

Deleted Call History.

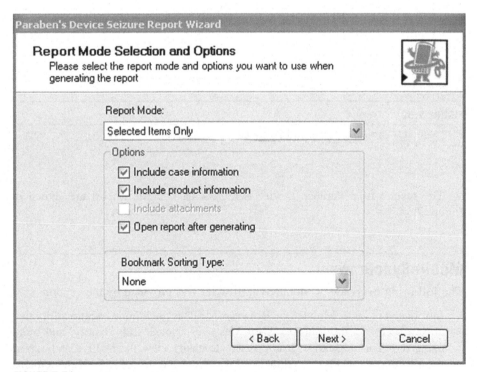

FIGURE 7.51

Report Wizard.

Parsed Data

Notes	
Creation date	18/05/2010 20:36:55:000
Summary	
Title	Check on loans

Calendar	
All day	No
Calendar ID	2
Description	
End date	22/07/2010 22:00:00:000
Location	
Start date	22/07/2010 21:00:00:000
Start timezone	America/Chicago
Summary	Jills birthday

FIGURE 7.52

PDF Report – Sample of Notes and Calendar.

The results from Paraben Device Seizure's backup file import are shown in Figure 7.53.

MobileSyncBrowser

The following overview of MobileSyncBrowser was provided by the vendor:

- Introduced in 2007, MobileSyncBrowser (MSB) is the iPhone backup utility that allows access to the iPhone's SMS Messages, Notes, Call History, and more using the iTunes backups. It is possible to easily view the archive and export the information contained within. MSB was the first utility of its kind and remains the most complete, cross-platform (Mac and Windows) solution available to the public. It is user friendly and presents a simple, iPhone-like interface. Licensing for law enforcement/forensic use is also available.

Scenario	Paraben Results	Ranking	Results
Call Logs	102	5	Above
SMS (allocated)	46	5	Above
SMS (unallocated)	0	0	Miss
MMS	2	4	Meet
Contacts	2483	4	Meet
Email	Content in webkit database	3	Below
Calendar	4	4	Meet
Notes	2 (1 deleted)	5	Above
Pictures (allocated)	5	5	Above
Pictures (unallocated	0	0	Miss
Screenshots	0	0	Miss
Songs	0	0	Miss
Web History	Yes	4	Meet
Bookmarks	2	4	Meet
Cookies	Yes	4	Meet
Applications	7 (found in .plist)	4	Meet
Google Maps	2 histories	4	Meet
Voicemail	voicemail.db but no actual .amr files	1	Below
Passwords	No	0	Miss
Plists/XML	Yes (77 plists)	4	Meet
Phone Information	Yes	4	Meet
Video	filenames only (no .mov or .wav files)	1	Below
Speed Dials	1	4	Meet
GPS	Yes	4	Meet
File Hashes	Yes	4	Meet
YouTube	Video Searches and history	4	Meet
HTML	0	0	Miss
Office Documents	0	0	Miss
Wifi	Yes	4	Meet

FIGURE 7.53

Paraben Matrix of Results.

Installation

In order to install the MSB, the files first need to be downloaded from the website. For this test, the Windows version was downloaded, but Mac was also an option. After running the installation file and stepping through the wizard, the application was installed within seconds. The next step was to enter registration information. To do this, within the MSB, one needs to go to Edit >> Preferences >> and enter the e-mail address and activation key sent to the user via e-mail. In order for MSB to operate successfully, iTunes also needs to be installed. The most recent version (9.1.1) was downloaded and installed.

Forensic acquisition

Rather than creating an image of the device, MSB reads the backup file of the iPhone created by iTunes while syncing the device to the computer. This backup file is read and then displayed within the MSB application. To acquire the data, the examiner first has to connect the iPhone to the computer and create a backup file using iTunes. Once the phone was disconnected, the software was started and it immediately found the backup file. The acquisition was extremely quick and easy, and located SMS Messages, Call History, Notes, Contacts, Calendars, Photos, and Other Files.

Results and reporting

The acquired information was displayed in a user-friendly window that simulated the look of the device itself, and the files were easy to navigate. MSB permits the user to export any file in order to view it using the necessary software. Figure 7.54 displays an overview of the iPhone's backup file.

All the standard application data can be viewed, including Call Logs, SMS, and Calendar. The Notes displayed only the one undeleted note, but by digging a little deeper into the notes.idx files (located in "Other Files" discussed later in this section), the deleted note was also found. Both the notes.idx and notes.db files are located in Photos and Other Files >> Library >> Notes (see Figure 7.55).

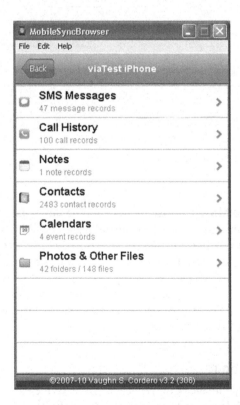

FIGURE 7.54

iPhone Data.

FIGURE 7.55

File Containing Deleted Note.

The next section displayed each of the contacts. However, in order to view details related to each contact, the file had to be exported as a "vCard File." The file must be exported and then opened within Microsoft Outlook.

The remaining categories included Calendar, which displayed all four events, as well as Photos and Other Files. The "Photos and Other Files" category contains an array of data including movies, applications, database files, plists, voicemails, and many others (see Figure 7.56). Each of these files/folders can also be exported so as to be viewed more easily. A large amount of data can be found in this section as the "Other Files" contain the raw data acquired directly from the device.

The "Documents" folder contained any videos/movies that were on the device, as well as some files related to other downloaded applications. The "Media" folder contains the photos that were stored on the device, including multimedia messages that were sent and received. A hash value is also calculated for each of these files.

The "Library" folder is where a significant amount of data can be found. It is in this folder that plists, database files, web history, maps data, and many other types of information are stored.

The results from the MSB tests are shown in Figure 7.57.

CellDEK

The following overview of CellDEK was provided by the vendor:

- The portable CellDEK is compatible with 1800 cell phones, PDAs, and satellite navigation devices. This cellphone data extraction device is a self-contained system with a touch-screen display and allows the user to identify devices by brand, model number, dimensions, and/or photographs. When the device type is selected, a "smart adapter" feature illuminates the correct USB adapter. Connectivity by Infrared and Bluetooth are also built in. Up to 40 adapters may be stored in the system's built-in rack.
- The CellDEK captures standard data within approximately 5 min. The CellDEK software automatically performs forensic extraction of the following data:

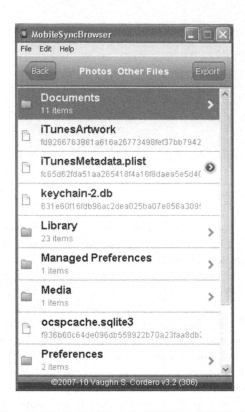

FIGURE 7.56

Photos and Other Files.

handset time and date, serial numbers (IMEI, IMSI), dialed calls, received calls, phonebook (both handset and SIM), SMS (both handset and SIM), MMS messages (not available from all handsets), deleted SMS from SIM, calendar, memos, to-do lists, pictures, video, and audio. The CellDEK features real-time data acquisition and allows one to view data captured on scene. Users can download data to a portable USB device. Easy-to-read reports are available on demand. The CellDEK also includes a "Secure Erase" feature that allows you to completely remove sensitive data from the laptop hard drive and an NIC (network isolation card) to isolate the suspect handset from the cellular network.

Installation

CellDEK is a completely self-enclosed extraction device; therefore, installation is minimal. The small suitcase-sized device contains all the necessary connectors and an internal computer with a 4.5×7.5-in. touch screen. The software is preloaded on the internal computer and starts immediately after signing in and agreeing to the user agreement. The touch screen includes an on-screen touch keyboard.

Scenario	MobileSyncBrowser Results	Ranking	Results
Call Logs	100	4	Meet
SMS	46	4	Meet
MMS	1	2	Below
Contacts	2483	4	Meet
Email	Content from Webkit database	3	Below
Calendar	4	4	Meet
Notes	2 (1 deleted)	5	Above
Pictures	5	4	Meet
Songs	0	0	Miss
Web History	Yes	4	Meet
Bookmarks	2	4	Meet
Cookies	Yes	4	Meet
Applications	7 (found in plist)	4	Meet
Google Maps	2 histories	4	Meet
Voicemail	5	4	Meet
Passwords	No	0	Miss
Plists/XML	Yes, ~70	4	Meet
Phone Information	Name and version	1	Below
Video	1 (no iTunes videos)	2	Below
Speed Dials	1	4	Meet
GPS	Yes	4	Meet
File Hashes	Yes	4	Meet
YouTube	Searches and history	4	Meet
HTML	0	0	Miss
Office Documents	0	0	Miss
WIFI	Yes	4	Meet

FIGURE 7.57

MobileSyncBrowser Matrix of Results.

However, updates may be necessary, as they were in this test. Like most extraction devices, updates to support new mobile devices may be needed from time to time. The update needed for this test was iTunes. To extract information from an iPhone using CellDEK, iTunes must be downloaded from Apple. This is done by logging onto the Apple website with a separate computer and saving the iTunes download to a USB Flash drive.

After downloading iTunes to the USB flash drive, the device was inserted into the USB port on the CellDEK. Simple on-screen prompts guide the user through the iTunes installation process.

This entire process was made easy by the detailed manual that was included with the CellDEK. Many of the images in this review are from the manual because taking screen shots on the self-contained computer of the CellDEK was not possible.

Forensic acquisition

After installing iTunes, the acquisition process took less than 5 min. After the user agreement, CellDEK loads to its main applications screen. From this screen the user can choose to manage files, view previous extractions, update software, and read a new device. After selecting to read a new device, the user is asked which kind of device is going to be read. In this case, the iPhone was selected.

Next, an on-screen prompt tells the user which cable to use by lighting up the cable connector. The examiner is instructed to insert this cable into the device bed near the screen. Once successfully connected, the next on-screen prompt instructs the user to connect the iPhone. After this is done, an information screen is displayed listing the useful files that are to be extracted and the information they contain.

There was one error that occurred during the acquisition: "Couldn't find lockdown plist file." On contacting technical support, it was learned that this error is displayed when iTunes does not detect the iPhone (as the lockdown plist files are created by iTunes). To resolve this, tech support suggested rebooting the CellDEK, and instead of accepting the End User License Agreement (EULA), to leave it and instead open iTunes. Once iTunes was running, the iPhone was reconnected until the device was shown on the left-hand side. The EULA could then be accepted and the acquisition ran successfully.

Results and reporting

The report from the extraction process is immediately displayed on the built-in screen. The report viewer allows the user to select the area of the report they would like to view, including Contacts, Call Log, Messages, Other, Extended Data, and Case Details.

The built-in screen and report viewer are very convenient. However, the small size of the screen makes looking through large amounts of data tedious. To overcome this, CellDEK allows the user to copy the files. The files may be copied to a USB Flash drive or can be written to a CD if a CD writer is attached to the CellDEK via the USB connection.

For this test, the files were copied to a USB Flash drive. After choosing "Manage Files" from the main application page, the user is prompted to choose between copying files or deleting files. The next prompt gives the user the option of copying all or a single file. If copying a single file is chosen, a list displaying all reports stored on the CellDEK is displayed organizing the reports by date.

Once the report is saved on a USB Flash drive, it can be transferred to other computers. Unlike other extraction devices, CellDEK does not require that

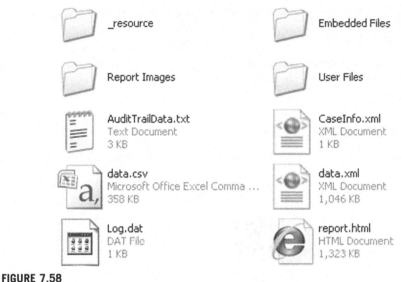

FIGURE 7.58

Transferred Files.

proprietary software be downloaded to view the extraction report. Instead, the report can be viewed as an HTML document. The folder containing the transferred files includes a .csv and .xml version of the extraction report. The extracted files also include images and a folder of user files (see Figure 7.58). The transferred files also include an Audit Trail text file that shows the exact time of the extraction.

The HTML version of the report is similar to the on-screen version. It includes a table of contents, allowing the user to jump to a specific part of the report. Images are available for viewing in both the .html version of the report as well as in a separate "Report Images" folder. The .html report lists various .plist and .db files but does not display their contents. To do this, the user must use a viewer that can read these files and view them separately. These files can be found in the "User Files" folder that was transferred from the CellDEK (see Figure 7.59).

The results of the CellDEK extraction are shown in Figure 7.60.

ENCASE NEUTRINO

The following overview of Encase Neutrino was provided by the vendor:

- EnCase® Neutrino® is designed for law enforcement, security analysts, and eDiscovery specialists, who need to forensically collect and review data from mobile devices. Investigators can process and analyze mobile device data alongside other types of digital evidence within any EnCase product.

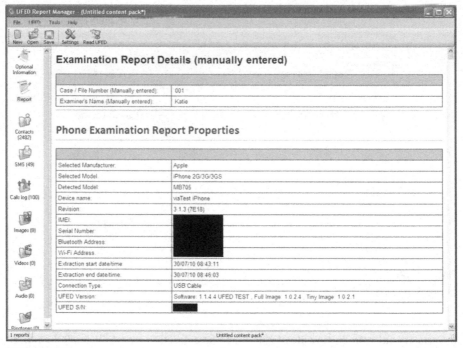

FIGURE 7.59

User Files.

- The solution features hardware support and parsing capabilities for the most common mobile devices and Smartphone operating systems including iPhone, Palm, BlackBerry®, Android, Windows Mobile, Motorola, Nokia, Samsung, and many more. Investigators can collect, analyze, and preserve all potentially relevant data including the following:

  - Device settings
  - Contacts
  - Call logs
  - E-mail
  - Images
  - SMS/MMS
  - Calendars
  - Other files stored on the device

- With EnCase Neutrino, an investigator can collect data from a wide variety of devices following an easy-to-use wizard, correlate data from multiple devices and computer media, seamlessly integrate collected data into EnCase Forensic or EnCase Enterprise for analysis, parse data quickly to improve the speed of the investigation process, and access more data on selected devices in comparison to similar products.

Scenario	CellDEK Results	Ranking	Results
Call Logs	100	4	Meet
SMS (allocated)	46	5	Above
SMS (unallocated)	0	0	Miss
MMS	2 attachments (only 1 picture)	2	Below
Contacts	2483	4	Meet
Email	0	0	Miss
Calendar	4	4	Meet
Notes	2 (1 deleted)	5	Above
Pictures (allocated)	5	5	Above
Pictures (unallocated)	0	0	Miss
Screenshots	0	0	Miss
Songs	0	0	Miss
Web History	Yes	4	Meet
Bookmarks	2	4	Meet
Cookies	Yes	4	Meet
Applications	7; only info found	2	Below
Google Maps	2 histories	4	Meet
Voicemail	5	4	Meet
Passwords	No	0	Miss
Plists/XML	Yes, 68	4	Meet
Phone Information	Yes, but missing firmware version, model #, serial #	2	Below
Video	1 (no iTunes videos)	2	Below
Speed Dials	1	4	Meet
GPS	Yes	4	Meet
File Hashes	Yes	4	Meet
YouTube	Searches and history	4	Meet
HTML	0	0	Miss
Office Documents	0	0	Miss
Wifi	Yes	4	Meet

FIGURE 7.60

CellDEK Matrix of Results.

Installation

EnCase Neutrino arrived in a package including an EnCase Forensic installation DVD, an EnCase Neutrino installation CD-ROM, a Neutrino interface cable for the Apple iPhone, and a USB security key. First, the DVD was inserted, whereupon the user was prompted to begin installation of EnCase Forensic (in this test, version 6.16.2 was installed). When the installation was complete, the DVD was removed and the CD inserted. EnCase Neutrino v2.7 was then installed. Following the install for both pieces of software, the user must restart the forensic machine. After the reboot, the USB dongle which came with the software was connected, and EnCase Neutrino was launched. Be sure to launch Neutrino and not EnCase Forensics, as they serve different purposes.

Forensic acquisition

Once Neutrino was launched, the iPhone was connected and the type of acquisition selected from the menu options – Apple >> iPhone 2G. The iPhone 2G was the only model listed and, because a 3G was being used for this test, EnCase was contacted to make sure that the 3G was supported. Despite what appeared on the screen, the 3G was supported, and the contact at EnCase suggested that all files from . . .\Program Files\Common Files\Apple\Mobile Device Support\ be copied to . . .\Program Files \Common Files\Apple\Mobile Device Support\bin. The next step in the acquisition was "Configuration." Here, the examiner is asked to enter evidence information and make sure to select the type of data he or she wishes to acquire (see Figure 7.61).

On the next screen, "Acquire Current Item" was selected and the acquisition began. Upon completion, the screen displayed a message saying "Successfully acquired Phone to viaTest iPhon.L01," which was the file that could be opened within the EnCase software at a later time.

Results and reporting

The acquisition resulted in a .L01 file, which was stored in the location specified in the "configuration" screen shown in Figure 7.61. When this file is double-clicked, the data are imported into EnCase in the form of a directory. The categories of data were displayed after expanding the "viaTest iPhone" folder. Text Messages, Call Logs, Calendar Events, Web History, and others are contained in their own folders, as displayed in Figure 7.62. The "Raw data" directory contains the rest of the files, such as applications, pictures, videos, and .plist files. This is where most of the data are going to be found as it contains all the original files from the iPhone backup.

Expanding the "SMS" folder from the original screen displays all the text and multimedia messages. The image is not attached to the MMS, so there is no easy way to differentiate between a text and multimedia messages, other than a lack of content. Once a message is selected, the user has a variety of options on how to display it. In Figure 7.63, the "transcript" option, which displays the phone number and message in the viewing pane, was selected. Other options include text, hex, or a report providing the size of the file as well as its physical location, sector, and hash value.

The "Notes" folder contained only one undeleted note, but the deleted note was also recovered within the notes.idx file, which was found under raw data/Home-Domain/Library/Notes. To do this, the "Search" function was tested. The first step was to navigate to the "Keywords" menu to add a searchable term. In this case, the

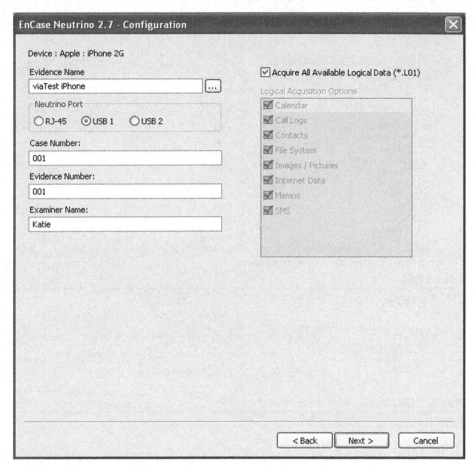

FIGURE 7.61

Neutrino Acquisition – Configuration.

FIGURE 7.62

iPhone Data.

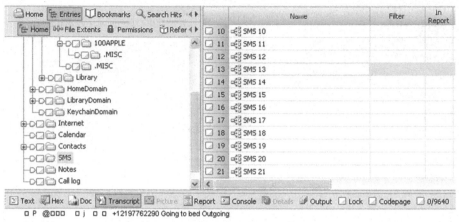

FIGURE 7.63

SMS Messages.

FIGURE 7.64

Keywords.

content of the deleted note was known to contain the text "pick prescription up," so the keyword "prescription" was entered (see Figure 7.64). Next, Tools > Search was selected, and the default settings were kept as is. Once this is completed, the user can select the "Search Hits" menu, which displays the results of the recent search for "prescription." As shown in Figure 7.65, the deleted note was found in the notes.db file as well as in notes.idx. The contents of these files were also displayed in the viewing pane at the bottom.

Within the raw data folder, the "MediaDomain" folder, which contains photos from the device, was reviewed. As with the SMS messages, once a picture is selected, there are several options to viewing it. The "Picture" option can be selected in order to view the actual image. Also displayed in the MediaDomain folder under Library >> SMS >> Parts is one of the two MMS pictures sent. The second MMS was unable to be recovered.

Many other types of data were found within the raw data folder, including the plist and SQLite database files containing data relevant to an iPhone investigation. Internet history and bookmark files as well as the keychain-2.db file, which contains e-mail, Wi-Fi, and Bluetooth account information, were located. Another point to be noted is that voicemail messages (.amr files) and videos were located, but in order to launch them with the appropriate application, the file must first be exported to the

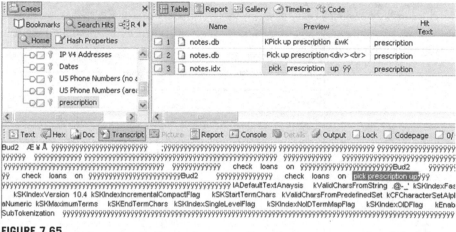

FIGURE 7.65

Search Results - Deleted Note.

workstation. This can be done not by right-clicking and selecting "Export," but by right-clicking and selecting "Copy/Unerase." This will copy the entire physical file and allow the examiner to play the voicemail messages and videos using the appropriate application on the forensic machine.

The results from EnCase Neutrino's test are displayed in Figure 7.66.

iPHONE ANALYZER

The following overview of iPhone Analyzer was provided by the vendor:

- iPhone Analyzer is a newcomer to the iPhone forensics market and provides a cross-platform software solution. With both open-source and low-cost commercial options, it provides a cost-effective way of exploiting iPhone data in a forensically safe way or simply exploring the usually hidden files on an iPhone, iTouch, or iPad.
- Based on a robust Java library, it provides an extensible framework for parsing plist and sqlite file types, including the backup files produced by iTunes. This framework can be used through the rich user interface, from the command line or as a Java library for use in other products. The typical mode of operation is working with entire backup files such as those from seized computers or nonintrusively examining a seized device. In either case, the entire directory tree is available for browsing, with multiple views on each file (including text, hex, plist browser, sqlite browser, and file-specific browsing). Alternatively, individual files can be examined using the same rich browser, or an entire live device can be accessed over SSH if it has been jailbroken.

Scenario	EnCase Results	Ranking	Results
Call Logs	100	4	Meet
SMS (allocated)	46	5	Above
SMS (unallocated)	0	0	Miss
MMS	2	4	Meet
Contacts	2483	4	Meet
Email	Content in webkit database	3	Below
Calendar	4	4	Meet
Notes	2 (1 deleted)	5	Above
Pictures (allocated)	5	5	Above
Pictures (unallocated)	0	0	Miss
Screenshots	0	0	Miss
Songs	0	0	Miss
Web History	Yes	4	Meet
Bookmarks	2	4	Meet
Cookies	Yes	4	Meet
Applications	7	4	Meet
Google Maps	2 histories	4	Meet
Voicemail	5	4	Meet
Passwords	0	0	Miss
Plists/XML	Yes, ~60	4	Meet
Phone Information	No	0	Miss
Video	1 (no iTunes videos)	2	Below
Speed Dials	1	4	Meet
GPS	Yes	4	Meet
File Hashes	Yes	4	Meet
YouTube	Searches and history	4	Meet
HTML	0	0	Miss
Office Documents	0	0	Miss
WIFI	Yes	4	Meet

FIGURE 7.66

EnCase Matrix of Results.

Currently, there is support for info.plist, manifest.plist, address book, calendar, sms, images (including meta-data such as geo location), and many other types.

- iPhone Analyzer can be used free as an open-source product; for more features (including rich searching and reporting), the professional version provides excellent value. Unlike many other products, this open-source model allows additional features at a reasonable consultancy rate, or it can be incorporated into other products for a license fee.

Installation

iPhone Analyzer was downloaded from http://sourceforge.net/projects/iphoneanaly-zer/. The resulting Java Archive (.jar) file was opened on a Macintosh computer, which immediately launched the application. Because this software is currently open source, no license or activation key was necessary.

Forensic acquisition

The iPhone Analyzer either reads the iPhone's backup files or, if the device is jailbroken, looks at the internal file structure of the phone through SSH. Because the test iPhone was not jailbroken, a backup file was created using iTunes. Once the backup was complete, iPhone Analyzer was launched and the backup was imported from the default iTunes backup location, as shown in Figure 7.67.

Results and reporting

After the backup file has been imported, two main screens are displayed: browse files and examine files (see Figure 7.68). The Device Info is immediately displayed on the main screen, while common bookmarks such as Contacts, Messages, and Photos are shown on the left-hand side. For each file selected, the examiner has the option to view it as it is displayed on the screen or to view it as an SQL database. Here, the file can be browsed based on name, phone number, etc.

For the address book, contacts were displayed in a somewhat unorganized format. One must be patient with larger files, as this particular file took 1–2 min to load as it contained over 2000 contacts. The file is in the form of a sqlitedb, and does not display cleanly on the screen. However, if you click on a contact, details of that individual will be displayed in a more organized format on the right-hand side. This particular file might be best displayed as a SQL database.

FIGURE 7.67

Import Backup File.

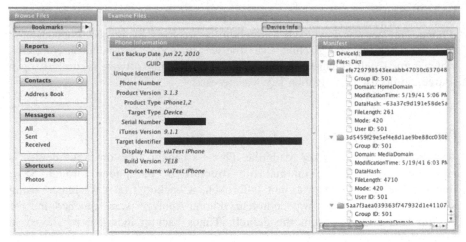

FIGURE 7.68

Device Info.

Under Messages, the user has the option to view Sent, Received, or All text messages. This section does include the MMS messages sent, but it is difficult to differentiate between an SMS and an MMS. In this test case, the two lines that have a blank "message" column are both multimedia messages. The images attached to these messages are displayed within the photos section.

Under the "Shortcuts" heading are the photos, which are displayed in thumbnails by default. Though not labeled, videos are also displayed in this section. The user can click on a particular photo or video to see a larger image as well as the EXIF data for that file (see Figure 7.69). There is also an "Export all images" option, but this option did not work successfully in this particular test.

Once the examiner has browsed through the bookmarks, there is the option to browse through the file system folders by selecting the arrow next to "bookmarks." Any database file or plist file within the file system directory can be viewed within the software itself. One issue is that a file type not supported by the software cannot be exported. For example, the voicemails are saved as .amr files on the device. This file was viewed as "unidentified" and it could not be exported and opened in a media player. The same issue occurred with a video (.mov file) located in the "Documents" folder.

Finally, the searching capabilities within the software were tested. To search for keywords, the user is to select Search >> Find, and enter a keyword. In this case, the name of one of the wireless access points that the device was synced with was entered. The search took less than 1 min, and provided the expected results as well as the original file location (see Figure 7.70).

The results from the iPhone Analyzer test are shown in Figure 7.71.

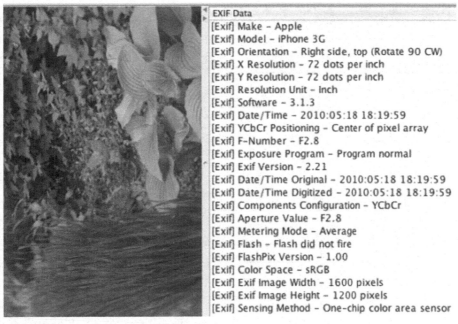

FIGURE 7.69

Photos/Videos.

FIGURE 7.70

Search Results.

SUMMARY

Digital forensics examiners are strongly encouraged to test and validate each tool that might be used as part of an investigation. In this chapter, several of the available iPhone forensics tools were tested in order to determine what type of data could be recovered from one tool to the next. Detailed steps on the installation of the software as well as the entire examination process were provided. Each section included the steps taken to perform an acquisition of the iPhone and where to locate potential evidence within each reporting tool. It is important to note that these tests were performed using specific software versions as well as one particular iPhone model and firmware version. Examiners should take further steps to validate and understand future software releases and tools prior to imaging a mobile device.

Scenario	iPhone Analyzer Results	Ranking	Results
Call Logs	100	4	Meet
SMS (allocated)	46	5	Above
SMS (unallocated)	0	0	Miss
MMS	2	4	Meet
Contacts	1000	1	Below
Email	Content from Webkit database	3	Below
Calendar	4	4	Meet
Notes	2 (1 deleted in .idx file)	5	Above
Pictures (allocated)	5	5	Above
Pictures (unallocated)	0	0	Miss
Screenshots	0	0	Miss
Songs	0	1	Below
Web History	Yes	4	Meet
Bookmarks	2	4	Meet
Cookies	Yes	4	Meet
Applications	2	1	Below
Google Maps	2 histories	4	Meet
Voicemail	Filenames and database only	1	Below
Passwords	No	0	Miss
Plists/XML	Yes, ~68	4	Meet
Phone Information	Yes	4	Meet
Video	1 - filename only	1	Below
Speed Dials	Yes	4	Meet
GPS	No	0	Miss
File Hashes	No	0	Miss
YouTube	YouTube Searches	4	Meet
HTML	0	0	Miss
Office Documents	0	0	Miss
Wifi	Yes	4	Meet

FIGURE 7.71

iPhone Analyzer Matrix of Results.

Reference

National Institute of Standards and Technology. (2010, November). Mobile Devices. NIST Computer Forensic Tool Testing Program. Retrieved January 10, 2011, from http://www.cftt.nist.gov/mobile_devices.htm

iTunes backup location

When a user initiates a backup of their iOS device through iTunes, these files are stored in a default location, depending on the operating system running on the workstation. The following table outlines the iTunes backup storage locations for various operating systems.

Table A.1 iTunes Backup Locations

Operating System	Location
Windows XP	C:\Documents and Settings\<user name>\Application Data \Apple Computer\MobileSync\Backup\
Windows Vista/ Windows 7	C:\Users\<user name>\AppData\Roaming\Apple Computer \MobileSync\Backup\
Mac OS X	Users/<user name>/Library/Application Support/MobileSync/ Backup/

Tools to analyze common file and data types

B

There are several file types and pieces of data that cannot be viewed using standard applications. The following lists out many of the common file and data types recovered from an iPhone as well as what applications can be used to view these files:

- *Property Lists (plists)*: Any text editor can be used to view a plist. Plutil can be used to convert from binary to XML (http://scw.us/iPhone/plutil/)
- *SQLite database*: SQLite Database Browser (http://sqlitebrowser.sourceforge .net/)
- *Unix Epoch Timestamps*: Epoch Converter Website (http://www.epochconverter .com/)
- *Mac OS X Epoch Timestamps*: CFAbsoluteTimeConverter (http://www.macup date.com/app/mac/37446/cfabsolutetimeconverter)
- *Disk Image File (.dmg)*: Can be mounted on a Mac using DiskImageMounter (double-clicking on this file will mount with this utility by default). Other forensic imaging tools that support the HFSX file system can also be used to mount an iPhone.dmg file, as well as mounting via command line (see Chapter 6 for details).

iPhone file system

```
.
├── CommCenter
│   └── spool
│       ├── MobileOriginated
│       └── MobileTerminated
├── db
│   ├── dhcpclient
│   │   └── leases
│   ├── launchd.db
│   │   └── com.apple.launchd
│   │       └── overrides.plist
│   │   ├── PanicReporter
│   │   └── timezone
├── ea
├── empty
├── folders
├── Keychains
│   ├── keychain-2.db
│   ├── ocspcache.sqlite3
│   └── TrustStore.sqlite3
├── log
│   ├── asl
│   ├── ppp
│   └── sa
├── logs
│   ├── AppleSupport
│   ├── Baseband
│   ├── CoreTelephonyTraceScratch
│   ├── CrashReporter
│   ├── fairplayd.log
│   ├── IQAgent
│   ├── lockdownd.log
│   ├── lockdownd.log.1
│   └── log-bb-live-stats.txt
├── Managed Preferences
│   └── mobile
│       └── com.apple.springboard.plist
```

```
├── mobile
│   ├── Applications
│   │   ├── 0ACAACB7-AC9A-4A12-87E3-F7BE8EEF26A5
│   │   │   ├── Documents
│   │   │   ├── Dropbox.app
│   │   │   ├── iTunesArtwork
│   │   │   ├── iTunesMetadata.plist
│   │   │   ├── Library
│   │   │   │   ├── Caches
│   │   │   │   ├── Preferences
│   │   │   └── tmp
│   ├── Library
│   │   ├── AddressBook
│   │   │   ├── AddressBookImages.sqlitedb
│   │   │   └── AddressBook.sqlitedb
│   │   ├── Caches
│   │   │   ├── AccessToMigrationLock
│   │   │   ├── AccountMigrationInProgress
│   │   │   ├── com.apple.AppStore
│   │   │   ├── com.apple.itunesstored
│   │   │   ├── com.apple.mobile.installation.plist
│   │   │   ├── com.apple.notes.sharedstore.lock
│   │   │   ├── com.apple.pep.configuration.plist
│   │   │   ├── com.apple.persistentconnection.cache.plist
│   │   │   ├── com.apple.springboard.displaystate.plist
│   │   │   ├── com.apple.UIKit.pboard
│   │   │   ├── com.apple.WebAppCache
│   │   │   ├── Maps
│   │   │   │   ├── MapTiles
│   │   │   │   │   └── MapTiles.sqlitedb
│   │   │   │   ├── TransitIcons
│   │   │   │   └── Info.plist
│   │   │   ├── MapTiles
│   │   │   │   └── MapTiles.sqlitedb
│   │   │   ├── Safari
│   │   │   │   ├── SafeBrowsing
│   │   │   │   │   └── SafeBrowsing.db
│   │   │   │   └── Thumbnails
│   │   │   ├── SBShutdownCookie
│   │   │   ├── Snapshots
│   │   │   │   ├── com.apple.mobilemail-Default.jpg
│   │   │   │   ├── com.apple.mobilenotes-Default.jpg
│   │   │   │   └── com.apple.mobilesafari-Default.jpg
│   │   │   ├── SpringBoardIconCache
│   │   │   └── SpringBoardIconCache-small
│   │   ├── Calendar
│   │   │   └── Calendar.sqlitedb
```

```
|   |       ├─ CallHistory
|   |       |   └─ call_history.db
|   |       ├─ Carrier Bundle.bundle -> /System/Library/Carrier Bundles/
310410
|   |       ├─ com.apple.iTunesStore
|   |       ├─ com.apple.itunesstored
|   |       |   ├─ itunesstored2.sqlitedb
|   |       |   └─ itunesstored_private.sqlitedb
|   |       ├─ ConfigurationProfiles
|   |       |   ├─ EASPolicies.plist
|   |       |   ├─ PasswordHistory.plist
|   |       |   └─ PayloadManifest.plist
|   |       ├─ Cookies
|   |       |   ├─ com.apple.itunesstored.plist
|   |       |   └─ Cookies.plist
|   |       ├─ DataAccess
|   |       |   ├─ AccountInformation.plist
|   |       |   ├─ ASFolders-492BF7DC-7739-47B8-9B5D-01111DF482C9
|   |       |   └─ ASFolders-D9D2E90A-5A76-4C92-B598-012C2BA348F6
|   |       ├─ Keyboard
|   |       |   └─ dynamic-text.dat
|   |       ├─ Logs
|   |       |   ├─ ADDataStore.sqlitedb
|   |       |   ├─ ADDataStore.sqlitedb-journal
|   |       |   ├─ AppleSupport
|   |       |   |   └─ general.log
|   |       |   ├─ CrashReporter
|   |       |   └─ MobileInstallation
|   |       ├─ Mail
|   |       |   ├─ AutoFetchEnabled
|   |       |   ├─ Envelope Index
|   |       |   ├─ IMAP-test@viaforensics.com
|   |       |   |   └─ INBOX.imapmbox
|   |       |   |       └─ Messages
|   |       |   |           ├─ 23.2.emlxpart
|   |       |   |           ├─ 23.4.emlxpart
|   |       |   |           ├─ 30.1.emlxpart
|   |       |   |           └─ 4.2.emlxpart
|   |       |   ├─ Mailboxes
|   |       |   ├─ metadata.plist
|   |       |   └─ MFData
|   |       ├─ Maps
|   |       |   ├─ Directions.plist
|   |       |   └─ History.plist
|   |       ├─ MobileInstallation
|   |       |   └─ ApplicationAttributes.plist
```

```
|   |   ├─ Notes
|   |   |   ├─ notes.db
|   |   |   └─ notes.idx
|   |   ├─ Operator Bundle.bundle -> /System/Library/Carrier Bundles/
310410
|   |   ├─ Preferences
|   |   |   ├─ com.apple.accountsettings.plist
|   |   |   ├─ com.apple.aggregated.plist
|   |   |   ├─ com.apple.AppStore.plist
|   |   |   ├─ com.apple.AppSupport.plist
|   |   |   ├─ com.apple.apsd.plist
|   |   |   ├─ com.apple.BTServer.airplane.plist
|   |   |   ├─ com.apple.BTServer.plist
|   |   |   ├─ com.apple.carrier.plist -> /System/Library/Carrier
Bundles/310410/carrier.plist
|   |   |   ├─ com.apple.commcenter.plist
|   |   |   ├─ com.apple.dataaccess.launchd
|   |   |   ├─ com.apple.GMM.plist
|   |   |   ├─ com.apple.iqagent.plist
|   |   |   ├─ com.apple.itunesstored.plist
|   |   |   ├─ com.apple.locationd.plist
|   |   |   ├─ com.apple.Maps.plist
|   |   |   ├─ com.apple.mobilecal.alarmengine.plist
|   |   |   ├─ com.apple.mobilecal.plist
|   |   |   ├─ com.apple.MobileInternetSharing.plist
|   |   |   ├─ com.apple.mobileipod.plist
|   |   |   ├─ com.apple.mobilemail.plist
|   |   |   ├─ com.apple.mobilenotes.plist
|   |   |   ├─ com.apple.mobilephone.plist
|   |   |   ├─ com.apple.mobilephone.speeddial.plist
|   |   |   ├─ com.apple.mobilesafari.plist
|   |   |   ├─ com.apple.mobileslideshow.plist
|   |   |   ├─ com.apple.MobileSMS.plist
|   |   |   ├─ com.apple.mobile.SyncMigrator.plist
|   |   |   ├─ com.apple.mobiletimer.plist
|   |   |   ├─ com.apple.operator.plist -> /System/Library/Carrier
Bundles/310410/carrier.plist
|   |   |   ├─ com.apple.PeoplePicker.plist
|   |   |   ├─ com.apple.persistentconnection.plist
|   |   |   ├─ com.apple.preferences.datetime.plist
|   |   |   ├─ com.apple.preferences.network.plist
|   |   |   ├─ com.apple.Preferences.plist
|   |   |   ├─ com.apple.springboard.plist
|   |   |   ├─ com.apple.voicemail.plist
|   |   |   ├─ com.apple.weather.plist
|   |   |   ├─ com.apple.youtubeframework.plist
|   |   |   ├─ com.apple.youtube.plist
|   |   |   └─ dataaccessd.plist
```

```
|   |   ├── RemoteNotification
|   |   |   └── Clients.plist
|   |   ├── Safari
|   |   |   ├── Bookmarks.plist
|   |   |   ├── History.plist
|   |   |   └── SuspendState.plist
|   |   ├── SMS
|   |   |   ├── Drafts
|   |   |   |   └── PENDING.draft
|   |   |   |   └── message.plist
|   |   |   ├── Parts
|   |   |   |   └── 02
|   |   |   |       └── 03
|   |   |   |           ├── 3-0.jpg
|   |   |   |           └── 3-0-preview
|   |   |   ├── sms.db
|   |   |   └── sms-legacy.db
|   |   ├── Voicemail
|   |   |   ├── 1.amr
|   |   |   ├── 4.amr
|   |   |   ├── _subscribed
|   |   |   └── voicemail.db
|   |   ├── Weather
|   |   ├── WebClips
|   |   ├── WebKit
|   |   |   ├── Databases
|   |   |   |   ├── Databases.db
|   |   |   |   ├── http_m.mg.mail.yahoo.com_0
|   |   |   |   |   └── 0000000000000004.db
|   |   |   |   ├── http_m.yahoo.com_0
|   |   |   |   |   └── 0000000000000002.db
|   |   |   |   ├── https_mail.google.com_0
|   |   |   |   |   └── 0000000000000001.db
|   |   |   |   └── https_mlogin.yahoo.com_0
|   |   |   |       └── 0000000000000003.db
|   |   |   └── LocalStorage
|   |   |       ├── http_m.mg.mail.yahoo.com_0.localstorage
|   |   |       ├── http_m.yahoo.com_0.localstorage
|   |   |       ├── https_mlogin.yahoo.com_0.localstorage
|   |   |       └── http_www.google.com_0.localstorage
|   |   └── YouTube
|   └── Media
├── com.apple.itdbprep.postprocess.lock
|   ├── com.apple.itunes.lock_sync
```

```
|      ├── DCIM
|      |    └── 100APPLE
|      |    ├── IMG_0001.JPG
|      |    ├── IMG_0002.JPG
|      |    ├── IMG_0003.JPG
|      |    └── IMG_0004.JPG
|      ├── Downloads
|      |    └── manifest.plist
|      ├── iTunes_Control
|      |    ├── iTunes
|      |    ├── Music
|      |    └── Ringtones
|      ├── Photos
|      |    ├── Photo Database
|      |    └── Thumbs
|      ├── Podcasts
|      ├── Purchases
|      ├── Recordings
|      └── Safari
├── MobileDevice
|      └── ProvisioningProfiles
├── msgs
├── preferences
|      ├── AeneasCustomFlags.plist
|      ├── csidata
|      └── SystemConfiguration
|      ├── com.apple.AutoWake.plist
|      ├── com.apple.network.identification.plist
|      ├── com.apple.wifi.plist
|      ├── NetworkInterfaces.plist
|      └── preferences.plist
├── root
|      └── Library
|      ├── Caches
|      |    ├── com.apple.pep.configuration.plist
|      |    └── locationd
|      |    ├── cache.plist
|      |    ├── cells-local.plist
|      |    ├── cells.plist
|      |    ├── clients-b.plist
|      |    ├── ephemeris
|      |    ├── h-cells.plist
|      |    ├── lto2.dat
|      |    ├── stats.plist
|      |    └── wifi
```

```
|    ├── Lockdown
|    |    ├── activation_records
|    |    ├── data_ark.plist
|    |    ├── device_private_key.pem
|    |    ├── device_public_key.pem
|    |    └── pair_records
|    └── Preferences
|         └── com.apple.locationd.config.plist
├── run
|    ├── asl_input
|    ├── configd.pid
|    ├── lockbot
|    ├── lockdown
|    |    ├── localcomm
|    |    └── syslog.sock
|    ├── mDNSResponder
|    ├── pppconfd
|    ├── SCHelper
|    ├── syslog
|    ├── syslog.pid
|    ├── utmpx
|    └── vpncontrol.sock
├── tmp
|    ├── DAAccountsLoading.lock
|    ├── launchd
|    |    └── sock
|    └── payloads
└── vm
```

Index

Note: Page numbers followed by *b* indicate boxes, *f* indicate figures and *t* indicate tables.

Made in the USA
Columbia, SC
10 January 2018